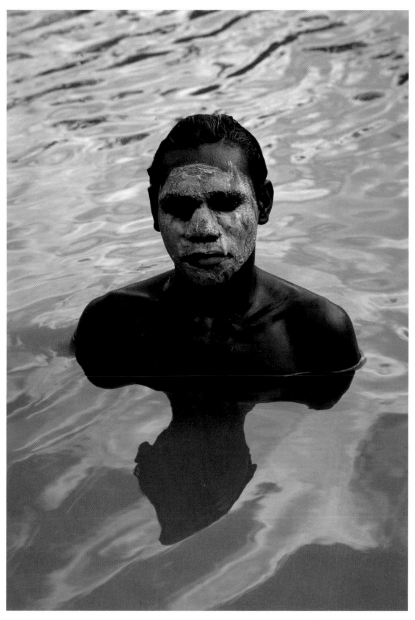

Heir to a culture that spans 60,000 years, an Aboriginal youth wears a mask of mud while swimming in a Cape York water hole.

Aust

Journey Through

Traces of a long-forgotten track dissolve in the haunting sands of Western Australia's Pinnacles Desert.

ralia
a Timeless Land

By Roff Smith

Photographs by Sam Abell

NATIONAL GEOGRAPHIC

WASHINGTON, D.C.

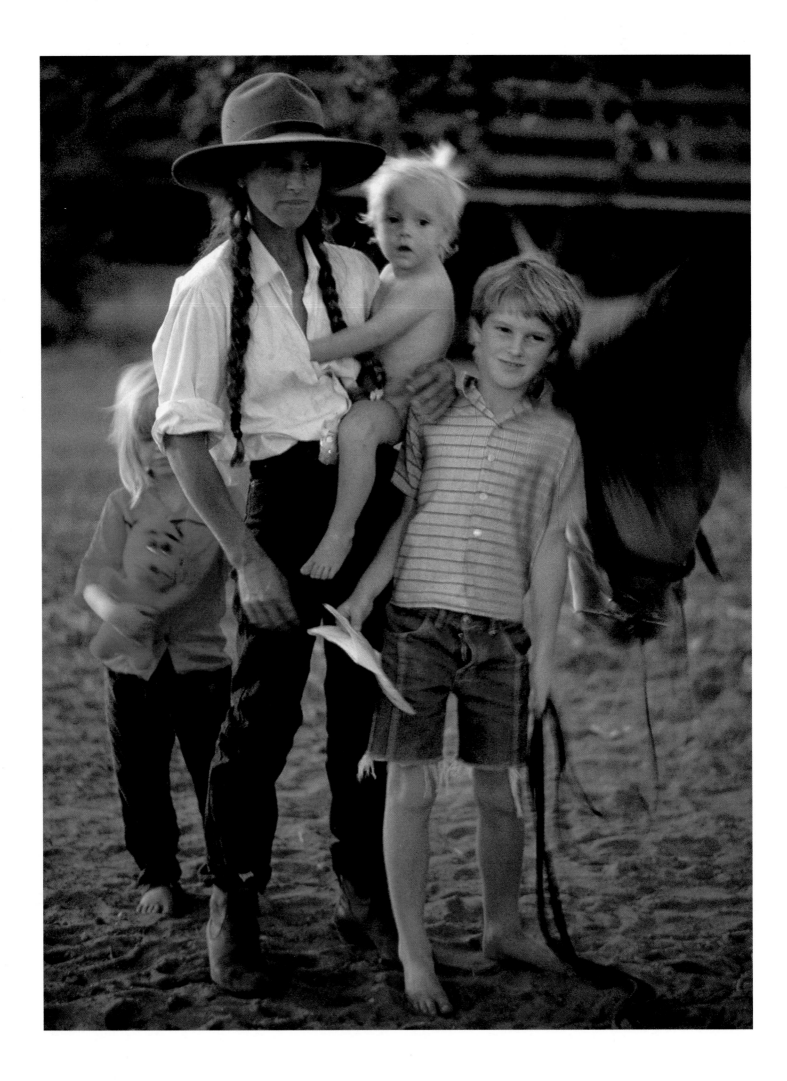

Contents

Cattle rancher Janice Bell and her children, like hundreds of other station folk, come in from the bush to take part in a Kimberley Championship Rodeo in the Western Australia town of Derby. With 28,000 inhabitants living in an area nearly twice as large as Britain, the Kimberley region of northwestern Australia is a surprisingly close-knit frontier. Events like the annual rodeo take on a family reunion quality.

Introduction

An island continent in a remote corner of the globe, Australia has tugged at the rest of the world's imagination since ancient Greek philosophers and geographers such as Aristotle and Pythagoras first postulated the existence of a Great Southern Land more than 2,000 years ago. They believed such a landmass must exist in order to keep the Earth in balance. Over the centuries lively medieval imaginations colored in this phantom continent with fabulous creatures and kingdoms. In 1606 Portuguese explorer Pedro Fernández de Quirós searched for it with the fervor of a Crusader, believing *Terra Australis Incognita* would prove to be a spiritual paradise. Different generations have different grails. To me, growing up in the snows of New England in the 1960s and '70s, Australia was a hazy collage of sunny images: The Sydney Opera House, Uluru, Bondi Beach, cricket matches, perpetual summers, and Land Rovers lurching down dusty red tracks. On my first trip to Australia, in 1982, I stepped off the plane marveling that autumn could be in March.

To the first European explorers the reality of Australia must have seemed as bizarre as fable. This was truly the land of upside down: Here the seasons were reversed, the swans were black, and strange trees lost their bark instead of their leaves. Marvels such as kangaroos, koalas, and platypuses lived in its fragrant bush, and the trees were so filled with raucous, brightly colored birds that early Spanish charts referred to the continent as *Terra Psittacorum*—land of parrots. When he wrote *Gulliver's Travels* in 1726, English author Jonathan Swift placed his fantasy country of Lilliput only a couple of days' journey, by canoe, from New Holland, as Australia was then known.

Forty-four years later, when James Cook's expedition sailed along Australia's luxuriant eastern shores, the profusion of strange plants and flowers they encountered in one inlet so excited the party's naturalists, Joseph Banks and Daniel Solander, that Cook named the place

6

E S I A

Arafura Sea

PAPUA NEW GUINEA

New Guinea

Torres Strait

SOLOMON
ISLANDS

Port Moresby ⊕

Thursday
Island
Somerset
Bamaga • Cape York

Melville Island
Dundas Strait
Cobourg Peninsula
• Victoria
Port Essington

Joseph
Bonaparte
Gulf
Cape Dussejour
Cambridge Gulf
Wyndham

Darwin ⊕
Oenpelli
Jabiru
KAKADU
NAT. PARK
ARNHEM LAND

Katherine
Ngukurr

Kununurra
Lake
Argyle
Y
Bungle Bungle
Range
PURNULULU
NAT. PARK
Alice
Downs
Halls
Creek
Balgo
Hill

Nhulunbuy

Borroloola

Newcastle
Waters

Tennant Creek •

NORTHERN

TERRITORY

Tanami Desert

Central Mt. Stuart +

Sandover

Macdonnell   Ranges
Alice
Springs

Mount
Olga
Yulara
ULURU-KATA TJUTA
NAT. PARK
ULURU

Finke

Simpson
Desert

Todd

A U S T R A L I A

Gulf
of
Carpentaria

Cape York

Weipa
ARCHER
NAT. PARK
Aurukun

JARDINE RIVER
NAT. PARK

IRON RANGE
NAT. PARK
Cape Weymouth
Lockhart River
ROKEBY
NAT. PARK
Coen

Shelburne Bay

Peninsula

MITCHELL
AND ALICE
RIVERS N.P.
Kowanyama

STAATEN RIVER
NAT. PARK

CAPE MELVILLE
NAT. PARK

LAKEFIELD
NAT. PARK

CAPT. COOK HWY.
Laura
Maytown
Cooktown
Cape Tribulation
Endeavour Reef
CAPE TRIBULATION NAT. PARK
DAINTREE N.P.
Kuranda
Port Douglas
BARRON
GORGE N.P.
Cairns
BELLENDEN KER NAT. PARK
Green Island
Atherton
Innisfail

Burketown
Karumba
Normanton

Georgetown

Tully

LUMHOLTZ
NAT. PARK
Ingham

Trinity Bay

Camooweal •

Julia Creek •

Mount
Isa
Cloncurry

Dajarra •

Dagworth •

Hughenden •

Charters
Towers

Magnetic Island
Townsville
Ayr
Bowen

Whitsunday Islands

GREAT BARRIER REEF MARINE PARK

CORAL SEA

ISLANDS

TERRITORY

C o r a l   S e a

P A C I F I C

Winton •

QUEENSLAND

Longreach •
Barcaldine •

Clermont •

Mackay

BRUCE HWY.

Swain
Reef

O C E A N

Rockhampton
Emerald •
Mount
Morgan •

Blackall •

Great Keppel Island
Heron Island
Gladstone

TROPIC OF CAPRICORN

Charleville •

Mitchell •
Roma •

Bundaberg

Maryborough

Gympie

Coolum Beach
Nambour
Maroochydore
Caloundra

Lady Elliot Island

GREAT SANDY
NAT. PARK
Fraser Island
Hervey Bay
Inskip Point
COOLOOLA   NAT. PARK
Laguna Bay
Noosa Head
Noosa Bay

SUNSHINE
COAST

Quilpie •

Cunnamulla •

Coongoola •

Toowoomba
Brisbane ⊛
Ipswich

Moreton Bay

S. Stradbroke Island
Coolangatta
Cape Byron
Byron Bay

Goondiwindi •

Darling
Downs

Gold
Coast +
Lismore
Mt. Warning

Birdsville •

Sturt
Stony
Desert

Oodnadatta •

SOUTH

AUSTRALIA

Coober Pedy •

Marree •

Lake
Eyre
North

Cooper Cr.

Lake Eyre
South

Strzelecki Cr.

Eyre Cr.

Diamantina

Georgina

Thomson

Barcoo

Warrego

Cooper Cr.

Collarenebri •
Moree •

Walgett •

Darling

Bourke •

Wilcannia •

Namoi

Dorrigo
Grafton

Armidale
Bellingen
Nambucca Heads

Tamworth
PACIFIC
HWY.

Coffs Harbour

Victoria Desert

Leigh Creek •
Beltana •

GAMMON RANGES
NAT. PARK

Ooldea •
Purple Downs •

Nullarbor Plain

ina

Eucla
Motel

EYRE HWY.

Ceduna •

Gawler Ranges

Whyalla •

Eyre
Peninsula
Port Lincoln •

West Point

Hawker •

FLINDERS
RANGES
NAT. PARK

Port Augusta •
Peterborough •
Terowie •
Clare •
Kapunda •
Adelaide ⊛

Silverton •

Broken Hill •

NEW SOUTH WALES

Scone •

Dubbo •

GREAT

Taree
BARRINGTON TOPS
NAT. PARK

Port Macquarie

Orange •
Bathurst •

Lord Howe
Island

Cessnock
Maitland
Newcastle

Morgan •
Waikerie •
Burra •
Renmark
Barmera
Berri

Wentworth •
Mildura

Griffith •

Katoomba
Jenolan Caves
BLUE MOUNTAINS N.P.

DIVIDING

KU-RING-GAI CHASE NAT. PARK
SYDNEY ⊛

Rowland Flat
Mannum
Murray Bridge

Port Pirie •

Goolwa

Wagga Wagga •

Goulburn •

Canberra ⊛

Wollongong
Nowra

Jervis Bay

Kingston •
South East

Flinders Island

Port Lincoln •

Kangaroo Island
Rocky River
FLINDERS CHASE
NAT. PARK

Spencer Gulf

Yorke Pen.
Gulf St. Vincent
Glenelg
Cape
Jervis
Penneshaw

Backstairs Passage

The
Coorong

Jerilderie •

Wangaratta •
Echuca •
Shepparton •
Albury •
Corryong •

Snowy
Mts.
Mt.
Kosciuszko

Cooma •

Queanbeyan •

AUSTRALIAN
CAPITAL
TERRITORY

Nepean River

Botany Bay

R A N G E

A u s t r a l i a n   B i g h t

Mount
Gambier •

Hamilton •

Warrnambool •

Horsham •

Beaufort •
Ballarat •
Creswick •

VICTORIA

Bendigo •
Euroa •

Omeo •
Mt.
Bogong •
ALPINE
N.P.
Australian
Alps

Snowy River

Geelong ⊛
MELBOURNE ⊛
Buninyong

Lorne •
Anglesea •
Traralgon •

Yarra

OTWAY
NAT. PARK

Port Phillip
Bay

WILSONS PROMONTORY NAT. PARK

King Island

Wilsons
Promontory

Bass Strait

Furneaux
Group

Cape Barren Island

King Island

George Town •
Burnie
Devonport

CRADLE MT. - LAKE ST. CLAIR NAT. PARK
Zeehan •
Queenstown •
Strahan •

Mt.
Ossa

Launceston
St. Helens

Evandale •
Ross •
Campbell Town •

FREYCINET NAT. PARK

TASMANIA

MARIA ISLAND NAT. PARK

Macquarie Harbour
MT. FIELD NAT.PARK
FRANKLIN-GORDON
WILD RIVERS   NAT. PARK
SOUTHWEST   NAT. PARK

Oatlands •
Richmond •
Hobart ⊛
Port Arthur

Tasman Pen.

Bruny Island

E R N   O C E A N

T a s m a n   S e a

130°   140°   150°   160°

Botany Bay. Later, when Cook's ship, the *Endeavour*, holed itself on the Great Barrier Reef along the coast of what is today far northern Queensland, the delighted Banks and Solander spent their enforced seven-week layover adding 180-odd new species of flora and fauna to their records.

Of course, Australia had quickened the imaginations of people eons before European explorers "discovered" the continent. Sixty thousand years ago an ancient Aboriginal people had come to these shores in what may well have been humanity's earliest major seafaring migration. Long before the Europeans' arrival they had mapped the land's great features, named its plants and birds and animals, recorded its history, come to understand its rhythms and seasons and complexities, and established their own unique metaphysical relationship with its warm, red earth. For thousands of generations they had passed on this knowledge, as well as their ethic of life, in a cycle of songs and dances, and had left rich legacies of rock art and engravings. Estimates vary. From 200,000 to 750,000 Aborigines were prospering in Australia at the time the 11 ships of the First Fleet sailed into Sydney Harbour in January 1788 to set up Britain's far-flung penal colony and political toehold in the South Pacific.

That landing brought irreparable changes to the Aborigines. Theirs was an ancient culture that treasured knowledge and skill above material possessions, but by the end of the 18th century they found themselves in conflict with a mighty European empire on the brink of the industrial revolution. Restless for land and fortune, gold and beef, wool for the textile mills, and coal to fire factory furnaces, the British shunted aside the original inhabitants and quickly took possession of the land. To the newcomers Australia was a primitive frontier, a rawboned continent to be tamed and brought to profitable service as resolutely British colonies.

On January 1, 1901, six Australian colonies united to form a new nation. Its constitution spelled out just what kind of nation it would be: White, xenophobic, Anglo-Saxon, and vigorously loyal to England, whose monarch would remain its head of state. One of the new federal government's first acts as a nation was to proclaim the infamous White Australia immigration policy, which shut the door on most of the world's peoples. The Aborigines, who had been living on the land for thousands of generations, were almost completely ignored: They couldn't vote or run for office, and they were not even granted citizenship until 1967.

For much of the 20th century Australia was a plummy colonial anachronism—thriving in its sunny isolation at the bottom of the world. But even as its Anglophile Prime Minister Robert Menzies was proudly proclaiming himself British to his bootstraps in the 50s and 60s, big changes were afoot that would change the face of Australia forever. The booming years after World War II and through the 60s and 70s brought tens of thousands of immigrants from Italy, Greece, Malta, Turkey, Lebanon, Poland, Yugoslavia, West Germany, and Romania. The 1980s and '90s saw large influxes of Asians as Australia embraced multiculturalism with the zeal of the freshly converted.

Australia has always been a land of promise. Even for the miserable convicts, who were brought to the colony in chains and filth, there were potential opportunities here they could never have had back in the London slums. They were on the ground floor of the making of a new nation. Many finished their sentences and went on to own prosperous shops or gentlemanly farms. Some went into politics. And a spectacular few, like Samuel Terry, went on to acquire huge fortunes. Terry was an illiterate stonemason's laborer who had been banished to Australia in 1800 for stealing 400 pairs of stockings. The young colony needed strong backs and good builders. After serving his term, the astute convict promptly started his own building firm. Then, as the city prospered around him, he branched into real estate. By 1820 he was one of the wealthiest men in New South Wales, where he was known as the "Botany Bay Rothschild." He enjoyed an income of more than £10,000 pounds a year, and when he died in 1838 he left an estate worth £250,000 pounds—almost unimaginable wealth in those days.

But Australia offers something more than the potential for sunny prosperity. Over the past 20 years in particular it has matured into one of the world's most cosmopolitan, confident, and tolerant societies. People from more than 200 nationalities now call Australia home, melting together with an unbuttoned easiness that would be impossible almost anywhere else. It is a nation of nearly 19 million people, the vast majority of whom live in cities and suburbs within a half hour's drive of a beach.

Today, almost a century after proclaiming its nationhood, a relaxed and multicultural Australia is undergoing a period of quiet, mature reflection. No longer England's bucolic country cousins, distracted by historic ties to a distant and musty Europe no more, Australians increasingly look to a vibrant Asia for their future. And as Australians become more comfortable with their own uniqueness and position on the Pacific Rim, they are questioning some of the old institutions they grew up with—the English monarchy and the Union Jack on their flag. A majority of Australians now favor the idea of becoming a republic, with a new constitution and an elected president rather than the reigning British monarch as head of state.

With growing maturity and self-confidence, Australians have also taken a collective deep breath and begun to confront some of the ugly truths about their past. And they are trying to do something about that history, however painful facing it might be. In 1992 the Australian High Court ruled that the continent had not been *terra nullius*—no man's land—when Captain Cook claimed Australia on behalf of the Crown in 1770: The Aborigines had held a valid native title to the land. Subsequent rulings affirming that Aborigines are entitled to claim vacant crown land have prompted a rash of land claims around Australia, as well as howls of protest from the nation's mining and pastoral interests. Whatever the outcome of the myriad legal tangles, it is obvious that it will never again be possible to ignore the wishes of the first Australians.

For all its worldly flair, international cities, and vibrant multiculturalism, it is Australia's physical uniqueness that most captures the world's imagination and its photographic lenses. This is an entire continent—almost three million square miles—that went walkabout around 65 million years ago, preserving in its splendid isolation entire branches of the evolutionary tree that vanished almost everywhere else: Marsupials, monotremes (egg-laying mammals) such as the platypus and the echidna, and living fossils such as the Jurassic period Wollemi pine that was found growing in a wild gorge little more than a hundred miles from downtown Sydney. The jewel-like Great Barrier Reef, the haunting monolith of Uluru, and the miracle of Kakadu National Park's wetlands are part of humanity's heritage.

Initiation rites in northern Australia's Arnhem Land tested the strength and will of young Aboriginal males. In the late 1920s candidates for manhood underwent a two-week-long series of trials. The third test demanded that they bake in the sun for a full day without food or water.

A trip to Australia remains one of the world's ultimate journeys. For many travelers it is an epoch-marking event in their lives, even if it goes unremarked at the time. I never came to this country expecting to be an immigrant, and although by now I've lived here almost all my adult life, until recently I still thought of myself as an American. So it came as a surprise to me several months ago when, after returning from a few months in the U.S., I gazed eagerly down at the barren South Australian landscape and the sight of Adelaide approaching in the distance and realized that the journey was taking me home.

Swollen by months of monsoon rain, the serpentine rivers of Australia's north turn dusty savanna into a vast wetland.

As dusk slips over the Kimberley, the monstrous eye of a saltwater crocodile gleams in marshes near the port of Wyndham.

Fresh rains and rows of lavender soften the hills of Tasmania, a counterpoint to mainland Australia's arid outback.

Catch in hand, an Aboriginal fisherman stalks rain-lashed shallows of the Gulf of Carpentaria in the Northern Territory

Moonshine casts a spell over Western Australia's ancient Bungle Bungle Range.

Schools of wrasse and damselfish swirl among corals at the foot of Lord Howe Island, in the South Pacific Ocean.

Scourge of the outback—fire. A bolt of lightning can transform tinder-dry scrub into shooting flames and glowing embers

Rock sentinels known as the Twelve Apostles—remnants of eroded cliffs—guard Victoria's storm-tossed Shipwreck Coast.

As day breaks at a station near Halls Creek, in the Kimberley, a jackaroo and his horses savor the predawn coolness.

Half-wild cattle forage hardscrabble earth dotted with termite mounds in Western Australia's rugged Kimberley.

CHAPTER ONE

The Far North

It was mid-September, near the end of the long dry season, and I was bouncing down a rough bush track toward the Gilbert and Staaten Rivers, extremely remote stretches of water that empty into far northern Queensland's Gulf of Carpentaria. I was traveling with local police constable Mick Jones; we were going fishing for barramundi. Northern Australia's finest, sweetest-eating game fish, barramundi lurk in the brackish mangroves and estuaries here—along with some of the world's largest and most dangerous saltwater crocodiles. It was the first time I had ever seen this part of Australia.

As I stared out the Land Cruiser window at miles of harsh scrub and endless savanna, I thought that even in a lifetime crowded with travel I had never seen any place more bleak and hostile. It had been seven months since the last rains fell. The ground was parched. Choking clouds of "bull dust," dust almost as fine as talc, drifted up from our footsteps and into our nostrils every time we stepped out to open gates along the track. Even with my lips clenched tight, I could taste it. The temperature was 110 degrees, the humidity was starting to build ahead of the coming monsoon, and the silvery leaves of the scrub hung limp in the torpid air. Insects whirred in the brittle grass. Farther out, the heat-warped horizon shimmered and wavered so much that it was impossible to tell where reality left off and mirage began. In another couple of months, when the monsoon hit, this would all be miles of marsh, mud, and riotous grass, and spectacular electrical storms would dance across purplish skies.

But now it was still and hazy and bright. Mick pulled over and stared out at one particularly desolate outlook.

After a few minutes of appreciative silence he slowly shook his head. "Beautiful, isn't it? I go away for a while but when I come back and see that, I know that I'm coming home." I smiled at him, wondering if he was joking. But, as I roamed Australia's far north over the next few months, I, too, began to appreciate its stark primal beauty: Its blood red sunsets, primeval mangrove swamps, ancient weathered gorges, the dangerous saltwater crocodiles that lurk in its brackish waters, and the eerie silhouettes of boab trees.

Australia's far north, also known as the Never Never in local parlance, is truly one of the planet's last great frontiers, stretching more than 3,000 miles from Queensland's Cape York Peninsula, through the Northern Territory's Arnhem Land, to the forbidding and little-known coasts of Western Australia's harsh Kimberley Plateau. It is a harsh and violent landscape, lashed by monsoons and tropical cyclones, swept by wild fires and floods of Biblical proportions, and roasted by summer temperatures that can soar to 120 degrees.

Few places on Earth are more treacherous. During the wet season a parched trickle like the Fitzroy River, in Western Australia, can turn almost overnight into a raging torrent 15 miles wide that washes away anything in its path. Old-time bushmen used to say that it was possible to die of thirst or drown in the same place, depending on what time of year a traveler was unlucky enough to be there. Other dangers await the unwary: Sharks and giant saltwater crocodiles and, in the hot summer months, the blood-warm seas can be awash with poisonous jellyfish. The tides up here are huge, fast, and powerful, and can rise nearly 40 feet in some places along the Kimberley coast. And everywhere in the dusty hinterland is a vast, almost conspiratorial silence reminiscent of the thousands of unexpected dangers or happenings that can make a luckless traveler disappear forever. As I bounced across the dusty gulf savanna in Mick's battered Land Cruiser that hot September afternoon, I couldn't help but notice how the hundreds of termite mounds dotting the land-scape looked like so many abandoned gravestones in the crackly grass.

Wild and unspoiled as it is, Australia's far north has been the continent's gateway to the world for thousands of years. It has the longest and most cosmopolitan human history of any place on the continent, dating back more than 60,000 years to the arrival of the first Aborigines. Macassar fishermen started probing these ragged coasts 800 years ago. Dutch, French, Portuguese, Spanish, and English explorers followed them beginning in 1606. Chinese prospectors flocked to the goldfields in the Cape York Peninsula, the Kimberley, and the Northern Territory in the 1870s. The pearling industry, in remote locales like Broome and Thursday Island, brought hundreds of Japanese pearl divers, Malay and Filipino seamen, Indian and Arab jewelers, and polyglot adventurers and drifters from every steamy port in Asia and around the world. In 1872 an undersea telegraph cable linking Australia with the rest of the world was dragged ashore at Darwin. In the 1930s Karumba, on the Gulf of Carpentaria, was a staging post for Qantas flying boat service from Australia to the United Kingdom.

For a time the far north was Australia's front line during World War II, and silent clearings dotting the scrub south of Darwin are all that remain of once-vital British and American air bases. In the 1970s and 1980s desperate refugees from Vietnam staggered ashore here after surviving weeks at sea in flimsy boats, risking pirates, sharks, and storms. Even today, refugees from all parts of Asia occasionally float up to these wild coasts, gambling everything to reach the promise of Australia.

In a land whose history is salted with tales of epic sea voyages and daring adventures, it is a pity that so little is known about the grandest and boldest venture of all. Sometime around 60,000 years ago, or possibly even earlier, a fragile boat ground to a halt on a wild and far-flung beach on what was then the northern frontier of Aus-

tralia, and a seafarer splashed ashore. This was the first time a human being set foot on an entirely new continent. Until that moment—as far as we know—all of humanity had lived on the largely interconnected land-masses of Africa, Europe, and Asia. The Americas were still unknown and untouched. It would be another 45,000 years or so before tribes from Asia would cross the land bridge now covered by the Bering Strait and venture into North America. By then Australia's Aboriginal culture was already older than any continuous culture known today.

No one knows what brought the first Aborigines to Australia—war, famine, climate changes, or swashbuckling curiosity—or where they landed. Anthropologists speculate that they originally came from somewhere in Asia and trekked and island-hopped their way south over the course of many generations. The precise route that brought the first Aborigines to Australia remains a mystery, too. They might have sailed from Timor, an island in the Indonesian archipelago, to the Kimberley coast in northwest Australia. Or they might have come down through the Philippines, made landfall in New Guinea, and walked across the rest of the way, camping on the low, flat plains where the Gulf of Carpentaria is today.

The world was a very different place then, much cooler, and locked in the grip of an ice age that blanketed the higher latitudes with sheets of ice as much as a mile thick. So much of the planet's water was locked away in glaciers that sea levels were more than 400 feet lower than they are today. In those days islands such as Java and Bali were joined to the Asian mainland instead of being separated by shallow seas. There was no Torres Strait between Australia and New Guinea, and Australia's coastline stretched almost to the edge of the continental shelf. In Ice Age days it was no more than perhaps 45 miles from Timor to what was then the northern coast of Australia.

What is intriguing about these early voyages is that even a 45-mile journey would have taken these ancient seafarers well out of the sight and safety of land—a remarkable act of faith, considering they would have had no idea what lay over the horizon. What would have made them do it? Did they have myths of lands beyond the sea? Were their frail crafts blown there by storms? No one knows. But an ancient campsite in a remote corner of Kakadu National Park in the Northern Territory's Arnhem Land dates back an estimated 55,000 to 60,000 years, showing that Aborigines had certainly arrived by then.

Whatever their reasons for leaving their old homes in Asia, the first Australians were quick to seize upon the promise of the new, spreading out across the continent in every direction and making it their own. Archaeologists have found campsites in the Nepean Valley, near Sydney, that date back 45,000 years. Another site, near Melbourne's Tullamarine Airport, is more than 40,000 years old. In those Ice Age days it was possible to walk to Tasmania without getting your feet wet. Skeletal remains found in a cave near Hobart go back 35,000 years.

Australia was a gentler place then, cooler and greener, dotted with inland lakes and carpeted with rich grasslands. Game was plentiful and included fabulous animals and birds that have long since become extinct: kangaroos that stood ten feet high and wombat-like creatures larger than a rhinoceros. Thylacines, marsupial "tigers," roamed the continent.

There were changes in the wind, though—literally. Sometime about 18,000 years ago the Earth began to grow warmer. In Europe and North America the ice sheets began to melt, and as they did the sea level began an inexorable rise, creeping higher on the beaches and slowly submerging the coastal lowlands. To individual Aborigines living on Australia's fertile shores, the changes would have been almost imperceptible: perhaps a grandfather's memories of childhood days when the beach was farther away from camp. Over many generations, however, the changes were profound. By 8,000 years ago a narrow but ever widening strait had begun to divide Australia from New Guinea; the broad shallow plain where hundreds of generations of Aborigines had camped, hunted, and danced was well on its way to becoming today's Gulf of Carpentaria. Parts of Arnhem Land, Queensland's Cape York Peninsula, and Western Australia's Kimberley region—all once more than 150 miles from the sea—were within

earshot of rhythmic rollers that washed against the sands. And as the coastline shifted inland, mangrove swamps grew up and replaced savanna, while the warmer, drier climate transformed the interior of the continent into a vast swath of arid scrub.

Aborigines have primarily an oral culture, handing down their ancient traditions and Dreamtime stories from generation to generation in a complex cycle of songs and dances. But they left behind a priceless illuminated history painted in vibrant reds, purples, and ochers in rock-shelter galleries scattered across Arnhem Land, the Kimberley, and Cape York Peninsula. Together they offer a unique illustration of the landscapes, flora, fauna, and social changes in tropical northern Australia over the past 12,000 years or so.

The earliest paintings are of animals. The first depictions of humans, done in what archaeologists call the Dynamic style of art, illustrate a life of plenty: Finely sketched biceps of hunters and dancers ripple with athleticism. Elaborate feather headdresses are worn. Primitive kangaroos and thylacines appear. Landscapes were open savanna, where boomerangs were the weapons of choice. As the centuries passed and sea levels rose, the paintings began to include trees, water lilies, yams, and fish. Boomerangs became obsolete as savanna gave way to forest and mangrove. Hunters used spears instead. The Rainbow Serpent—a deity associated with creation—as well as floods and rain appear in the art.

The monsoon climate represented in the paintings apparently heralded trouble. A rock shelter in a remote gorge in Kakadu contains what some art historians believe to be the earliest known depictions of human beings in battle. One spectacular mural, 4,000 to 6,000 years old, shows 111 stick figures charging each other, hurling spears. Eight of the figures are falling, pierced by spears and spurting blood. Archaeologists interpret these conflicts as the result of global warming, when rising seas forced coastal people off their ancestral lands and onto the higher ground of their neighbors. It was around this time, about 6,500 years ago, that the seas stopped rising.

By then, Australia's northern coastline looked much the way it does today. Rising seas had flooded the lowlands in Southeast Asia, creating the Indonesian archipelago. Timor, a likely jumping-off place for ancient mariners, was now more than 200 miles from the nearest Australian landfall—a much more formidable voyage than the earliest migrants had faced. Even so, a final migration apparently took place about 5,000 years ago, the latecomers bringing with them a half-wild Asian camp dog that was to become Australia's dingo. After that, the remote island continent was largely cut off from the rest of the world, and dozed for centuries.

The first Europeans known to have visited Australia landed in 1606 on the Cape York Peninsula, near where the town of Weipa is today. Dutch navigator Captain Willem Jansz, commander of the *Duyfken—Dove*—had been sent by the directors of the Dutch East India Company to see what sort of spices, gold, and rare woods might be found in the Great Southern Land. He was unimpressed, reportedly describing it as a "waste land…. inhabited in some places by wild, cruel, black men and barbarians who killed some of our sailors."

A second Dutch expedition into these waters, in 1623, also failed to find any promise in the crocodile-infested mangroves and vast stretches of flat, dusty scrub along this wild coast. "It is very dry and barren for, during all the time we have searched and examined this part of the coast to our best ability," wrote Capt. Jan Carstensz, who led the 1623 expedition, "we have not seen one fruit-bearing tree, nor anything that man could make use of: there are no mountains or even hills, so that it may be safely concluded that the land contains no metals, nor yields any precious woods, such as sandalwood, aloes or columba. In our judgment this is the most barren region that could be found anywhere on earth."

Whatever these Dutchmen thought of the scenery, they were certainly wrong about the Cape York Peninsula's lack of minerals. Ironically they had landed almost on top of the world's largest deposit of bauxite—the ore used to make aluminum. Since the mid-1960s the far-flung outpost of Weipa (population 2,200) has supported the giant Comalco bauxite mine, worth millions to the Australian economy.

If the early Dutch visitors were too dismissive, 19th-century British empire-builders held grandiose (and equally inaccurate) ambitions for this remote peninsula. Jutting into Torres Strait, only 150 miles from New Guinea and on what was then a major East Indies shipping route, the tip of Cape York seemed the ideal place to build a trading city—another Singapore. In 1863 the Queensland government sent John Jardine, a former police magistrate from Rockhampton, to the tip of the peninsula—at 10 degrees 41 minutes 21 seconds south latitude, the northernmost point in Australia—to establish the new city. It was called Somerset, after the Duke of Somerset, then Lord of the Admiralty.

To keep the outpost supplied, the Queensland government commissioned Jardine's two tough young sons, Frank and Alexander, to drive a mob of cattle from Rockhampton north through more than a thousand miles of uncharted bush, swamp, and jungle to Somerset. It was a formidable undertaking. The only previous attempt to travel the length of Cape York had been a disastrous expedition led by Edmund Kennedy in 1848. Of 13 men who set out, just three survived; only the group's Aboriginal guide had actually reached the tip. Kennedy had been killed by hostile Aborigines a few miles short of his goal.

The Jardine brothers set out in May 1864 with 8 men, 42 horses, 250 head of cattle, and a lot of ambition. Over the next few months they hacked their way north through the scrub. They lost most of their horses and cattle, but every man survived to reach Somerset the following March. Their remarkable achievement, however, was marred by the ferocity with which they treated Aborigines along the way. Adopting a shoot-first-and-don't-bother-asking-afterward policy, the gung ho party bulled their way up the peninsula leaving a trail of corpses. Their ruthlessness culminated in a bloody battle on the Mitchell River in which 30—and possibly more—Aborigines were gunned down.

Somerset, the would-be Singapore that was the focus of so much effort and bloodshed, never grew beyond 200 inhabitants. Termites, fevers, cyclones, and hostile Aborigines took their toll, and in 1877 the

Queensland government had the inhabitants evacuated to nearby Thursday Island, where a pearling industry was just getting started. Frank Jardine, however, remained in the area, running a string of cattle stations in northern Cape York. Much admired by colonial authorities, he was hated and feared by the Aborigines. Local legend has it that after he died of leprosy in 1919, the Aborigines secretly reburied him, head pointed downward, to make certain that his murderous spirit could never return.

Today, the Cape York Peninsula remains one of Australia's wildest and least inhabited frontiers. A gold rush in the southern part of the peninsula during the 1870s lured thousands of fortune hunters to this wilderness. They left, however, almost as quickly when the pay dirt grew scarce, and once rollicking settlements, such as Maytown and Laura, are virtually silent now. Most of the few people up here live in isolated Aboriginal communities and cattle stations. Roads are few and rough, and most residents receive mail once a week from a single-engine Cessna that flies out of Cairns. Only the mail run through South Australia's remote deserts is longer.

Traveling overland to the Tip, as the peninsula is known, is one of Australia's great four-wheel-drive adventures. The route stretches across 500 miles of wild, axle-breaking bush track from Cooktown to Bamaga, an isolated community perched just inland of the Torres Strait about a hundred miles from New Guinea. Challenging at any time of year, the roads become impassable during the wet season, and the handful of isolated towns and roadhouses along the way are cut off from the rest of the world. Even in the dry season, a number of challenging river crossings (beware of crocodiles!) have to be made. The swamps, rain forests, and marshes cursed by the likes of Kennedy and the Jardines more than a century ago are today cherished national parks.

Lakefield National Park, with its vast tidal mudflats, lagoons, and primeval marshes, is particularly noted for its conservation of saltwater crocodiles. About 120 miles farther north the track winds through the rain forests of the southern segment of Mungkan Kandju National Park,

a million acres of preserved wilderness where the Coen and Archer Rivers flow down from the jungle-clad McIlwrath Range. Near the northern end of the peninsula lies the magnificent Jardine River National Park, with its lush rain forests, the stately Jardine River and a large population of crocodiles. Fording the wide and sandy Jardine River is the last major barrier for travelers before reaching Bamaga—and ultimately the Tip. The ruins of Somerset and the lonely graves of Frank Jardine and his family lie just a few miles away. These relics of conquest and ruthless colonial ambition are today an easy day trip for visitors to the elegant Pajinka Lodge, a popular wilderness resort owned and operated by the local Injinoo Aborigines.

West along the rim of the Gulf of Carpentaria lies wide, hot gulf savanna country that has hardly changed since 1861, when explorers Robert O'Hara Burke and William John Wills struggled through it during the Wet on an epic south-to-north crossing of the continent. The harshness of the scenery came as a surprise to me when I first traveled through here. Since the south end of the Gulf of Carpentaria lies at roughly the same latitude as Cairns, I had expected this tropical coast to be green and lush with rain forests. Instead it was burned brown and shimmering with heat, except for mangrove swamps along the immediate coast.

The settlements out here have a tough, frontier atmosphere that isn't to everybody's taste. A remote refueling stop for Qantas flying boats in the 1930s, the outpost of Karumba today is a fishing port with a reputation for roughness and a pub known as the Animal Bar.

I went in for a drink one afternoon when the fleet was in and found myself talking with about six-foot-four inches of hardened, heavily-tattooed ex-con, one of about a dozen mallet-fisted drinkers loitering around the bar. Fortunately we got along. On a return visit the next afternoon I found myself confronted at the pool table by a weasely man who looked like his knife work would be efficient. My drinking buddy of the previous day drifted by and said hello. The other bloke went pale and remembered he had to be somewhere else.

Thirty miles east of Karumba is Normanton, another frontier town on the Norman River. The largest saltwater crocodile ever recorded—just over 28 feet long, with the build of a modest-size dinosaur—was reputedly shot on the banks of the Norman in 1957. There is no shortage of its snaggle-toothed relatives lurking in the river and mangrove swamps today.

A hundred and forty miles farther west on a rough and lonely gravel road is Burketown. One of outback Australia's most isolated communities, it is sometimes cut off from the rest of the world for weeks at a time when monsoon rains flood the low savanna. Burketown marks the western edge of the Gulf of Carpentaria's savanna grasslands and the beginning of the wetlands that stretch north and west towards the primeval wilderness of Arnhem Land and the frontier city of Darwin, capital of the Northern Territory.

Darwin surprises a lot of first time visitors, who typically step off the plane expecting to find themselves in a set for *Crocodile Dundee*. Instead, they discover a bright, modern cosmopolitan city of 80,000, with a spread of neat suburbs and shopping malls. At first glance only the tropical flowers in the gardens, the soporific heat, and the dazzling turquoise blue of the Timor Sea seem to give Darwin a sense of location; otherwise it could be a big Melbourne suburb. But look at a map. This toehold of suburbia is the only settlement of any size on Australia's entire 3,000-mile inhospitable northern coast, and it is the focus of activity for this region of the Northern Territory—an area known as the Top End. Less than an hour's drive south on Daly Street is desolate scrub; two hours east lie the primeval wetlands of Kakadu National Park—landscapes unchanged in thousands of years. Saltwater crocodiles still appear on occasion in the suburbs of Darwin, and in the summer its beaches are so full of deadly jellyfish that swimming is banned.

The reason the buildings and office blocksof this low-slung city appear so new is because they are: Darwin was nearly wiped off the map by Cyclone Tracy, which roared into the city on Christmas Day 1974 packing winds of up to 160 miles an hour. Most of the colonial buildings and wooden houses built, tropical style, on stilts are gone, replaced by (it is hoped) cyclone-proof architecture.

Darwin's history is a litany of tenacious rebuilding. It has been blown down by cyclones several times, bombed by the Japanese in World War II, and in its early days eaten by termites. A weather station in the city now tracks cyclones that might threaten it. Although Darwin is regarded as the last frontier, it was actually one of the first places settled by the British. After establishing convict colonies in Sydney, in 1788, and in Hobart, in 1804, the Colonial Office decided it would be prudent to plant the flag in the northern part of the continent to thwart French and Dutch ambitions in the area. Matthew Flinders, the English navigator who circumnavigated the continent in 1803, had repeatedly bumped into his French counterpart, Nicholas Baudin, on his travels. Baudin was also surveying the Great Southern Land. His charts were sprinkled with French names, Joseph Bonaparte Gulf, Cape Leveque, Cape Dussejour, and, most ominously in those days of empire, he referred to the continent as Terra Napoleon.

In 1818 the British established a settlement at Port Essington that was soon abandoned. In August 1824 Captain J. J. Gordon Bremer was dispatched from Sydney to set up a military outpost, Fort Dundas, on Melville Island. It was a miserable place. Tropical fevers, termites, the dreary monsoons, and hostility from the Tiwi Islanders, on whose land the colonists were trespassing, forced the British to abandon the outpost by 1829. Another attempt, Fort Wellington at nearby Raffles Bay, lasted only from 1827 to 1829.

Still fearing that the French would try to establish a colony here, the British reestablished the settlement at Port Essington in 1838. Sure enough, a few days after the Union Jack was run up the pole and the new outpost christened Victoria, after Britain's new queen, two French ships appeared on the horizon. They were the *Astrolabe* and the *Zelee,* under the command of Captain Dumont d'Urville, ostensibly on an exploratory expedition around Australia. Plagued by disease, termites, and the harsh tropical climate, Victoria fared no better than the other efforts. It was abandoned by 1849. Present-day Darwin dates from 1869. It was originally called Palmerston, but was known by sailors for the harbor on which it was sited: Port Darwin. It had been named after the celebrated naturalist who passed this way on the *Beagle* in 1839.

Soon the brawling seaport, which flourished on the back of a gold rush in the 1880s, became known around Southeast Asia as Port Darwin. It was officially renamed Darwin in 1911. The town might have taken its new name sooner, but until 1911 the administration of the Northern Territory was in the hands of prim and religious South Australians who had little regard for Charles Darwin and his evolutionary monkeys.

The town's residents had no such reservations. Certainly there was nothing particularly godly about early Darwin. Consider this description by poet and columnist Andrew Barton "Banjo" Paterson when he visited the Top End in 1898: "Palmerston on Port Darwin…is unique among Australian towns, inasmuch as it is filled with the boilings over of the great cauldron of Oriental humanity. Here comes the vagrant and shifting population of all the Eastern races…all sorts and conditions of men. Kipling tells what befell the man who 'tried to hustle the East,' but the man who tried to hustle Palmerston would get a knife in him quick and lively."

A century later Darwin is still a swirl of races and creeds, but the xenophobia and racism of Banjo Paterson's day has been replaced by a proud multiculturalism. Darwin is as much a gateway to Asia as it is a toehold on Australia's wild frontier. More than 60 nationalities can be found in this exotic city. Evenings I have spent strolling among the food stalls at Darwin's Mindil Beach markets felt as though I were in Asia rather than outback Australia. The warm tropical air is generally redolent with spices, scorched chilies, and hot cooking oil. Satay, *laksa,* and *nasi goring* are among the foods for sale. Families set up folding chairs and tables on the beach, and in a medley of Asian and European languages, chatter amongst themselves as they watch the sun sink into the Timor Sea.

Late in the spring, as thunderheads start to build ahead of the coming monsoon, the sunset markets close. The gregarious town becomes moody and introverted, battening down mental and physical hatches for the long, oppressive summer months of heat, humidity, torrential rains, and tropical cyclones. The Wet, as the monsoon season is known, can be as dreary and draining in its way as the long darkness of a Scandinavian winter. Life slows to a torpid, irascible crawl. Everything, it seems, is put on hold until after the Wet. Life in the far north is portioned into two main seasons—the Wet and the Dry. The dry season typically runs from May through October, the Australian winter, when the temperature drops into the low 80s and the skies are a taut blue for weeks at a time. Creeks dry up, savanna grasses wither, and water holes shrink to shimmering puddles of mud with cracks around the edges.

Then, through the spring months of October and November, the temperature and humidity start their inexorable rise. Over the Gulf of Carpentaria, spectacular tubular cloud formations called the "morning glory" appear at dawn. By the heat of the afternoon, all across the tropical north of the continent, towering cumulus clouds, built by thermals, are scudding across the horizon.

Hot nights pulse with distant flashes of lightning, promising but rarely delivering any stormy relief from the oppressive humidity. Occasionally, a stray bolt of lightning strikes the earth, sparking a wildfire in the tinder-dry brush that can blacken tens of thousands of acres and redden sunsets with its smoke. I have camped in the bush on such stifling nights, wondering whether the tickling I felt was ants or sweat (it was both) and watching an evil-looking fire ring a distant hillside. Locals call these relentlessly sweaty months the Build-up. A universal grumpiness seems to settle over the region. Mates snap at each other for no good reason, and police blotters fill up with cases of petty assaults and drunkenness of those who have "gone troppo." The rains usually start to fall late in December. Day after day of torrential monsoon, thunder, and purplish black skies grip the tropical northern towns with gloom. In Darwin the pace of life slows to a sullen crawl, and many of those who can afford to go elsewhere retreat to the sunny coolness of the south.

In the bush, however, the rains bring a celebration of life that would shame Hieronymus Bosch. Withered scrub is suddenly transformed into a fantasy of ferns, marsh, and riotous grasses that can grow more than 15 feet in a single month. Desert canyons sprout thundering cataracts and waterfalls. Flat, dusty plains become broad wetlands teeming with bird life. Nowhere is this miraculous transformation more spectacular than in Kakadu National Park, a World Heritage site about 80 air miles southeast of Darwin.

At nearly five million acres, Kakadu is Australia's largest national park and ranks with the Great Barrier Reef as one of the most popular. Kakadu encompasses almost the entire drainage basin of the South Alligator River and a little of every kind of habitat Australia's far north has to offer. It shelters a remarkable assemblage of flora and fauna that includes some 280 bird species, 128 species of reptiles, 64 native mammal species, 51 varieties of freshwater fish, 1,600 species of plants, and more than 4,500 species of insects.

Kakadu includes a portion of the 300 mile-long Arnem Land Escarpment and part of the Arnhem Land Plateau within its boundaries. The escarpment is a chain of sheer sandstone cliffs that rise hundreds of feet above the low, flat woodlands and form the edge of the Arnhem Land Plateau. When the monsoons arrive, typically dropping almost five feet of rain in a few torrential weeks, the waterlogged plains form vast freshwater wetlands, and the excess rainwater spills over the edge of the escarpment in a series of magnificent waterfalls. Two of the most spectacular—and frequently photographed—are Twin Falls and Jim Jim Falls. At Jim Jim the thundering water tumbles, including one sheer, heart-stopping pitch of 590 feet, more than 700 feet. Niagara Falls, by comparison, drops a paltry 167 feet.

One day, usually early in May, the rains cease; the sun breaks through the shredding clouds; and mists rise from the drenched earth. This is the start of the dry season. No more rains come. Day after day, week after week, there is nothing but faultless blue sky and dazzling sun. The waterfalls dry up; the water holes recede to little pools ringed by patches of shiny mud. By July the jungly undergrowth has withered and faded from lush arsenic green, through a suite of yellows, to brown, and finally black. Wildlife congregates around the shrinking water holes. Of these, one of the favorites among visitors to Kakadu, is Cooinda, an oasis of raucous flocks of birds, luxuriant water plants, and large crocodiles sunning themselves in the mud.

After six months of dry weather, the humidity starts to rise. Lightning dances once again on the horizon. The sun rises red from the smoke of distant bushfires. It is time for the cycle to begin anew.

Farther west, in the corner of the continent, lies an ancient, gnarled region known as the Kimberley: a place so vast and remote it is virtually a world unto itself. It is immense—about 139,000 square miles of dramatic mountain ranges, sweeping tidal flats, and a ragged, treacherous coast that has hardly changed since Dutch navigator Abel Tasman skirted it in 1644.

Despite its size—almost twice as large as Great Britain—there are only three towns of more than 2,000 people in all of the Kimberley: Derby, Kununurra, and the colorful old pearling port of Broome. The biggest of these towns, Broome, has about 9,000 inhabitants. The remainder of the Kimberley's population of 25,000 live in isolated cattle stations, mining camps, Aboriginal communities, and dusty towns scattered like a landlocked archipelago across this craggy, billion-year-old wilderness. The nearest big city, Perth, lies more than a thousand miles to the south, far beyond the implacable void of the Great Sandy Desert that makes up the Kimberley's southern flank. To the north lie the turquoise blue waters of the Timor Sea, over which Australia's first inhabitants came about 60,000 years ago. The original coastline they knew was long ago submerged by rising seas after the Ice Age, erasing forever their earliest settlements and sacred sites. But the secluded caves and rock shelters across the Kimberley hinterland are rich in vibrant rock art galleries and murals.

My first glimpse of the Kimberley came several years ago from the window of a chartered twin-engine turboprop. It was flying workers into the secluded Argyle Diamond Mine, which is nestled in the Ragged Ranges about a hundred miles south of Kununurra. It was a hot and humid morning early in March, near the end of the wet season. As we droned through the clear, blue Kimberley sky, the plane pitched and bounced in the thermals. Now the diamond miners drive to the Argyle for two-week shifts, but then this flight from Kununurra was a daily routine for them. They resolutely read their dog-eared novels, but I was glued to the spectacle spreading out beneath the little plane's wings. Recent rains had made the desert bloom. Luxuriant tropical grasses rioted where only a few weeks earlier there had been nothing but reddish blistered stone. Magnificent waterfalls tumbled over cliffs, and cataracts sparkled in far off gorges.

The sense of adventure and the romance was heightened by the knowledge that ahead, in the hazy distance, lay the world's largest diamond mine: A craggy, well-guarded hilltop where more than 38 million carats of raw diamonds are produced each year, more than one-third of the planet's entire output. Jewels from the Argyle come in a range of exotic colors: Champagne, cognac, green, blue, and, rarest of all, pinks that have fetched up to one million dollars a carat in the hushed showrooms of New York and Amsterdam. These are diamonds so remote, according to the company's marketing blurb, "that it took three billion years to find them."

Forty-five minutes after taking off from Kununurra, the little plane touched down at the mine's private airfield. The workers trundled off to their jobs, and I began a fascination with the Kimberley that has brought me back time and again.

The Kimberley contains some of Australia's most spectacular and least visited natural wonders: Roaring tidal waterfalls at Talbot Bay, fossilized remains of a huge Devonian Age coral reef, and the dramatic Wolfe Creek Meteorite Crater. Perhaps the most magnificent sight in the Kimberley is the haunting maze of tiger-striped sandstone domes known as the Bungle Bungles. Although sacred to local Aborigines for more than 20,000 years and known to a handful of Kimberley pastoralists for the past century, the ancient formations were virtually unknown to the outside world until the early 1980s. A filmmaker shooting a documentary about the splendor of the Kimberley captured some aerial footage of the Bungle Bungles glowing coppery bronze in the warmth of an afternoon. The stunning images immediately captured the public's imagination. Today, the timeless spectacle of the Bungle Bungles epitomizes the primeval power and grandeur of the Kimberley. In 1987 they were included in Purnululu National Park. Like most places in the Kimberley, much of it must be explored by four-wheel drive or seen by air.

Because of its remoteness, the Kimberley was the last region of Australia to be explored by European settlers, and until relatively recently it was still a land only for outback-hardened prospectors, pioneers, and adventurers. Mail deliveries by packhorse, the sails of the pearling luggers setting out to sea, the much anticipated steamer that came up the coast from Fremantle every few weeks—images that seem to come straight from the pages of a Joseph Conrad novel—are within the memories of people still living. Telephone service and television did not arrive in the outlying stations and communities until the 1980s. The region's main highway, which skirts its southern edge, wasn't paved until 1986. The Kimberley's earliest European history—the explorers, gold rushes, epic cattle drives—is no further removed than the parents and grandparents of families such as the Emanuels, the McDonalds, and the Duracks.

The region was named the Kimberley by the West Australian government in 1880 to honor Britain's Secretary of State for the Colonies, the first Earl of Kimberley. Its hinterland was first crossed by explorer Alexander Forrest in 1879-1880. His glowing reports of good grazing country drew a rush of cattlemen in the 1880s, some of whom drove mobs of cattle across the stony heart of the continent to stake their claims.

One of the most dramatic cattle drives in history—and, at 3,500 miles, the world's longest—was made by the McDonald family, whose descendants still own the million-acre Fossil Downs cattle station in the heart of the Kimberley. Starting near Goulburn, New South Wales, with just over 700 head of cattle, the family headed northwest in March 1883, taking three years to cross the continent.

That same year the Durack family left their homes in the Cooper Creek region of southwest Queensland bound for the Kimberley. The story of their epic two-year cattle drive and early struggles to settle along the giant Ord River and near the Bungle Bungles is chronicled in Dame Mary Durack's outback classics *Kings in Grass Castles* and *Sons in the Saddle*.

A short-lived gold rush near Halls Creek in 1885 brought a rapid influx of 10,000 prospectors and fortune seekers to the Kimberley. Most were disappointed. Faced with the harsh conditions, tropical heat, and summer monsoons, they left as rapidly as they had come, but some stayed on.

In the 1860s the discovery of rich pearling grounds off the coast of Broome had lured adventurers from all around southeast Asia. The fledgling port was gazetted as a town in 1883. Ironically, the man for whom Broome was named, West Australia Governor Sir Frederick Napier Broome, was deeply offended that his name had been given to such a rough shantytown. He was sure the settlement wouldn't last more than a few years. Few Australians today remember who or what Sir Frederick was, but almost everybody aspires to visit the famed "port of pearls" that bears his name.

Broome, in the region's far southwest, is without doubt the prettiest town in the Kimberley. Its oasis-like setting, turquoise seas, and exotic Asian atmosphere reflect its colorful past as a pearling port. From the tourist point of view, Broome is the only town in the Kimberley to have a beach rather than looking out on miles of grim-looking tidal mudflats. And what a beach. Some two miles west of the town center are the vast white sands of Cable Beach, so named because this is where an undersea telegraph cable from Java was dragged ashore in 1889. Several hundred yards wide at low tide, and stretching for more than 15 miles, Cable is often rated one of the world's most beautiful and unspoiled beaches, and the low-key luxury resort built nearby in the 1980s is frequently ranked among Australia's best.

But it was pearls, not scenery, that gave Broome its start in the 1860s. By 1900 the rich seabeds of Roebuck Bay had made Broome the world's pearling capital. It boasted a polyglot population of more than 5,000 and a fleet of some 400 pearling luggers putting out to sea. The boisterous community was a bewildering swirl of races and cultures: Japanese, Malays, Filipinos, Chinese, Indonesians, Aborigines, Indians, Melanesians, Pacific

Islanders, and an assortment of European adventurers, drifters, and rapscallions from all over the world. Pearling was a fast-money, dangerous occupation, as the crowded Japanese cemetery on the edge of town can attest. Many of the occupants were young men, killed by the bends, cyclones, or sharks.

The Great Depression and World War II—during which Broome was bombed by the Japanese—put Broome's pearling industry into a long decline. The introduction of plastic buttons during the war nearly killed it off, since there was no longer a market for the mother-of-pearl that had been the town's mainstay. A small but reliable demand for pearls kept the fading town alive until it was "discovered" in the 1980s. An Englishman, Lord McAlpine, became so enamored of Broome that he poured millions into the town and developed the prestigious Cable Beach Resort.

His lordship later fell onto financial hard times, but Broome's nascent tourist industry prospered on his investments and today is one of Australia's most cherished and romantic destinations. Visitors range from backpack travelers and drifters to well-heeled tourists who apparently can afford the five- and six-figure price tags on the fine pearl jewelry offered by the cluster of boutiques in town.

Yet for all Broome's big-money resort development, its streets shaded by mango and palm trees, the slow pace of life locals call "Broome time," and quaint institutions such as the Sun Picture Gardens exert a lazy, tropical charm. Billed as the world's oldest open-air movie theater, the Sun is little changed since it opened in 1916. Patrons sit in canvas sling chairs under a wooden shelter and watch an outdoor screen framed by palm fronds. I watched W. C. Fields and Mae West in *My Little Chickadee* there a few years ago, munching popcorn and watching fruit bats chase night insects across the screen.

A hundred miles farther north is Derby, a remote town of about 3,000 perched on the edge of a vast sprawl of mudflats in King Sound. Despite its lonely, almost apocalyptic setting, when the town was declared in 1883, Derby entertained lofty ambitions as a commercial center for the pastoralists of the West Kimberley. It was named for then Secretary of State for the Colonies, the 15th Earl of Derby. A jetty was built in 1885, and thousands of prospectors passed through here on their way to the Halls Creek goldfields about 300 miles inland.

Treacherous and powerful tidal currents at the entrance to the sound made Derby a difficult and dangerous port, and a phenomenal 36-foot tidal range in the harbor left ships sitting on the mud at low tide. Today cargoes are loaded onto shallow-draft barges and relayed to bulk carriers anchored in deep water well offshore, and Derby is better known as an airfreight and communications center for the West Kimberley.

Derby was the northern terminus for Australia's first airmail service, which began flying between Geraldton and the isolated Kimberley seaport in 1921. Later Derby became a base for the Royal Flying Doctor Service, and its hospital is the biggest and best equipped in the Kimberley. For many visitors, however, the town is best known as a terminus of the Gibb River Road, famed as one of the most dramatic four-wheel driving adventures in Australia. A dubious shortcut, about 150 miles shorter than the paved highway, the Gibb River Road stretches from Derby nearly 450 miles through the heart of the Kimberley to the old port of Wyndham.

The route crosses the dramatic King Leopold Range and skirts some of Australia's most remote national parks. The highway was begun in the 1960s to help isolated cattle stations bring their livestock to market. Locals still refer to it as the Beef Road, and travelers along it are warned to be careful of the huge triple-rigged road trains that rumble along in a shower of gravel and bull dust.

For tourists venturing along it in the dry season, the Gibb is the road back through time to a fossilized coral reef that once would probably have rivaled today's Great Barrier Reef. At Windjana Gorge, about 80 miles east of Derby, the Lennard River cuts a narrow three-mile path through this ancient limestone complex, lush with palms, rife with freshwater crocodiles, and noisy with a wide variety of birds.

In the 1890s this lost world was the hideout of Jandamarra, a famously elusive Aborigine guerrilla fighter who conducted a spirited campaign to stave off white occupation of the Kimberley. Known to the settlers as Pigeon, he tried to organize local Aboriginal groups to march on Derby and drive the whites out of the Kimberley. Jandamarra was eventually tracked down and killed

near Tunnel Creek Gorge in 1897, but Aboriginal resistance to the takeover of their lands continued long after his death. As late as the 1930s Aborigines occasionally speared unwary travelers in the Kimberley.

Not all Kimberley Aborigines were hostile to the pioneers, however. Many offered their remarkable bush skills to the newcomers, and although they had never raised cattle before, Aborigines quickly became known as some of the finest riders and wranglers on the range. Indeed, many early pioneers owed their success to the hard work of Aborigines.

About a third of the way along the Gibb River Road is a turn-off for an isolated mission at Kalumburu, on the ragged northern edge of the Kimberley coast. The mission is about 165 miles north along a rough bush track made impassable much of the year by heavy monsoon rains.

This wild, northern fringe of Australia contains some of the Kimberley's most magnificent scenery: Gorges thick with ancient fan palms and rare species of plants found nowhere else, giant cascades that form Mitchell Falls, and the hidden splendor of 4,000-square-mile Drysdale River National Park. This pristine wilderness is possibly Australia's most remote national park, an untouched wonderland of swamps, ranges, and pockets of rain forest that are accessible only by helicopter or by canoe down the wild Drysdale River. A scientific expedition to this hidden corner of the Kimberley in 1975 turned up dozens of new species of plants.

The Gibb River Road joins the main highway near Wyndham, an isolated cattle-shipping port of 700 at the mouth of the King River. "The thermometers, and the mosquitoes are three feet high," wrote travel writer Ernestine Hill when she passed through here in the 1930s. Nestled at the foot of Mount Bastion, Wyndham is the most hauntingly remote settlement I have ever seen. Forbidding hills behind the town seem to shoulder out the rest of the world. The view from Five Rivers Lookout, at the top of the mountain, however, is as breathtaking as it is timeless: A shimmering expanse of crocodile-infested tidal flats where five of the biggest rivers in the Kimberley—the Ord, Pentecost, Durack, Forrest, and King—sluggishly meet the Cambridge Gulf.

For most of the past century Wyndham's main industry was the meat works, where Kimberley cattle were slaughtered before export. Until it closed in 1985, this frontier abattoir offered the few sightseers that came up this way one of the Kimberley's most gruesome spectacles: The snouts of scores of giant saltwater crocodiles waiting expectantly in the marshes near the outflow of the blood drain. The closure of the meat works hit the town—and, presumably, its population of crocodiles—hard, but in the past few years its fortunes have picked up. Today Wyndham is an export center for the Kimberley's live-cattle trade with Asia and the Middle East. It is also a shipping port for the burgeoning sugar industry and market gardens in the giant Ord River Irrigation Scheme that is centered around the town of Kununurra, some 50 miles east. The site of the old meat works is now a successful crocodile farm.

Kununurra is by far the youngest town in the Kimberley, laid out in 1961 as part of an ambitious plan to create fertile farmland from remote tropical scrub. For the better part of a century the West Australian government had been trying to figure out what to do with its grand northwest frontier.

Despite its year-round warmth, sunshine, and vast tracts of rich clay soil, the Kimberley's savagely lopsided climate of torrential monsoon rains followed by months of earth-cracking drought had defeated every attempt to grow crops. During the wet season the Ord River is Australia's most powerful flow of water, roaring down the flanks of the Durack Range and uselessly dumping more than 13 million gallons of water each second into the Cambridge Gulf. Why not dam the Ord? If the water could be rationed throughout the year, it was reasoned, the river's broad floodplain could be turned into an irrigated garden. Experimental farms during the 1930s and 1940s successfully grew cotton, sorghum, maize, rice, sugar, and linseed along the Ord.

In 1958 the Ord River project was born. Millions of dollars were poured into dams, irrigation systems, and the building of the township of Kununurra. A small diversionary dam got the project under way, and by 1966 there were 31 farms along the Ord River.

In 1972 the centerpiece of the project, the huge Ord River Dam, was completed, inundating an 18,000-year-old Aboriginal campsite as well as the pioneering Argyle Downs Station. In their place was the giant 380-square-mile Lake Argyle; a small inland sea that holds more than 18 times the volume of Sydney Harbour. An impressive feat of remote-area engineering, the Ord River project was also for many years Australia's most expensive white elephant. Nothing seemed to go right. Crop prices were unexpectedly low, and costs were unexpectedly high. Silt problems threatened to clog the dam. Caterpillars ate the cotton crops, while thousands of magpie geese flocked to the area to feast at the fledgling rice fields. Many farmers sold out and quit.

But those who managed to stay are today reaping the rewards. The Ord River's nearly 35,000 acres of irrigated farmland produce rich crops of peanuts, mangoes, melons, cucumbers, bananas, sunflowers, and sorghum. In 1996 Australia's first new sugar mill in almost 70 years was built near Kununurra to handle the Kimberley's burgeoning sugar industry. Kelly's Knob, a rocky promontory that towers over Kununurra, looks over a microcosm of what the early settlers hoped outback Australia would be like—lush green cane fields, orchards, and the blue waters of Lake Argyle in the distance.

The reality, however, lies beyond these surveyed and irrigated edges—in the harsh and dusty immensity of earth and sky.

Following pages: *A massive boab tree braces against the might of the Fitzroy River in full flood. Close relative of African and Madagascan baobabs, boabs are largely confined to Australia's northwest coast.*

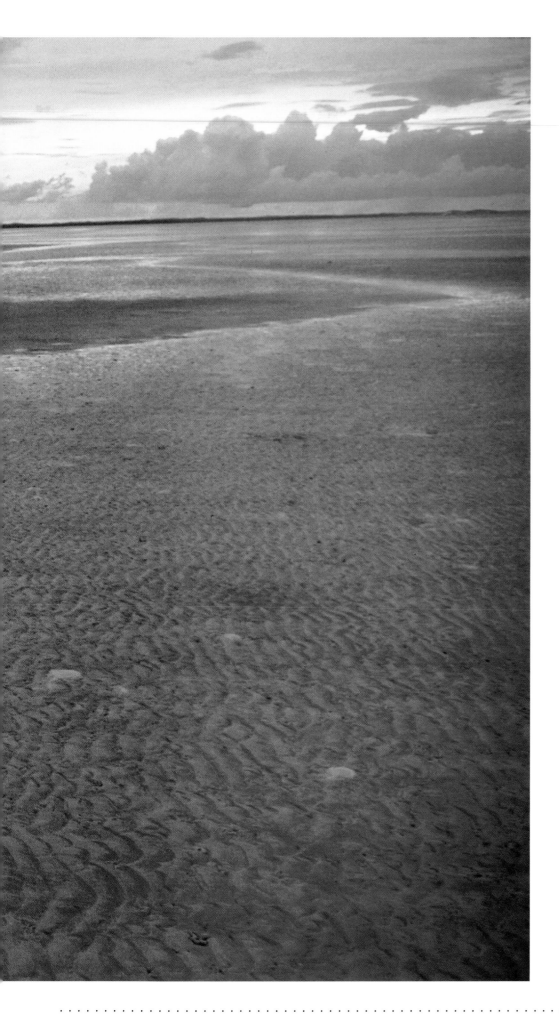

Largest and most feared of all Australian creatures, a saltwater crocodile warms itself in the shallows of Cape York Peninsula's Shelburne Bay. "Salties," as these reptiles are called, can grow to more than 20 feet in length and can weigh well over a ton. Occasionally, they make a meal of an unwary human.

In the Jardine River of Cape York a
saltie swims beneath water lily pads.
An estimated 150,000 of these
reptiles once lurked in the mangrove
swamps and rivers of northern
Australia, but hunting beginning in
the 1940s whittled that number.
Today, salties are protected, and
their numbers are on the rise.
An estimated 65,000 survive in the
Northern Territory.

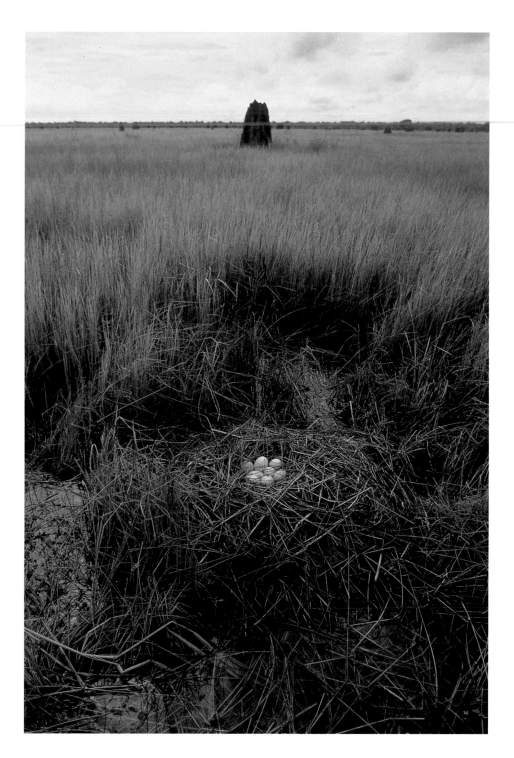

Vast and remote, the marshes of Cape York's Lakefield National Park conceal their own lost worlds. A termite mound rises from grassland that shelters a nest of magpie goose eggs. Scores of bird species call the park home. From April to November, after wet-season flooding, swamps and water holes that cover the lowlands shelter thousands of migratory birds.

Following pages: *Like weather-worn tombstones, termite mounds pock charred earth of the Cape York Peninsula. Both fire and termites play life-giving roles in the area's ecology. Termites break down dead wood and grasses, while intense dry-season fires release nutrients. Monsoon rains will redraft the scene, creating a tropical fantasia.*

Red-winged parrot perches on rain-battered spear grass stalks in the savanna near Nhulunbuy, a remote community in the ancient Aboriginal homeland known as Arnhem Land. A product of the wet season, spear grass can grow as much as 15 feet a month, but as the monsoons gather tempo, the grasses are slowly beaten down into a watery mat. Aborigines called these fiercest torrents bang-gereng—the knock'em down rains.

Following pages: Spiky barricade against the outside world, a dead mangrove on a lonely beach in the Northern Territory evokes the harshness of Australia's forbidding northern coast. Battered by tropical cyclones, washed by treacherous tides, steamed in tropical heat, and haunted by crocodiles, this ragged coast remains a wild frontier 60,000 years after the first Aborigines stepped ashore here.

by Frank Brennan, S.J.

The Aboriginal Struggle for Land, Life, and Culture

For decades European explorers had sailed past the coastline of the Great South Land. Meanwhile, Macassan sailors from the Indonesian archipelago made frequent visits to the northern shores of Australia, meeting and trading with the Aborigines. In 1770 Captain James Cook sailed up the east coast of Australia. He then went ashore on a small island in the Torres Strait, north of Cape York. In the name of His Majesty, the British King, he claimed possession of the continent he had sailed past and named the island Possession Island. In 1788 Captain Arthur Phillip established a penal colony at Sydney Cove, asserting British sovereignty over the east of the Australian continent. It could then be lawfully settled in the name of King George III.

The Aborigines were treated as if they had no rights to their traditional lands—lands that they had occupied and used for tens of thousands of years for hunting, camping, and ceremony. To European eyes, the Aborigines were nomadic hunters and gatherers who had no regard for the biblical injunction to fill the Earth and subdue it. They were not seen as owners of the land. Even Europeans who had some concern for the well-being of the Aborigines presumed that they could be moved from their traditional lands close to settlements. The Aborigines, settlers assumed, could hunt and camp just as happily on other land not required for European development.

The Aborigines enjoyed tens of thousands of years in splendid isolation and were spared foreign aggression until 1788. The continent held plenty of room and food for everyone. The Aboriginal population was probably fewer than one million spread throughout the entire continent. The Aborigines did not see themselves as one united people. Without a common foe there was no need for that. They had time to develop hundreds of languages and elaborate religious beliefs about their origins and relationships. Land was central to any group's identity and religious beliefs. The members of an Aboriginal group saw themselves as belonging to their land. While Europeans considered themselves the future owners of the land, Aborigines saw themselves as being owned by the land. Distinctive landforms were the story book of the activities of ancestral beings of the Dreamtime—the eternally present past. To the Aborigines dispossession meant much more than the loss of real estate. It meant the loss of their whole world of meaning.

As the frontier of European settlement expanded, the Aborigines were dispossessed of their traditional country. They often suffered the devastating effects of first contact, including smallpox and murder. Eventually, the British claimed sovereignty over the entire Australian continent, establishing six colonies. In London, the Secretary of State for Colonies issued periodic instructions urging the colonists to respect the Aborigines' rights to continuing use and occupation of their hunting and camping grounds. But the colonists' greed and convenience always took precedence over the claims of the Aborigines.

Colonial expansion continued into the remotest regions of the continent. The settlers claimed that they were simply occupying land that was *terra nullius,* land belonging to nobody. The local colonial authorities, who were a world away from their masters in London, permitted settlers to take over vast tracts of land for farming and grazing. The colonies were moving toward self-government, and the new landholders were most unsympathetic to any directives from Sydney or London that urged them to accommodate the Aborigines. They were a threat to the sheep, cattle, and families of the settlers. The lands being claimed for sheep runs were vast areas in the style of American ranches. Land grants half the size of Wales were incomprehensible to civil servants sitting at their desks in London. They had, however, humanitarian concern for the well-being of the natives. Secretary of State Henry Grey, the third Earl Grey, wrote to the Governor of New South Wales in 1848:

It should be generally understood that Leases granted for this purpose give the grantees only an exclusive right of pasturage for their cattle, and of cultivating such Land as they may require within the large limits thus assigned to them, but that these Leases are not intended to deprive the Natives of their former right to hunt over these Districts, or to wander over them in search of subsistence, in the manner to which they have been heretofore accustomed, from the spontaneous produce of the soil except over land actually cultivated or fenced in for that purpose.

On the frontier massacres occurred, and the dispossession continued. While many coastal areas were settled by the newcomers, especially in the south, where the weather was more appealing to Europeans, the remoter regions and the northern areas remained untouched by them for another hundred years. The hot climate and the unproductive soil provided the Aborigines in these parts with a shield from the colonizers. Australia's other indigenous people, the Torres Strait Islanders, did not experience European settlement until the arrival of the London Missionary Society in the 1870s, the islands having been included in the colony of Queensland in 1869. On the mainland a few Aboriginal tribes were spared any sustained European contact until well into this century. The Yolngu people in Arnhem Land had their first contact with the arrival of Methodist missionaries in 1935. No matter how late the contact came, however, the indigenous people of Australia were treated as if they had no rights to their land.

In 1901 the six colonies formed a federation, the Commonwealth of Australia. A constitution listed the powers of the Commonwealth Parliament, the equivalent of the U.S. Congress, leaving all other legislative powers to the states. The Commonwealth Parliament did not have power to make laws with respect to Aborigines. The states maintained sole power in relation to Aborigines. Land issues were also the exclusive concern of the states. There was no equivalent provision to one in the United States Constitution that empowers Congress to regulate commerce with Indian tribes. There were no treaties with the Aborigines. Though reserves of public land were set aside for Aborigines, these reserves were governed by state authorities. The reserves were public land that could be dedicated to other purposes by state governments without compensating or consulting with the Aborigines. And they could be moved to other places at the state's convenience.

It was not until the 1960s that Aborigines and their supporters were heard on the streets and on the airwaves campaigning for civil rights and land rights. Much of the attention focused on the Northern Territory. Unlike the states of Australia, the territory was under federal control. Much of it was still inhabited only by Aborigines. In 1963 the Yolngu people of Arnhem Land, who had tolerated the presence of a few Methodist missionaries for some 30 years, were informed that the national government was going to allow a Swiss consortium to mine bauxite on their traditional lands. The Aborigines objected strongly, and, with assistance from the missionaries, drafted petitions to the Commonwealth Parliament. The Yolngu demanded that they be consulted and that no arrangements be made with any company that would destroy their livelihood and independence. Their pleas fell on deaf ears, and they decided to claim their land rights in court.

The social policies affecting Aborigines were starting to change. There had been many state-implemented race-based laws and policies that treated Aborigines differently from other people. Aborigines had been banned from consuming alcohol. They had been paid low wages on cattle stations. Aborigines under the age of 21 had been automatically treated as wards of the state. Children, especially those of mixed descent, were often separated from their parents and brought up in institutions run by government or churches. These children became known as the "stolen generations." Some of these policies were benignly administered in a protective way, but often they were racist. When Aborigines pushed their claim for equal wages on cattle stations, the European owners warned that equal wages would mean fewer jobs for Aborigines. The cattle station owners were not prepared to allow Aboriginal families to stay on the stations unless family members were employed. So the benign policy of equal wages resulted in even more Aborigines having to leave their traditional country. Dispossession and dislocation continued.

In 1967 the Australian people voted overwhelmingly to amend the constitution so that the Commonwealth Parliament would have power to make laws with respect to Aborigines throughout the nation and not only in Commonwealth territories. The issue of Aboriginal rights was no longer just a domestic issue of concern only to state governments. It was now a national issue, with international ramifications. The national government, however, suspecting that Aboriginal claims to land were Communist inspired, proceeded very cautiously. The government would not even grant the Aborigines a lease over eight square miles of their traditional country at Lord Vestey's Wave Hill Station lest this be a precedent for other claims and encourage the Aborigines to set up permanent facilities on the land.

In 1971 the Yolngu people from Arnhem Land who had opposed bauxite mining lost their land-rights claim in the Northern Territory court. The judge decided that British common law did not recognize any communal interests in land and that any Aboriginal rights to land would have been extinguished by the assertion of sovereignty by the British authorities at the time of their arrival and settlement.

During the election year of 1972 Aborigines set up a tent embassy outside Parliament House in Canberra. The Australian Labor Party's Gough Whitlam, Leader of the Opposition, pledged his party to granting land rights if elected. After the election the Whitlam government held an inquiry into Aboriginal land rights and drafted a federal law for the Northern Territory. This government, which lasted only three years, also passed through Parliament the Racial Discrimination Act. That act banned state governments and parliaments from acting in a racially discriminatory way. This new law was to become the Aboriginal bill of rights because it would strike down any law or policy of state governments that singled out Aborigines for special treatment without their consent. This would mean an end to the old laws and policies that discriminated against Aborigines. Aborigines could now go to court when they could not win popular support for their rights from politicians. In 1977 the Northern Territory's land-rights law went into effect, and some states also passed laws allowing the governments to grant land title to Aboriginal communities. The states of Queensland and Western Australia, covering the northern parts of Australia, were very slow to respond.

Queensland was host for the Commonwealth Games in 1982. These games are a mini-Olympics in which countries from the British Commonwealth of Nations compete. The international spotlight turned on Queensland's treatment of indigenous people when Eddie Mabo, a Torres Strait Islander, sued the state of Queensland in the High Court of Australia, claiming land rights on his traditional island of Mer. This was the first time Australia's highest court had been asked to consider whether indigenous people had any surviving rights to land that was theirs at the time of colonization. The Queensland government attempted to short circuit the court proceedings by passing a law through the Queensland parliament. That law declared retrospectively that any native title rights had been extinguished without compensation in 1879 when the Torres Strait islands were made part of Queensland. The High Court struck down this state law because it was inconsistent with the Racial Discrimination Act.

In 1988 Australia celebrated its bicentennial. But the political question was: the bicentennial of what? The foundation of the nation did not occur in 1788; that did not take place until 1901. It was not the date of British sovereignty over the whole continent, but only over the eastern half. Aborigines said 1988 was the bicentennial of the commencement of their dispossession. Aboriginal claims for land rights and self-determination were heard more loudly and more clearly by Australians during this year of celebration. Indeed, it became a year of soul-searching about national identity.

In 1992 Eddie Mabo and his fellow Torres Strait Islanders won their claim for land rights in the High Court. It ruled that Australian common law recognized the native title of indigenous people. The native title rights survived until they were taken away by government's granting the land to someone else. But the government would have to respect Aboriginal land rights in the same way as any other land owner's rights.

The Mabo decision gave Aborigines real bargaining power in the political process. Thirty-six percent of the Australian landmass was still "vacant crown land" or "Aboriginal reserve" where native title could still exist. If mining companies wanted access to that land for exploration or development, they had to act in a non-discriminatory way toward any native title holders. But there was no register of native title holders. The miners did not know with whom to deal, and they thought it unfair that they bear the cost of ascertaining the identity and claims of native title holders. The Australian government and key Aboriginal leaders negotiated a solution that was then made law: All actions taken on land since the Racial Discrimination Act would be valid only if compensation was paid when there had been interference with native title rights. If mining companies in future wanted access to land subject to native title claim, they would need to negotiate with the claimant.

One matter remained unresolved: Could native title survive in some form on cattle stations when a "pastoral lease" had been granted with the understanding that Aborigines would have access to the land for hunting, fishing, camping, and ceremony? A pastoral lease was a special title over a vast area of land that permitted the grazing of cattle but did not grant ownership of the land. In 1996 the High Court ruled in favor of the Wik peoples from Cape York. The Wik claimed ongoing native title rights on land that had been subject to pastoral lease. The mining industry was perturbed because pastoral leases cover another 42 percent of the continent. The effect of the decision was that future mining activity on 78 percent of the continent (the 42 percent pastoral lease land and 36 percent vacant crown land or Aboriginal reserve) could not proceed unless there was first an assessment made of native title.

The 1993 Native Title Act set up the machinery for dealing with native title. It was proposed by Paul Keating, who, as prime minister, placed great emphasis on including Aborigines in the consultations. Keating appreciated the need for the country to reach a just and lasting agreement with the indigenous leadership after two centuries of terra nullius. The Keating government readily acknowledged that most Aborigines could never establish a native title claim because they had been dispossessed of their land or lost all contact and association with the land. A land fund administered by indigenous Australians to allow the purchase of land on the open market was set up as some compensation for all that had been lost.

In 1998 the government had to deal with the effects of the High Court's Wik decision. Prime Minister John Howard proposed changes to the Native Title Act that wound back the gains that Aborigines had made under Paul Keating's laws. The Howard government was sympathetic to business interests, having thought that the previous Keating government and the High Court had gone too far in accommodating Aboriginal claims. The Howard government thought that too much Aboriginal policy had been moved on to the national stage and should be returned to the states. The Native Title Act has now been amended so that states can set up their own tribunals for the determination of native title claims. States can also reduce the Aboriginal right to negotiate with mining companies on pastoral leases. The changes made by the Howard government did not have the support of the indigenous leaders.

The Aboriginal campaign for rights, recognition, and reconciliation has broadened beyond the issues of land rights. The topic of land rights is not just about the preservation of culture and identity: It is also about political and economic power in Australian society. Many Aborigines want to manage their own affairs on their traditional lands in the way that the Indian tribes do on their reservations in the United States. There it is readily accepted that tribes will maintain some jurisdiction over law and order on tribal land and some economic advantages such as the power to run casinos or to conduct mining. Many Australians, however, still think that equality demands that Aborigines be subject to the same law on their land as any other Australians.

Aborigines want the Australian Parliament to apologize for past government policies that separated so many Aboriginal children from their families and their lands. While Aborigines over the last 30 years have won the battle against adverse legal discrimination, they have not yet won the hearts and minds of other Australians about their entitlements to special recognition as the indigenous people of the continent. Though there is now broad support for giving Aborigines some favorable mention in the constitution, there is no agreement about the constitutional recognition of indigenous rights. During the 1988 bicentennial, the Aborigines issued the Barunga Statement. It now hangs in the parliament building in Canberra. They called on the Commonwealth Parliament "to negotiate with us a Treaty or Compact recognising our prior ownership, continued occupation and sovereignty and affirming our human rights and freedoms." When the eyes of the world turn to Sydney during the Olympic Games in the year 2000, that treaty will still be only a dream. All social indicators will still place Aborigines on the bottom of the social ladder. Many of them will still be fringe-dwellers in the Great South Land that has been their country for tens of thousands of years.

Australians are still undecided about the terms of recognition and equality for Aborigines who have maintained connection with their traditional lands and culture despite two centuries of dispossession and assimilation. In 1996, marking the 20th anniversary of Australia's recognition of his people's land rights, Mr. Galarrwuy Yunupingu, Chairman of the Northern Land Council in the Northern Territory, said to his people: "This land is something that is always yours; it doesn't matter what nature or politics do to change it. We believe the land is all life. So it comes to us that we are part of the land and the land is part of us."

The Aboriginal struggle to put right the wrongs of the past continues.

Sanctified by pungent fumes from the smoldering leaves of a conkerberry bush, a newborn named Veronica receives a traditional Aboriginal baptism as her grandmother, Rita Sturt, passes her over a ritual fire. The smoke is believed to clear an infant's chest and head and launch the baby into a healthy life.

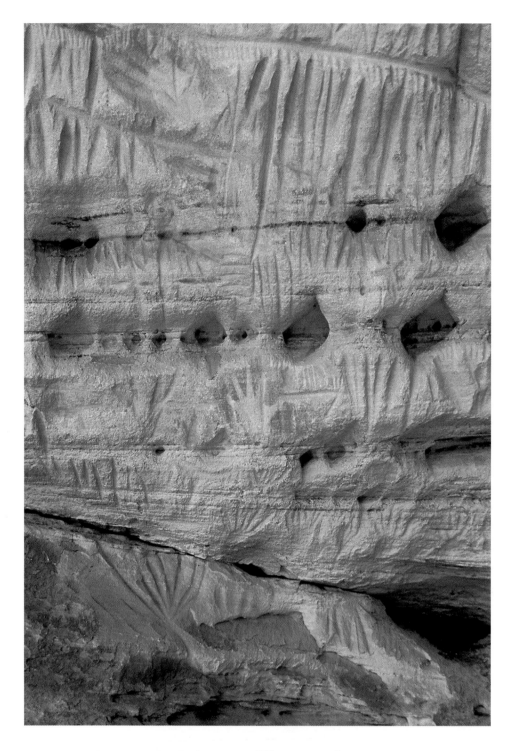

*Handprints on a cliff near Wynd-
ham evoke the 2,000 generations of
Aborigines who dwelled in the Kimberley's labyrinthine canyons and
gorges. Stencils were made by spray-
ing a mouthful of pigment over the
artist's hand. Millennia of spear
sharpening left gouges and grooves
in the sandstone. Thousands of such
rock art galleries lie scattered
throughout the far north.*

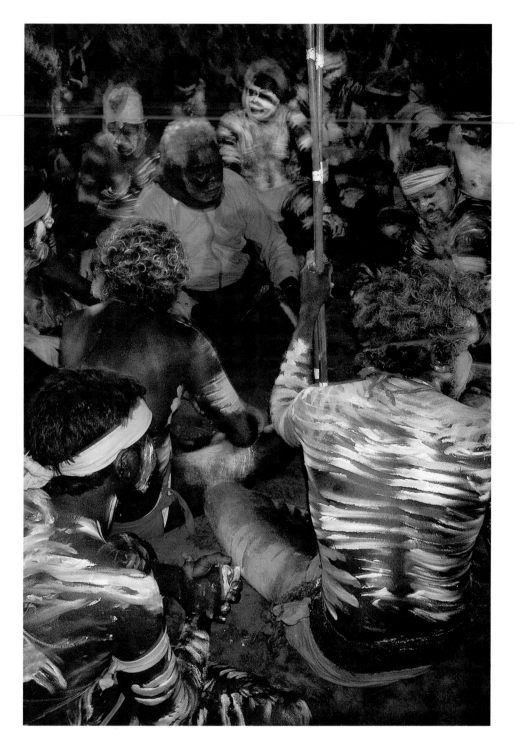

*Aboriginal dancers daubed with clay
and ocher prepare for a tribal
corroboree, or ceremonial dance,
near Derby in the Kimberley. The
139,000-square-mile wilderness of
ancient gorges and mountain ranges
in Western Australia's remote northwest frontier remains a stronghold of
Aboriginal culture and rock art.*

Bogged in beach sand, stranded travelers on Queensland's Cape York Peninsula signal a passing light plane. The pilot radioed for help, and rescuers from a nearby Aboriginal community winched the truck out before high tide swamped it. Monsoons, crocodiles, and incredible isolation can make travel in Australia's far north an exhilarating adventure—or a trap for the unwary.

Following pages: Master of a *610,000-acre cattle station on the Cape York Peninsula of Queensland, John Fraser poses with his son and grandchildren in front of their homestead. In addition to running 4,000 cattle, Fraser guides hunts for feral bulls and wild pigs. The horns of a rogue bull and trophy tusks line the hood of his battered Land Rover.*

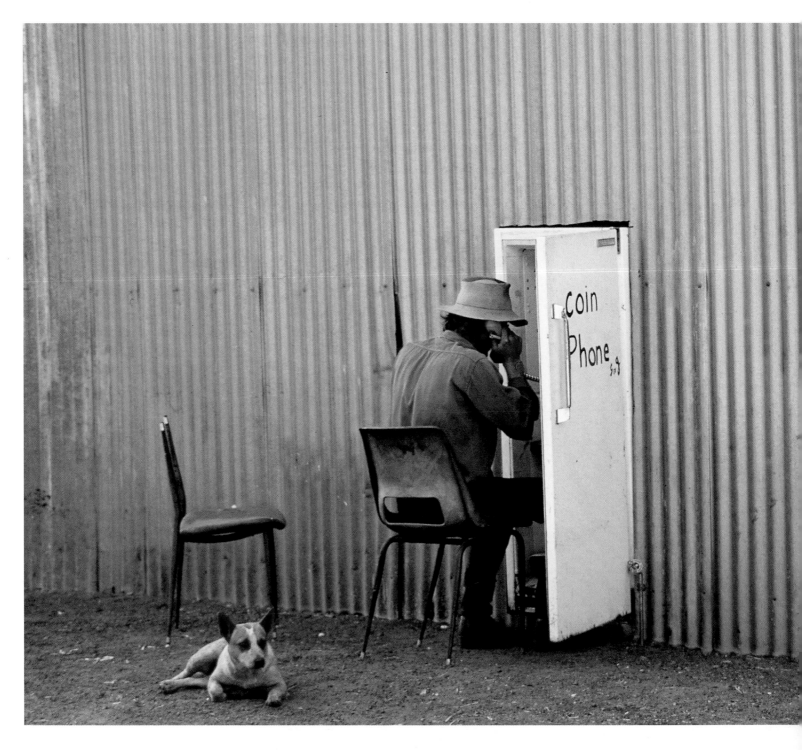

Offbeat humor pervades the outback, where many conveniences must be built by hand. Jackaroos at Drysdale River Station joke that they have to keep the telephone in the fridge so that it doesn't melt. Phones replaced static-filled radio chat sessions in the Kimberley only about 20 years ago.

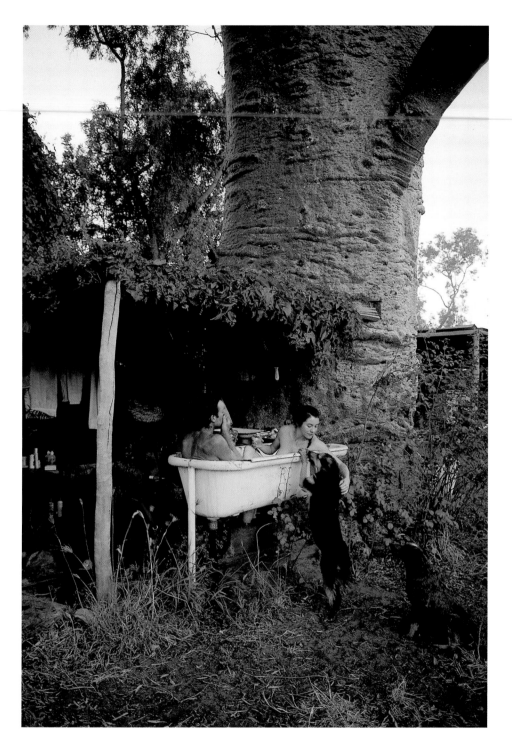

Isolation and rugged individualism have bred a unique and whimsical inventiveness in the Australian bush. At Ellenbrae Station, in the heart of the Kimberley, New Age residents built an outdoor tub and plumbing into the massive trunk of an old boab tree. In fact, the boab remains a traditional source of water in the Kimberley bush.

Following pages: *John Koeyers and his children unwind in the homesteader's Drysdale River Station auto-repair shop and playroom— his garage. Drysdale's isolation, more than 200 air miles from the nearest town, means that the children receive their education through the School of the Air, with lessons beamed daily by radio from Derby.*

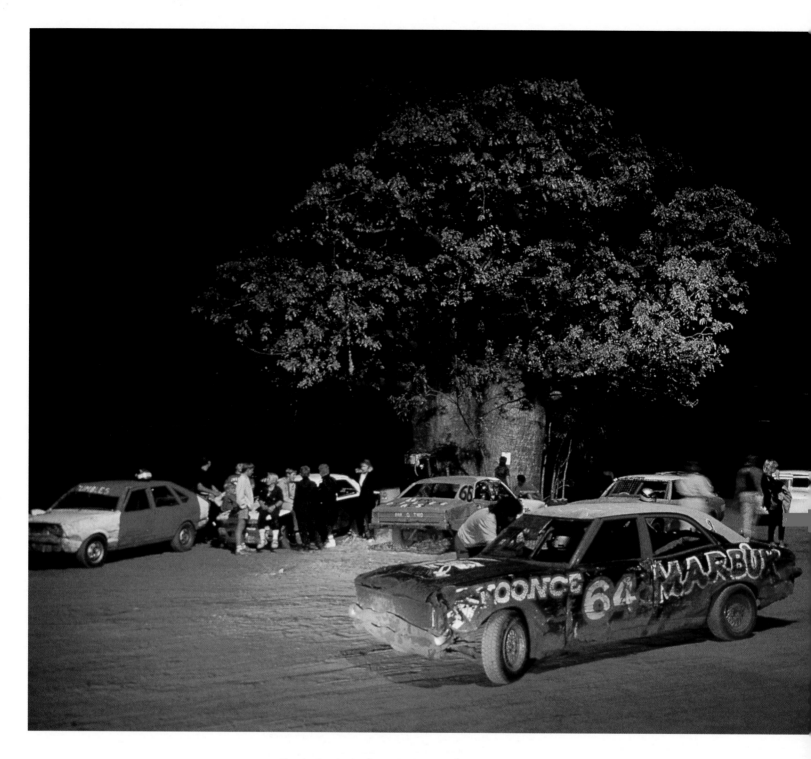

Contestants and spectactors gather
around a massive boab tree at a
demolition derby in the Western
Australia town of Derby. The competition forms part of the Boab Annual
Festival, which runs for two weeks
each July in the town on the west
Kimberley coast.

Weary but watchful, a jockey at a race in Broome cradles his saddle as he studies the proceedings. Race meetings take place each June and July in the old pearling port on the Indian Ocean.

Ready to ride, an Aboriginal stock-man awaits his turn during a Kim-berley Championship Rodeo. Already masters of outback bush craft, by the turn of the century Aborigines had earned renown as the finest riders and wranglers on the range despite never having seen horses or cattle until the arrival of Europeans.

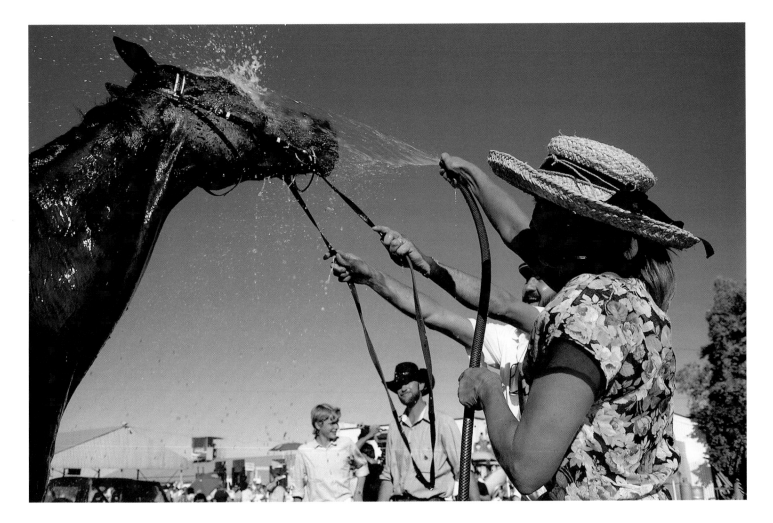

Cooling water eases the heat at an
annual race meeting in Broome.
Tourism based on its beaches grows
in the rambunctious old pearling
port, but its brawling saloons and
hard-drinking stockmen keep a
frontier flavor alive.

Beef for the "barbie" fills a truck bed at a cattle station near Halls Creek in the Kimberley. Served outback style—in huge blood red chunks— the beef will feed the crew during the annual roundup. Stations in the Kimberley average more than half a million wild acres. Helicopters often drive cattle into pens for shipment to market.

Following pages: *Largest diamond producer in the world, the secluded Argyle Diamond Mine glows pink in a Kimberley sunset. Each year some 38 million carats of raw diamonds— more than one third of the world's total production—come from this well-guarded pit in the Ragged Ranges. The world's sole reliable source of intense pink diamonds, the Argyle produces only a handful of the ultrarare stones each year.*

CHAPTER TWO

The Outback

Explorer Charles Sturt headed into the burning deserts in South Australia in 1830, optimistically towing a boat behind him. Sturt and his party had ventured into the outback to answer once and for all one of the Victorian era's burning geographical questions: Does Australia have an inland sea? Visions of water and fertile plains in the heart of their country had been tugging at Australian imaginations since the first explorers crossed the Blue Mountains, 75 miles west of Sydney, in 1813.

Sturt's trek was a journey into hell. For months he and his men were tormented by thirst, flies, dust, and temperatures that soared to more than 150 degrees before winter rains finally came and offered some relief. Sturt was eventually forced back, his sadly useless boat abandoned like a forlorn hope.

Determined to succeed, Sturt mounted another expedition in 1844. A young John MacDouall Stuart went along on that expedition. It taught him a lot about travel in the harsh outback and fired his own enthusiasm to find the elusive watery heartland. Fifteen years later, on a desolate hill in what he believed to be the exact center of the continent, he laconically noted in his journal:

Took Kekwick and the flag, and went to the top of the mount, but found it to be much higher and more difficult of ascent than I anticipated. After a deal of labour, slips and knocks, we at last arrived on the top.... Built a large cone of stones, in the centre of which I placed a pole with the British flag nailed to it. Near the top of the cone I placed a small bottle, in which there is a slip of paper, with our signatures to it, stating by whom

it was raised. We then gave three hearty cheers for the flag, the emblem of civil and religious liberty, and may it be a sign to the natives that the dawn of liberty, civilisation and Christianity is about to break upon them. We can see no water from the top.

Imagine that lonely scene. Two sunburned explorers on a stony hilltop surrounded by a dusty immensity of earth and sky that seemed to stretch for more than a thousand miles in every direction, their dry-throated hurrahs swallowed up in the profound outback stillness.

The truth was slowly dawning. Stuart had named the stony hilltop Central Mount Sturt, after his mentor, during an expedition in 1860. In 1861 he returned. This time he pressed on toward the top end of the continent. Instead of an inland sea and a fertile heartland, there was only outback: Arid plains dotted with spinifex, vast stretches of burning sand dunes, and miles upon miles of dazzling salt flats.

Stuart crossed the continent successfully, but he returned in 1862 a broken man. His body was wracked with scurvy, and he was nearly blind from months of glare, flies, and dust. His health irretrievably ruined, he returned to London and died three years later.

Today the hilltop on which Stuart and Kekwick hoisted the Union Jack has been renamed Central Mount Stuart in honor of his accomplishments. It lies just off the lonely Stuart Highway, Australia's main outback route, which crosses the continent in the explorer's footsteps. Stuart was a tad off the mark, though, in his reckoning when he placed his hilltop in the center of Australia; today's navigational aids put the geographical center of the continent about 250 miles south, close to Alice Springs. With the exception of the long strip of asphalt stretching from horizon to horizon, little has changed out here since Stuart's time.

A couple of years ago I bicycled 600 miles of the lonely Stuart Highway, from Tennant Creek north to Darwin. I used to think of the great South Australian explorer as I set up my little camps in the fragrant bush beneath the blaze of outback stars. Although I was on a bicycle and had the happy advantage of covering a hundred miles a day on a mapped highway, our days had a lot in common. Like the early explorers I had to rise before dawn to take advantage of the relative morning cool, then find a patch of shade by ten o'clock to escape the outback's blinding midday heat, dozing away the motionless hours while flies hummed overhead. And in the evenings, as I watched a blood red sun sink into the timeless scrub, I rationed out my stale warm water for the next day's ride and longed for a cool drink. Obviously I had it a lot easier than Stuart and his colleagues: At least I knew where I was and what lay ahead. But even with the benefit of road maps, satellite photos, and views from the windows of a plane passing over the continent at 37,000 feet, the sheer size, harshness, and emptiness of outback Australia is hard to comprehend.

How big is it? Well, I estimate that the outback covers more than 70 percent of the continent, an area of more than two million square miles. But numbers hardly do it justice. Put it another way: You could lose Texas out there with barely a ripple. Western Australia alone is about the size of India. Outback doctors and priests and magistrates get about in light aircraft, and their "local" territories may be larger than the whole of the United Kingdom. Ranchers measure their properties— they call them stations—by the square mile, or even by the hundreds of square miles. The world's biggest cattle station is in South Australia: Anna Creek, all 7 million plus acres of it, or about 12,000 square miles, perched on the edge of the vast Simpson Desert. Anna Creek is run by the Kidman family, one of Australia's oldest grazing

dynasties. The Kidmans lease several other multi-million-acre spreads in the area for a total of about 45,000 square miles. For sheer size that is like owning Pennsylvania. It makes the Kidmans *one* of outback Australia's biggest landowners.

Children growing up on these lonely stations attend school by radio, since the nearest town may be several hours drive away. And they grow up fast. I've ridden down a rough track on a sheep station in central Queensland in a Land Cruiser steered by a three-year-old girl who was sitting on her father's lap, getting practice. And she was a good, assertive driver, too. "You never know, out here, one of us adults might be injured and she might be the only one able to go off for help," he explained. Confidence and competence are doubly important qualities out here. In addition to horses, graziers use light aircraft to look over their properties or go to town, and they round up their livestock with helicopters.

Until 1928 the incredible isolation of Australia's outback meant that anyone who lived out on the remote stations or Aboriginal communities had little or no access to medical facilities. Life in the bush is hard and often dangerous, and those who were unlucky enough to become seriously ill or injured could expect to wait many days for a doctor to come up a rough bush track by pack horse or camel. That is, if a doctor was available.

It took the twin 20th-century miracles of radio and airplane, and a compassionate Presbyterian missionary named John Flynn, to bring medicine to the bush. In 1912 Flynn established the first hospital in the outback, in the remote South Australian town of Oodnadatta. But there was still no way for many outback dwellers to reach the hospital or to alert doctors to any medical crisis in the bush. In 1927 an electrical engineer named Alfred Traeger invented a simple but effective pedal-powered radio transmitter that would allow people living on lonely outback stations to send messages to towns or neighbors up to 300 miles away. This device, coupled with larger aircraft capable of transporting stretcher-bound patients, opened the door to aerial medical service.

The first base opened in 1928, in Cloncurry, an old mining town in Queensland's rugged northwest that by then had become a stop for the Queensland & Northern Territory Aerial Service (Qantas). The medical service was based out of the Qantas aerodrome and leased its planes and pilots to ferry doctors to their outback patients. The first call was to an injured stockman near Julia Creek, about 80 miles east of the new base.

As word spread, other outback regions asked to have an aerial medical service as well. The Presbyterian Church couldn't afford to expand the operation, and in 1934 a nonprofit organization—the Australian Aerial Medical Service—was formed to serve the outback. Today, the organization, called the Royal Flying Doctor Service, is one of Australia's proudest and most remarkable traditions. There are 20 RFDS bases scattered around the country. Dentists, specialists, physiotherapists, and psychologists make the rounds of outback communities. Dashes to outlying stations and dramatic evacuations on isolated dirt strips are still a big part of life in the RFDS, but it performs a comprehensive range of less heralded medical services as well. It runs regular medical clinics at distant stations and Aboriginal communities, offering immunizations and checkups. Even in the outback, anyone in Australia is now no more than about two hours from emergency medical assistance.

Like medical service, mail delivery must cope with the enormous distances in the outback. The world's longest mail run leaves Port Augusta, in South Australia, at 8:30 every Saturday morning. It is a two-day, 28-stop marathon by light aircraft to isolated stations and settlements scattered for hundreds of miles along the Strezleki and Birdsville Tracks.

On Australia's vast cattle and sheep stations themselves, four-wheel drives assigned to checking the water holes clock up 60,000 miles a year—without ever leaving the property. Even the towns are huge. Mount Isa, a silver- and lead-mining town of 22,000 in northwest Queensland, is the world's biggest municipality. It sprawls over an area almost the size of Switzerland.

Everything is oversize out here. To protect their sheep from dingoes, outback graziers built the longest fence in the world, 3,307 miles from Queensland's Darling Downs to South Australia's cliff-lined coast on the Great Australian Bight—a thousand miles longer than the Great Wall of China. The trucks that hammer down empty outback highways are road trains, which can weigh more than 140 tons and haul three trailers. Allow at least a mile of open highway to pass one. Fortunately, long stretches of straight open highway are fairly easy to find. The longest of these is on the Eyre Highway, between Balladonia station and the lonely Caiguna roadhouse. It runs dead straight for 53 empty miles.

Surprisingly, given its immense size, Australia's outback is a little hard to delineate on a map. Ask around, as I did on a 10,000-mile bicycle trek around Australia, and you'll soon find that no two Australians can agree on exactly where the outback starts. As a rule of thumb, it's anywhere west of the Great Dividing Range, the rugged spine of mountains than runs along Australia's eastern seaboard, and covers the vast stretch of open land across the continent to the Indian Ocean. It includes the wide-open arid grazing lands in western Queensland and New South Wales—the mythical outback Australia of "Waltzing Matilda" and the Flying Doctor Service and Big Jackie Howe, the champion shearer who sheared 321 sheep one day at Alice Downs Station in 1892. It is also the harsh red center, near Alice Springs, with its colorful history of Afghan camel drivers, the Overland Telegraph line, and the haunting spectacle of Uluru. It is the blinding white salt pans and inhospitable wastelands of South Australia, where Burke and Wills perished in 1861. It is the saltbush and mallee scrub along the Murray-Darling Rivers and the mining town of Broken Hill. And it is the vast and silent desert in Western Australia, where the prospector Lasseter perished while trying to find his way back to his fabulous lost gold strike.

Nevertheless, a traveler can amble down thousands of miles of lonely bush tracks, through endless harsh and lonely landscapes, without ever reaching the outback. In nine months of hard riding, through lonely outback wastes, from the gulf savanna in the north to the waterless expanses of the Nullarbor Plain in the south, I never heard anyone tell me that, yes, you are now in the outback. The outback was farther out still, somewhere beyond the next elusive—and usually heat-warped—horizon. That's because to most Australians the outback is a sort of state of grace, a nation's soul. Part myth and part ballad, it can't be fettered by the here and now, or reached in any four-wheel drive. It is a sort of rootless, ornery freedom, of frayed cuffs and laconic humor and the swag, the canvas bedroll slung over the shoulders of drifters roving the open country looking for work, the next meal or anything else that might turn up. "The Australian swag," declared writer Henry Lawson, "was born of Australia and no other land—of the Great Lone Land of magnificent distances and bright heat; the land of self-reliance, and never-give-in, and help-your-mate. The grave of many of the world's tragedies and comedies—royal and otherwise. The land where a man out of employment might shoulder his swag in Adelaide and take the track, and years later walk into a hut on the Gulf, or never be heard of any more, or a body be found in the bush and buried by the mounted police, or never found and never buried—what does it matter?"

Whatever it is and wherever it is, the outback is certainly no place for the fainthearted. Out here is some of the toughest and most inhospitable terrain in the world—the Simpson Desert, the Gibson Desert, the Great Victoria Desert, the Great Sandy Desert, Sturt Stony Desert, and the Tanami Desert, to name a few of the better known wastelands. There are vast, dusty, anonymous plains dotted with saltbush or covered with tangled mallee scrub—a gnarled and stunted species of euca-lypt—or, farther north, mile upon mile of spinifex, a prickly type of clump grass that looks like so many millions of huddled porcupines in the distance. Yes, some of the cattle and sheep stations out here might be the size of small European countries or American states, but the browse is so lean that it can take more than 50 acres to support a single animal. Droughts are frequent and can last for years. The dramatic storms that break the droughts can leave vast areas flooded for weeks at a time. The blinding summer heat and roasting northerly winds are almost beyond belief to anyone who has never experienced them.

"At noon I took a thermometer, graduated to 127°, out of my box and observed that the mercury was up to 125°," wrote an amazed Capt. Charles Sturt on his expedition in 1844. "Thinking that it had been unduly influenced, I put it in the fork of a tree close to me, sheltered alike from the wind and the sun. In this position I went to examine it about an hour afterwards, when I found that the mercury had risen to the top of the instrument, and that its further expansion had burst the bulb, a circumstance that I believe no traveller has ever before had to record."

The journals of most of the early European explorers are punctuated with starvation, scurvy, thirst, desperation, sunstroke and blindness. For all their misery and torment, Sturt and his crew were lucky. Most of them survived, staggering into Adelaide looking like living skeletons, after having long been given up for dead. Less fortunate was the Prussian explorer, Ludwig Leichhardt, who set off in 1848 from Roma, Queensland, on an attempt to be the first to cross the heart of the continent east to west. His entire party vanished. Many others owed their lives to Aborigines, to whom these seemingly hostile wastes were a comfortable home.

The classic symbol of the Australian outback is the hypnotically beautiful monolith known as Uluru—formerly Ayers Rock—in the Northern Territory. It rises abruptly almost 1,200 feet above the desert at the heart of the continent, throwing the surrounding flatness and desolation into hauntingly sharp relief. Uluru—the name means "great pebble" in the Pitjantjatjara language—is a single chunk of hardened sandstone more than 600 million years old.

Eons of wind, rain, and shifting seasons exposed it, wearing away the softer earth around it. Geologists believe that only the top 10 percent of Uluru is visible. Much more is still buried under the desert. Even so, it is a six-mile hike all the way around the base of this "great pebble." This excursion is far more than merely a scenic approach to a geologic marvel, with up-close looks at its ancient striated flanks, sculpted gullies, and overhangs, and the rioting wildflowers that spring up at its base thanks to runoff rains. Uluru is an epicenter of Aboriginal spiritual life, and the path circling it is a journey into a Dreamtime culture with ancient roots.

Aboriginal spiritual life revolves around ancestral spirit beings, which dwelled on Earth during a prehistoric

Dreamtime era before human beings were created. These beings originally had human form, but later changed into other creatures—magpies, snakes, wallabies, and caterpillars. As they wandered the continent in search of food and water, they fashioned the landscape and, over time, became the ancestors of all living things. The paths they followed in their time on Earth are full of power and are celebrated in elaborate cycles of song, ritual, and painting. These activities keep alive many forms of ancient wisdom, such as advising hunters when and where to search for game and how to find water in the dry years, and giving details about the origins of complex kinship and marriage customs. Many of these powerful, invisible Aboriginal pathways intersect at Uluru—such as those of Mala, the hare wallaby; Kuniya, the python; and Kiru, the viper—giving this haunting desert monolith immense spiritual significance. The sculpted crevices and overhangs around its base are filled with rock paintings and engravings dating back thousands of years.

Many of these are sacred sites—some set aside strictly for women, others set aside strictly for men—and today's visitors to Uluru are expected to respect these ancient Aboriginal customs. While specific spiritual aspects of the rock remain closely guarded secrets known only to the initiated, the grandeur and mystique of Uluru are as obvious as the rock itself.

It is one of the most recognized Australian icons in the world and the centerpiece of 327,570-acre Uluru-Kata Tjuta National Park, about 200 miles southwest of Alice Springs. Australia formally returned Uluru to the Aborigines in 1985, and they leased it back to the government for 99 years as a national park, with Aborigines taking a majority of seats on the park's board of directors. The Lasseter Highway, which only a few years ago was a dirt track, is now a smoothly paved two-lane highway, and the airstrip, near a luxury resort at Yulara, handles daily jet traffic from most of Australia's cities. Tourists come to wonder and to be moved—to admire the play of light and shadow on the rock's grooved face, and to marvel at the way it subtly shifts colors as the sun arches through the sky. Over the course of a day Uluru grades from pale, desert pink through a spectrum of mauves and coppery browns, and finishes, in the dying rays of an outback sunset, in a fiery and luminous crimson.

Oddly, all this magnificence was lost on the first European to visit Uluru back in 1873. He was a singularly unimaginative surveyor named William Gosse whose laconic journal entry that night remarks that he had climbed "a high hill east of Mount Olga, which I named Ayers Rock...."

But Gosse did start a tradition. About two-thirds of today's visitors make the same climb up the incredibly steep and exposed flank of the rock. This hike is only for those with a good head for heights and strong thighs. I did it in 1989, and it left my legs feeling like jelly. The heart-stopping descent left blisters on my toes from being jammed into the ends of my boots. I wouldn't do it again, although not because it was so strenuous. Over the years the local Aborigines have politely let it be known that the route the tourists use to climb the rock follows a spiritual track, and that they would very much prefer visitors to admire Uluru from its base.

As custodians of this ancient marvel, the Aborigines are deeply saddened when a visitor is injured on the climb. This is an event that occurs about once a year, usually from heart attacks or something silly like chasing a windblown hat over an exposed ledge. For a time the park service tried putting white crosses at the base of Uluru to discourage the old and unfit. The only result was that a lot of fat, middle-aged men began mugging for the camera in front of these somber warnings—and then starting up the rock anyway. And so the crosses were removed. So far the Aborigines have shown a remarkable tolerance for tourists' foibles and have not yet banned the climb, although they are considering it.

The Aboriginal owners are more guarded about the jumble of 36 enormous sandstone domes known as Kata Tjuta—the name means "many heads"—that are about 20 miles west of Uluru. Tourists to this sacred spot—which for visual spectacle is as least as good as Uluru—are restricted to just a couple of short trails. Like Uluru, this ancient range was hewn out of a single Precambrian sandstone block. It used to be known to European travelers as the Olgas. Explorer Ernest Giles, who camped here in 1872, christened them in honor of Queen Olga of Württemberg. "The appearance of Mt Olga from this camp is truly wonderful," he wrote. "It displayed to our astonished eyes rounded minarets, giant cupolas and monstrous domes. They have stood as huge memorials from the ancient times of earth, for ages, countless eons of ages since creation first had birth. Time, the old, the dim magician, has ineffectually labored here…Mount Olga has remained as it was born."

In the red heart of Australia about 200 miles northeast of Uluru, Alice Springs, affectionately known as "the Alice," nestles in the craggy Macdonnell Ranges. More than any other town, it has come to symbolize the rough-and-ready Aussie outback. As Uluru is a crossroads of Aboriginal song lines, so the town of Alice Springs is the hub of modern outback legends, myths, and creation stories. The Alice started out as a relay station for the Overland Telegraph—aptly nicknamed "the singing string"—which passed through here in 1872 and connected Australia, via Java, Singapore, and India, with London.

Over the years a dusty settlement sprang up around the telegraph station, serving as a sort of staging post for stockmen, prospectors, telegraph men, and camel drivers heading north or into the vast western deserts. In the early days and up until 1933, the settlement was called Stuart, after the outback explorer who passed near here in 1860. It was the year-round spring out by the telegraph station, two miles north of town, that was named Alice, in honor of Alice Todd, wife of Sir Charles Todd, the South Australian postmaster general who supervised the building of the Overland Telegraph.

Hardly anyone outside Australia had ever even heard of the place until 1950, when Nevil Shute's best-selling *A Town Like Alice* put the rough outback town on the world's literary map. Although it is much larger now—at around 30,000 residents—the Alice retains its frontier rawness: "a grid of scorching streets where men in long white socks were forever getting in and out of Land Cruisers," wrote English travel writer Bruce Chatwin, who visited Alice Springs in 1986. Residents are mostly geologists, drill rig operators, railway workers, or jackaroos in from one of the stations. Although it rates high on the tourist map, Alice Springs still earns most of its keep from mining, oil, cattle, and transport. There's a modest export industry in shipping wild camels to the Middle East, and even a winery on the outskirts of town.

This is a restless hard-drinking oasis of transients and tourists, known for such rowdy events as its camel races and the riotous Henley-on-Todd boat regatta in which competitors carry their boats down the dusty bed of the Todd River. The Alice Springs rodeo is one of the most respected on the Australian circuit. But behind all the blokey gaiety and the cavalcade of motels, fast-food joints, tacky souvenir shops, and travel agents touting excursions to Uluru and Kings Canyon is a sense of a smoldering, hard-boiled little town. Its society of rednecks, drunks, drifters, and the sad spectacle of outcast Aborigines living in squalor along the riverbank suggest a not-too-pretty raffishness just below the surface. Few people get sentimental about Alice Springs. It is what it always has been—a springboard to someplace else, somewhere over the horizon: the outback.

Every Tuesday and Friday, in the early afternoon, one of Australia's most romantic trains leaves the Alice on a 966-mile journey south through the desert and mulga scrub to Adelaide. The train is known affectionately as the *Ghan,* named in honor of the tough Afghan camel drivers who, together with their pack animals, kept the remote desert town supplied and were the unsung heroes of Australia's outback exploration.

Camels are not native to Australia, but they are ideal for traveling in the outback. Their broad, soft feet do not sink in sandy soils the way horses hoofs do; they could thrive on tough desert scrub; carry enormous loads; and, of course, they are famed for their abilities to travel long distances between water holes. A few experimental camels were imported as early as the 1840s, but it wasn't until the Victorian government bought 25 camels for the Burke and Wills expedition, in 1860, that the possibilities of using these ships of the desert to open up the outback began to be understood.

In 1866 South Australian pastoralist Thomas Elder imported 120 camels and began breeding them at his Beltana Station. Thousands more were imported. Within a few years and well into the 1930s, camel trains and their Afghan handlers were the mainstays of outback transportation. Some settlements, such as the Western Australia gold rush town of Kalgoorlie, made their main streets especially wide to accommodate the turning radius of these long strings of vital pack animals. Camels were used for virtually everything: Hauling ore from remote mines; taking wool clips to market; carrying the mail; and transporting men and equipment during the construction of the Overland Telegraph, the railroad to Alice Springs, and the trans-Australian railroad across the Nullarbor Plain to Perth.

Vital though camels were to opening up their vast arid country, rank-and-file Australians never warmed to them as they did to horses. Camels were regarded as dirty, ill-tempered, and dangerous. They spat, they stank at both ends, and they seemed to take delight in causing mischief. Harry, a cantankerous camel with John Horrocks' 1846 expedition into the South Australian outback, savagely bit expedition members, chased the other animals, and chewed holes in precious bags of flour. Relations between camel and human were eventually strained to the breaking point when Harry shot to death the expedition leader. Horrocks had been loading a rifle when Harry lurched, caught one of his traces around the weapon's cocking mechanism, and discharged it into Horrocks' face. Harry was shot, but not before he'd bitten another stockman.

The skilled camel drivers from Afghanistan and India's North-West Frontier, who had been brought to Australia to handle the beasts, were similarly misunderstood. Mysterious, silent, dark, and turbaned, they were regarded with suspicion by the British community and were forced to live in separate camps and squalid shanties. Known as ghantowns, these sprang up on the outskirts of far-flung settlements such as Bourke, Oodnadatta, Broken Hill, Port Hedland, and Cloncurry. Among the other jobs the cameleers undertook was carrying supplies and building materials to the isolated construction camps of the men building the outback railways.

By the 1930s these railways had made camel trains obsolete. The once-valuable pack animals were simply turned loose in the bush, where their descendants run wild today. There are an estimated 100,000 feral camels in Australia, which is the last country to have herds of the

animals. Each year many are captured and exported to the Middle East, or are tamed and used for tourist rides in exotic outback towns such as Broome.

As for the Afghan cameleers, they, too, dispersed. Some returned to the subcontinent; others took jobs on lonely railway maintenance gangs or found their way into the cities, where they blended into Australia's increasingly polyglot population. Today, little more than lonely Muslim grave sites, abandoned mosques, groves of date palms planted in out-of-the-way oases, and the name of the famous train remain to remind outback travelers of this exotic chapter of Australian history.

The episode that inspired the importation of camels to Australia is still remembered throughout the country. More than 10,000 well-wishers lined the streets of Melbourne on August, 20, 1860, to watch Robert O'Hara Burke and William John Wills lead 17 other men and a cavalcade of camels, horses, and wagons northward on a grand adventure to cross the continent. A brass band played, people cheered, and children and dogs ran alongside the parade. It was colonial Australia's equivalent of a moon shot. Lavishly funded by the Victorian government, the expedition's brief was to see "if there really existed in their great continent a Sahara…great lakes…or watered plains which might tempt men to build new cities."

The leader of the expedition, 40-year-old Robert O'Hara Burke was a hot-tempered Irishman and former cavalry officer who had been working as a policeman in rural Victoria. Wills was a starry-eyed 26-year-old surveyor. The expedition carried more than 21 tons of supplies and camp furniture, including an oak table and a dozen beds—and 60 gallons of rum for their camels! The camels themselves had been imported especially for the expedition; the start of the long and proud tradition of using dromedaries and Afghan camel drivers in opening up the outback. Astonishingly, though, given the importance the Victorian government put on the expedition's success, neither Burke nor Wills nor anyone else on the team had had any previous exploration experience or knew much about the Australian outback. By the time the carnival-like procession had reached the outskirts of Melbourne, it was already in trouble. Heavy rains bogged the overburdened wagons. Ahead lay almost 1,400 miles of the hottest, driest, harshest, and loneliest landscape on the planet.

Over the next few weeks the men traveled slowly through the rolling plains, goldfields, and tough mallee scrub of northern Victoria, bickering with each other along the way and pausing periodically to ditch excess gear. Mallee is a gnarled and stunted variety of eucalypt that grows in dense clumps on loose, sandy soils. Horses, camels, and men all found it tough going. At the outback settlement at Menindee, on the lower Darling River, the group divided.

Menindee was a well-known jumping-off place for the outback: Major Thomas Mitchell and Charles Sturt had both camped here during their expeditions in 1835 and 1844. The Menindee hotel—which is still standing today—was regarded as a sort of rough-and-tumble explorers' club. It was here Burke learned that South Australian explorer John Mac-Douall Stuart was about to depart from Adelaide on his third attempt to cross the continent. Suddenly Burke saw his own expedition as a race against that of the tough and vastly more experienced Stuart.

By this time summer was nigh. Ignoring locals' advice that the hot season was a risky time for tenderfeet to head into the desert, Burke set off briskly for Cooper Creek, an isolated string of water holes more than 400 miles away. The plan was to establish a base camp there, from which he and a handpicked team could make a quick push over the final 700 miles to reach the Gulf of Carpentaria. They arrived at Cooper Creek in mid-November—in 110 degree heat.

After waiting a month at Cooper Creek for the slow-moving wagons to catch up, Burke grew impatient. He decided to split his party. Four men would remain at the water hole while Burke, Wills, and two others—Charlie Gray and John King—would make the final push for the gulf. They set off in mid-December—high summer in the outback, when water holes shrink and disappear and a brassy sun flares overhead, bleaching out colors and warping the horizons in shimmering waves of heat.

Several times local Aborigines approached Burke and his men and might have given them invaluable advice, but the neophyte explorers weren't interested. "A large tribe of blacks came pestering us to go to their camp and have a dance, which we declined" wrote Wills in his diary. "They were very troublesome and nothing but the threat to shoot them will keep them away. They are, however, easily frightened and, although fine looking men, decidedly not of a war-like disposition…from the little we have seen of them they appear to be mean spirited and contemptible in every respect." He was to eat those words several brutal months later; unfortunately, by then, they were all he had to eat.

Much of the time the four men traveled by moonlight to escape the searing daytime temperatures. They crossed the Sturt Stony Desert, an apocalyptic landscape of bare, pebbly earth and, farther north, trudged across vast plains dotted with clumps of prickly spinifex.

Over the years spinifex has proved the bane of many outback travelers, myself included. Its sharp, quill-like needles are easily able to penetrate trouser legs, chafing and irritating flesh. As the party traveled farther north, the climate grew hotter and muggier. The monsoon season was imminent. A few miles short of the Gulf of Carpentaria the team's camels became too bogged in the mud to continue.

Burke left King and Gray with the camels while he and Wills pushed on, reaching their farthest point north on February 11, 1861. Impenetrable, crocodile-infested mangrove swamps prevented them from getting a clear view of the ocean, but the taste of saltwater in the creeks told Burke and Wills that they had effectively reached their goal. They rejoined King and Gray and began the long, slow, dreary trudge back to their base camp at Cooper Creek, more than 700 miles away. They were exhausted, provisions were running low, and the heat and humidity never let up. On April 17, just a few days away from base camp, Charlie Gray dropped dead of exhaustion and malnutrition.

Meanwhile, back at Cooper Creek, the rest of the party had given up waiting. Before he left, Burke had said he and his men would be back in three months or less. By now nearly four months had passed, in heat and flies and dust and idleness, without any word of the party. Supplies were running low, and on the morning of April 21 the men pulled out of Cooper Creek and headed south. Before they left, they buried some food and a message in a bottle in case Burke should still be alive and make it to Cooper Creek. They carved instructions—DIG 3FT N.W. APR. 21 1861—onto the bark of a giant coolabah tree that had shaded the camp—and left.

A fateful nine-and-a-half hours later Burke, Wills, and King staggered up to Cooper Creek—and found their camp deserted and the message that the party had left only that morning. "Our disappointment at finding the depot deserted may be easily imagined," wrote Wills, "returning in an exhausted state, after four months of the severest travelling and privation, our legs almost para-lyzed so that each of us found it a most trying task only to walk a few yards."

Deciding that they could not possibly overtake the retreating party, the men dug up the provisions left for them, ate, rested overnight, and then set off for the out-back police depot at aptly named Mount Hopeless, in South Australia. Before they left, they reburied some pro-visions, carefully but foolishly erasing their tracks from around the big coolabah tree.

Foolishly, because fate had more tricks to play on the hapless explorers. While they headed off to Mount Hopeless, apparently unaware that there was no water en route, their colleagues had had a change of heart and returned to Cooper Creek for one final check. Seeing the site apparently undisturbed, they left again—this time for good. Ironically, Burke, Wills and King were less than 30 miles away and on their way back, having given up the attempt to reach Mount Hopeless. Too weak to attempt to follow their colleagues, they now had to throw them-selves on the good graces of the Aborigines.

Considering the earlier attitudes of the explorers, the Aborigines were remarkably charitable and forgiving, giving the starving white men cakes made from seedlike parts of nardoo, a local drought-resistant fern. But the Aborigines had their own business to attend to and were often gone for days at a time. The explorers tried to make their own nardoo bread, but they lacked the Aborigines'

thousands of years of experience and failed to prepare the mix properly. What they didn't know was that there is an enzyme in the nardoo that robs the body of vitamin B and prevents digestion. The Aborigines' skillful prepara-tion removed these enzymes. The explorers didn't, and they gradually starved on full stomachs.

"I am weaker than ever," Wills wrote in his final journal entry, dated June 29, 1861, "although I have a good appetite and relish the nardoo much; but it seems to give us no nutriment…. Nothing now but the greatest good luck can save any of us; and as for myself I may live four or five days if the weather continues warm. My pulse is at forty-eight, and very weak, and my legs and arms are nearly skin and bone. I can only look out, like Mr. Micawber, 'for something to turn up'." Nothing did. Burke and Wills both perished. Twenty-year-old John King might have followed them into the grave but for the intervention of kindly Aborigines who, "seemed to look upon me as one of themselves, and supplied me with fish and nardoo regularly."

Meanwhile, Burke and Will's redoubtable South Australian rival, John MacDouall Stuart, had met with defeat on his latest attempt to cross the continent. He arrived back in Adelaide in time to hear of Burke and Wills lonely deaths. Neither that somber news nor his own broken health deterred him in the least. Three weeks later he volunteered to lead another expedition. The South Australian government backed him, and on Octo-ber 25, 1861, he and his men set off on a final attempt to cross the continent.

They reached the sea on July 24 the following year and returned triumphantly to Adelaide in December, without the loss of a single member of the group. Ironi-cally Stuart arrived in the city, a broken but successful explorer, on the very day the bodies of Burke and Wills passed through Adelaide on the way to Melbourne and Victoria's first state funeral.

While the inland explorers and their camel trains were gone for months at a time out over the shimmering horizons, the settlers, prospectors, and graziers they left behind were busily staking out claims and opening up vast tracts of land to sheep, cattle, and the plow. In this, the Burke and Wills expedition achieved an ironic success in its goal of opening up new grazing land. Although the neophyte explorers did not discover much, search parties sent to find them, led by experienced bushmen did. Australia's landed gentry was not far behind. Within a few short years, these wealthy squatters had snapped up much of the best grazing land, laying the foundations for some of Australia's great pastoral dynasties. And while the squatters built their fortunes and elegant homesteads, the rank-and-file Australians began taking imaginative possession of their new country.

The lyrical outback myth was born; its heroes were the rugged, bronzed footloose Aussie swagmen who knocked about the countryside, were always loyal to their mates, and who liked a drink or three at the pub or a bet on the horses. They were proud, good-hearted, immensely competent, none too well fixed for cash, had a laconic sense of humor, and generally lived a better, freer life than their confined city cousins. The *Bulletin* magazine, launched in Sydney in 1880, helped establish these romantic images of the Australian bush, showcasing poems and folksy vignettes of bush life by the likes of Andrew Barton "Banjo" Paterson and his dour and down-at-the-heels contemporary, Henry Lawson.

There was certainly no shortage of material or colorful characters. One such bloke was Henry Redford, a stockman who drifted around the sprawling cattle stations in the dusty central Queensland outback in 1870. Redford was a skilled bushman who had taken the trouble to learn the rhythms of the land from the Aborigines and how to find food and water. Redford spoke several of their languages. Equipped with these formidable talents, he and his gang spirited away a thousand cattle from the giant Bowen Downs Station. Their getaway was one of the great cattle drives of all time: More than a thousand miles through the same harsh, arid, little known country that had killed Burke and Wills only decades earlier. The rustlers moved the herd all the way to Adelaide, where they sold the cattle for £5,000.

They might have got away with it, except that a conspicuous white shorthorn bull—imported from England for stud duties—had tagged along behind them like a faithful puppy. Its distinctive appearance ultimately betrayed them. Later Redford was arrested and hauled back to Roma, Queensland, for trial—the white shorthorn bull accompanied him as a witness for the prosecution—

but his daring cattle drive had so fired the public's imagination that no jury of his outback peers would convict him. Rural Queenslanders—who love to tell this story—have it that the jury returned a quixotic verdict of: "Not guilty, but he's got to give the cattle back!" And when the outraged magistrate ordered them to reconsider, they did—this time supposedly returning with an ornery: "Not guilty, and he can keep the bloody cattle!"

The Brisbane *Courier* reported that "they have a curious practice in the far west of this colony of pulling fellows for cattle stealing and taking them to Roma to be tried by a jury of their peers, who enjoy the fun amazingly and after going through a form of evidence and making a few bovine jokes, bring in a verdict of 'Not Guilty'." After Redford's remarkable acquittal, the court at Roma lost its jurisdiction to hear cattle rustling cases for two years.

While Redford went on to more adventures—and further rustling charges—in the tropical north, his old stomping ground in central Queensland went on to midwife some of Australia's most enduring and defining legends. They were men like Big Jackie Howe, Australia's real-life answer to Paul Bunyan and steel-driving John Henry, a champion shearer who lived near Blackall.

Born in 1861, Howe was the son of a circus acrobat. A strapping young athlete in his own right, he learned the skills for which he was to become so famous from Chinese shearers. Shearing sheds are intensely competitive places, with an emphasis on speed and endurance, and Howe quickly established a reputation as Australia's greatest shearer, regularly notching up tallies of 250 sheep in a day. At Alice Downs station in October 1892, Howe chalked up his greatest ever tally: 321 lambs in a union-prescribed day of 7 hours and 40 minutes.

It is a record that has never been beaten, at least not by anyone using the kind of old-fashioned hand-powered shears Howe used. (And it was 1942 before anyone topped it using electric shears.) Howe left behind another legacy that went well beyond the shearing shed: The style of sleeveless navy blue singlet his wife made for him, to give him ease of movement, was adopted by working class Australians everywhere and is known to this day as a Jackie Howe.

More outback legends were forged 60 miles farther north, in the town of Barcaldine, which became the strike headquarters for more than a thousand shearers during a bitter strike in 1891. Their fiery gatherings beneath the limbs of a 200-year-old gum tree, still standing and known as the "tree of knowledge," provided the catalyst for the founding of the Australian Labor Party the following year.

About a 170 miles northwest of Barcaldine is the town of Winton, the birthplace in 1920 of another Aussie emblem, the Queensland & Northern Territory Aerial Service, the airline known today the world over by its acronym: Qantas. Perhaps the most stirring bit of Aussie folklore came out of Winton. It is where Banjo Paterson reputedly wrote the lyrics to "Waltzing Matilda," Australia's unofficial national anthem.

One story has it that Paterson wrote "Waltzing Matilda" while visiting a lady friend named Christina Macpherson at nearby Dagworth Station in 1895. The exact history behind the song and the tune has been lost over the decades in claim, counterclaim, wishful thinking, and myth. The lyrics, which are so freighted with outback slang that they are almost incomprehensible to non-Australians, tell the story of a happy-go-lucky vagabond who, while camped beneath a coolabah tree, butchers a stolen sheep for his dinner. As he is cooking it, three mounted troopers ride up. Rather than be arrested and lose his cherished freedom, the hobo dives into a nearby pond and defiantly drowns himself.

A century later the song still tugs on Australian imaginations. Some listeners believe "Waltzing Matilda" has its roots in the pro-labor politics of the day, a sympathetic note for the defiant striking shearers who were to help form the Australian Labor Party. Others believe it was simply a folksy local story put to rhyme by Paterson in order to please his hostess, who in turn put it to an old English military tune. Some believe the source of the melody is an old Scottish ballad. Whatever its origins, within a very few years after Paterson wrote it, the evocative "Waltzing Matilda" became—and remains—Australia's best loved tune.

There is more to the outback myth than lean and lanky riders, roving crews of shearers, and ne'er-do-well swagmen. Some of the world biggest mineral deposits have been found in the Precambrian rocks of Australia's outback, and they've inspired some of the most colorful towns in the outback: Mount Isa, Broken Hill, Kalgoorlie, and the rollicking opal fields of Coober Pedy, in the remote South Australian outback.

Coober Pedy—a corruption of an Aboriginal phrase *kupa piti*, or white man in a hole—was discovered by chance by a teenage boy in 1915, and over the past 80 years a unique community of hardened adventurers, drifters, and fortune hunters from 45 nations has sprung up around it.

The first time I drove into the town along the desolate Stuart Highway, I had a feeling I was approaching a set from one of the apocalyptic *Mad Max* movies. Indeed, much of *Mad Max III* was shot here. For miles around the landscape is dotted with eerie conical piles of rubble from the more than 250,000 holes made by opal miners. They look somehow evil in fading desert twilight. People here live underground: Many of its residents live in caves to escape the burning heat of summer. These cave homes, hotels, and businesses are surprisingly pleasant and airy, and their well-insulated rooms remain a constant and comfortable 72 degrees. Home expansion is a simple matter of digging out a new room in the dense clay, with perhaps the occasional opal find to help defray your costs. That is one of the joys of Coober Pedy: Anyone with a prospecting permit has an equal chance of striking it rich. Opals are randomly distributed throughout the rich red earth. One hole has as good a chance as another at striking a band of fiery black opal, the most valuable type, which can be worth tens of thousands of dollars.

Perhaps Australia's most colorful mining town is Broken Hill, New South Wales, near the South Australia border. In 1883 Charles Rasp, a German-born drover on a remote sheep station, stumbled onto an enormous mineral-rich formation with the aid of a how-to-prospect guidebook he'd purchased while on holiday in Adelaide.

it out, found some backers, and went into mining. Later the investors realized they had found a mountain of galena-sphalerite ore, almost unimaginably rich in silver, lead, and zinc. At 280 million tons, the six-mile-long, boomerang-shaped ore body remains to this day the biggest and richest of its type ever found.

Rasp and his partners became incredibly rich, and their company, Broken Hill Proprietary (BHP), became Australia's largest corporation. Several more of Australia's great mining houses—such as CRA and North Limited—also sprang from these metal-rich rocks about 570 miles west of Sydney.

By the early years of the century, Broken Hill had a rowdy population of more than 30,000 and supported more than a hundred hotels and pubs. It was known throughout the world for its quick wealth, wild living, and the increasingly bitter conflicts between labor and management. The town of Broken Hill became a honey pot for prospectors, adventurers, radical American unionists who had been chased out of Chicago, strong-backed miners, and company men. A mining engineer named Herbert Hoover, who later became President of the United States, was another visitor who passed through "the Hill."

Vast wealth and the mines' enormous staying power created an architecturally rich town. Argent Street, the city's main thoroughfare, is crammed with elegant Victorian two- and three-story pubs, their balconies embellished with traceries of ornamental iron lace. Broken Hill's town hall is opulently Italianate, the trades-hall building is an effusive mix of baroque styles, while the headquarters of the North Broken Hill Mine is a stunning piece of art deco.

More than a century after Rasp discovered it, the Broken Hill orebody continues to produce enormous wealth. It is now waning, however, and by 2006 mining is expected to cease. Today, the "silver city" is looking to the silver screen for jobs. Broken Hill's 300-plus days of sunshine, clear desert air, and its regular air links with Sydney have made it a hot location for filmmakers and the advertising industry. Set designers, casting agencies, and location scouts have set up businesses here, and bemused locals often get work as extras.

Movies such as *Mad Max II* and *Priscilla, Queen of the Desert* were filmed here. Coca-Cola's famous sky-surfing commercial was shot over the Mundi Mundi plains, an hour's drive north of Broken Hill. Levi's, Pepsi, Toyota, and XXXX Beer have all filmed high-profile commercials in and around Broken Hill, and rock groups such as INXS have shot video clips here. The ghost town of Silverton, about 15 miles north of Broken Hill, is an especially popular filming venue. Its colorful pub, the Silverton Hotel, has been renamed more than a dozen times for its film, commercial, and TV mini-series appearances.

The same fragile desert light and dramatic outback scenery that attract the film industry have also brought some of Australia's best artists to Broken Hill. Known as the "brushmen of the bush," the group includes such nationally prominent names as Pro Hart and Jack Absalom. The once rough mining town is now dotted with art galleries and bright with murals. And on a hilltop on the northern outskirts of town are 12 sandstone sculptures. Created by sculptors from around Australia and overseas, they exude a kind of Stonehenge quality in the ancient landscape.

I went out there one evening around sundown, walking among the haunting statues. I looked out across the desert and the delicate mauves and pinks in the western sky. Early lights twinkled in Broken Hill. Far off in the distance I watched the high beams of a truck booming along the Barrier Highway bound for a distant Sydney.

Following pages: *Sunlight shimmers on the ancient, wind-scoured rocks of the Balgo Hills in Western Australia's Great Sandy Desert. Recent rains have freshened the trees and grasses huddled in the normally dry watercourses.*

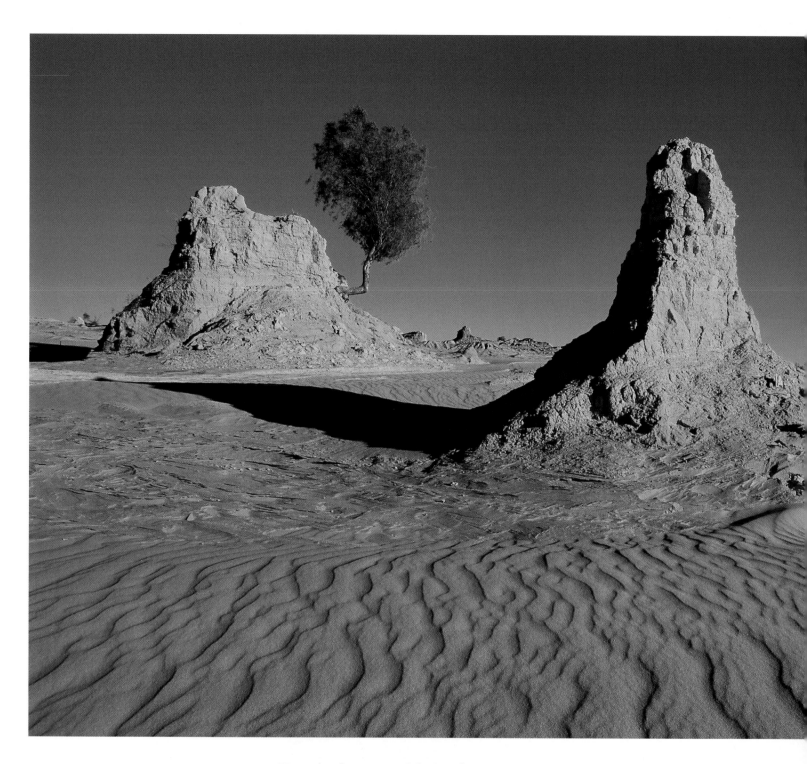

Haunting lunette sand dunes of Mungo National Park, in western New South Wales, conceal an almost unbroken record of more than 60,000 years of Aboriginal history. Among the discoveries: The remains of the world's earliest known cremation were unearthed here, a simple ceremony that took place about 26,000 years ago on the shore of what was then a chain of freshwater lakes.

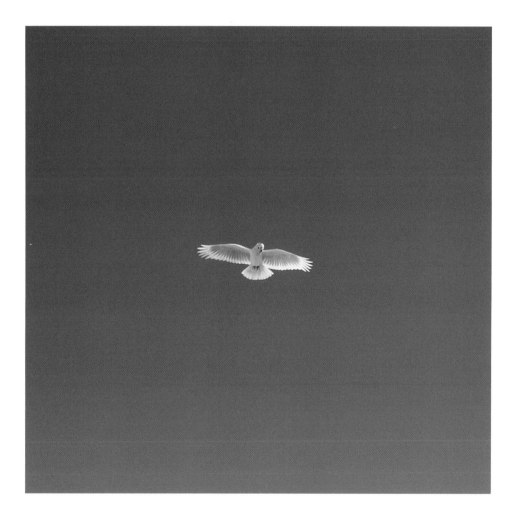

Early morning sun catches the brilliantly hued wings of a pink cockatoo as it soars into blue skies over Lake Mungo. These raucous birds—known colloquially as desert cockatoos—flit around the outback in flocks of 30 or more, often erupting from the bush in a rush of noise and color.

Following pages: *A lonely cattle station known as Old Andado appears lost in the timeless waves of sand dunes that cover the vast Simpson Desert. This hostile void defied early explorers' attempts to cross it, and it was not until 1929, when aerial surveys began, that the thousand parallel dunes of the Simpson Desert were finally mapped. Rains can transform the seemingly lifeless desert into waving grasslands almost overnight.*

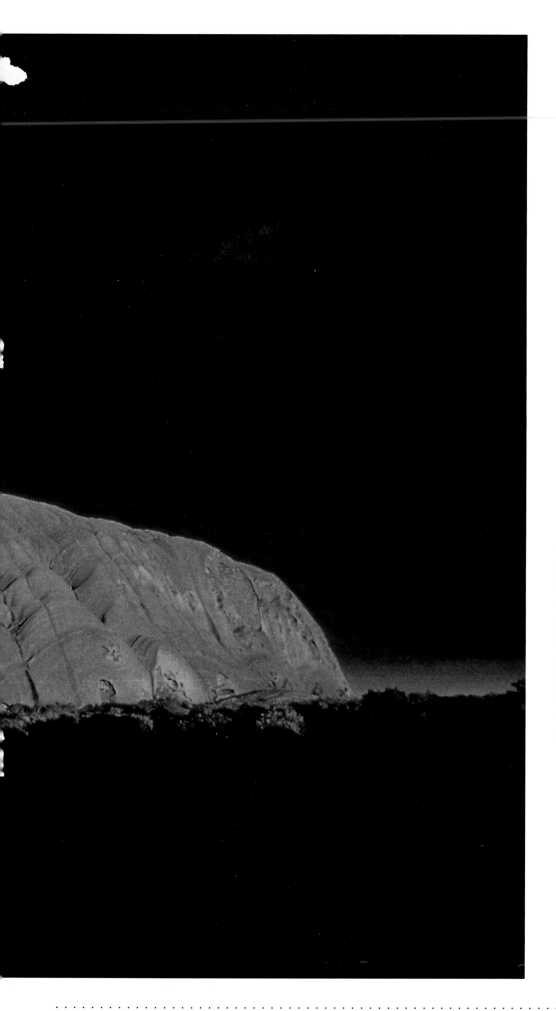

Rising eerily from the flat plains in Australia's red center, the 600 million-year-old sandstone monolith known as Uluru casts a hypnotic spell that has drawn travelers toward it for thousands of years. Once known only to the Anangu Aborigines, it is now one of Australia's most universally recognized symbols. Perhaps a quarter-of-a-million visitors make the pilgrimage here each year.

Out for an evening joyride, a group of Aborigines bounce along a dusty track near the community of Balgo, on the eastern fringe of Western Australia's Great Sandy Desert. Open-air excursions in the back of a truck are both social events and a popular way to defeat the desert's heat at the end of the day.

*An Aboriginal family unwinds in
front of a television in the warmth of
a desert evening at the Balgo community in remote Western Australia.
Although the government provides
housing, many Aborigines prefer the
traditional open-air lifestyles of their
ancestors, sleeping and eating in
their yards until winter arrives.*

Desperate and determined, a wild horse lands headfirst after leaping a gate to escape a stockman's rope at Innaminka Station. The ranch, spread along Cooper Creek in the northeastern corner of Queensland, covers 5,500 square miles.

Cooked in the coals of a dying camp-fire, goanna—a sand monitor lizard—is a prized delicacy in Yagga Yagga, a remote Aboriginal community near the Great Sandy Desert. The Aborigines of Yagga Yagga have broken away from social problems in other communities and have returned to the traditional lifestyle of their ancestors.

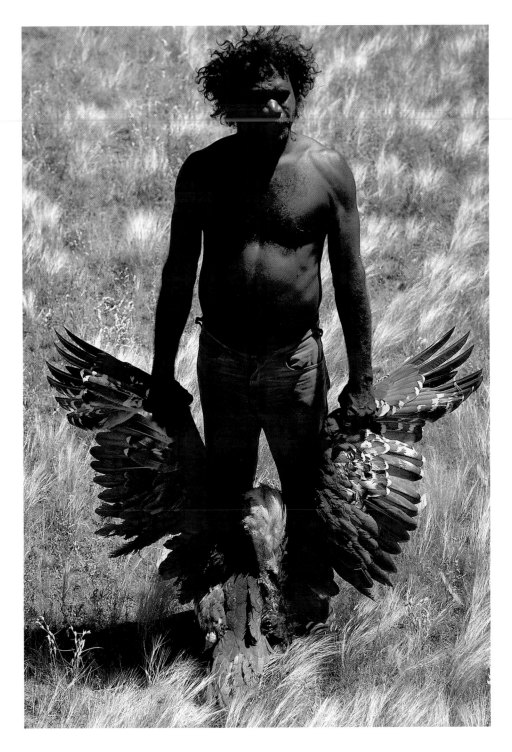

Aboriginal hunter Mark Moora returns victorious from the bush with his kill—a wild turkey. Although the last of the purely nomadic Aborigines quit the desert in 1984 in favor of a more Western style of life in communities, a growing number of Aborigines, such as Moora, are returning at least part-time to some of the old traditions.

Following pages: *Guided by the domes of Kata Tjuta, Robyn Davidson leads her camel train westward across broad spinifex plains in central Australia. Davidson made an epic camel trek across the outback in 1977. Until the early 1930s camels carried freight in the outback. Today, their descendants run wild in the bush.*

*Sly predator: A dingo slinks away
from a water hole. Believed to have
been brought to Australia from
Southeast Asia by seafarers about
3,500 years ago, these slightly built
feral dogs hunt kangaroos, rodents,
and lizards. For the past two centuries, however, their easiest pickings
have been slow-moving sheep, setting
the stage for a ceaseless war between
humans and dingoes.*

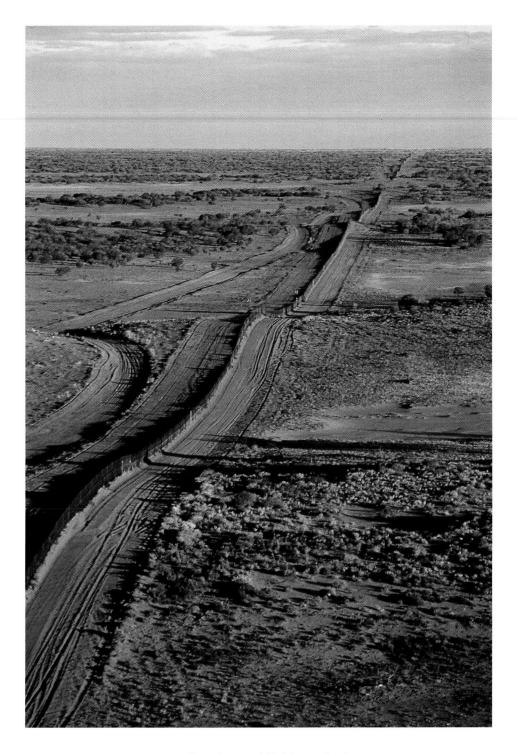

Bounding the world's biggest back-
yard, the Dog Fence stretches 3,307
miles through the outback from
Queensland to the west coast of
South Australia. Conceived in 1880
to protect sheep from dingoes, the
fence requires vigilant patrolling
and constant maintenance. Dingoes
inside the fence are classed as vermin
and can be shot on sight. Bounties
for dingoes run as high $500.

Sudden rock slides can crush vehicles working in the pit of a gold mine; fortunately no one was injured in the accident at the giant Telfer Mine, in Western Australia, that crumpled this cab. Although vastly safer than it was in the old days, mining remains one of Australia's riskier occupations. Nevertheless, fat pay checks and the prospect of adventure lure thousands of Australians into the outback each year.

King of outback highways, a double-decker road train hauls about 200 cattle to the Mareeba saleyards from Dunbar Station in the Cape York Peninsula. These massive triple-trailer rigs can weigh as much as 140 tons and be half as long as a football field. As they thunder along the remote desert tracks they throw up gravel and clouds of talc-fine bull dust.

Following pages: *In a swirl of dust a pack of snarling Australian cattle dogs musters a shorthorn bullock into a drafting pen on Sandringham Station in Queensland's Simpson Desert. Once this scene would have been preceded by a several-month-long cattle drive through the outback. Now massive road trains haul beef to market in a day or so.*

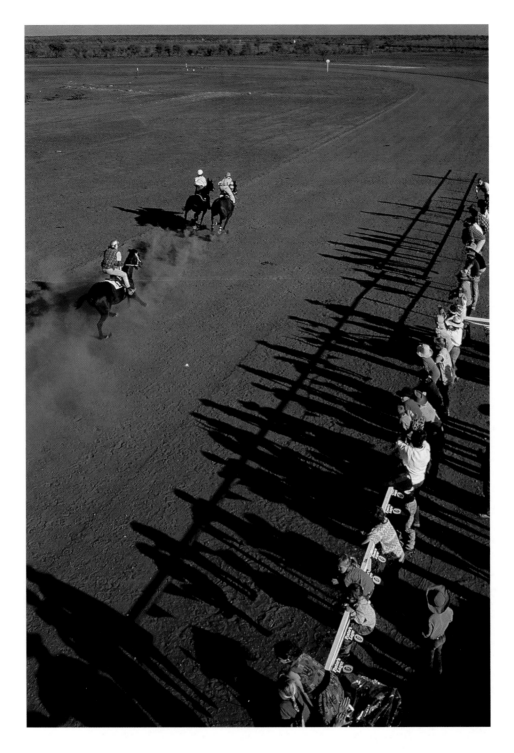

Rodeos, stock trials, and horse races, such as this one in the outback South Australian town of Marla, draw crowds from stations hundreds of miles away. A rough-hewn cama-raderie prevails at these events, with range gossip, shouted beers, the occa-sional punch, and thousands of dol-lars in wagers exchanging hands.

Bruised but unconquered, champion rider Richard Nunn (above, at right), head stockman for the giant Anna Creek Station, rests beneath laurels won at a stock trial in nearby Marla. Although road trains have replaced old-time cattle drives, horses still play a role in roundups on the big stations.

Tank-topped local hero throws a haymaker at a member of Fred Brophy's Boxing Troupe, which visited town for the races in Birdsville, Queensland. Traveling boxing shows, in which locals test their mettle against a pro, have long been a feature of outback entertainment. In this case the 30-dollar purse went to the challenger.

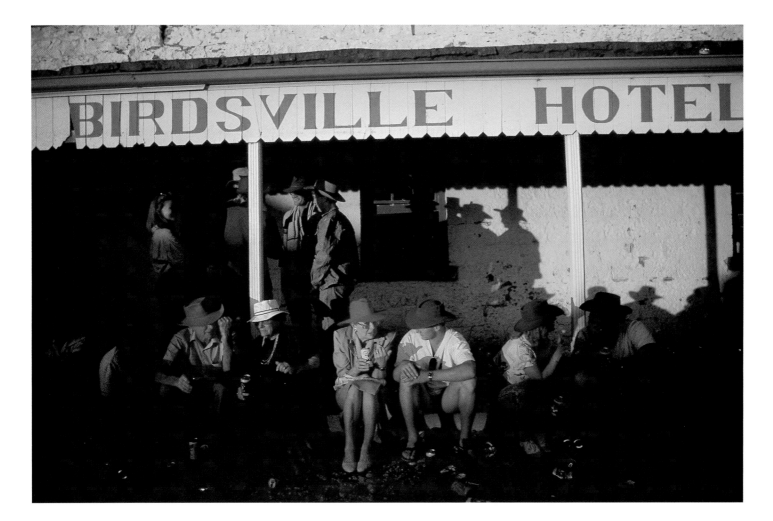

The Birdsville Races, held the first weekend in September, are one of the high points of the outback social calendar. Almost overnight the population of the remote community swells from 80 to more than 6,000, and so many light aircraft empty skies that the Civil Aviation Safety Authority has had to impose special race weekend flight regulations to control traffic on the town's landing strip.

Following pages: *Irrigation from the Murray-Darling River system has transformed the harsh outback scrub of Queensland's Darling Downs into vast—and lucrative—cotton fields. Bales await tarpaulins and shipment to distant city markets.*

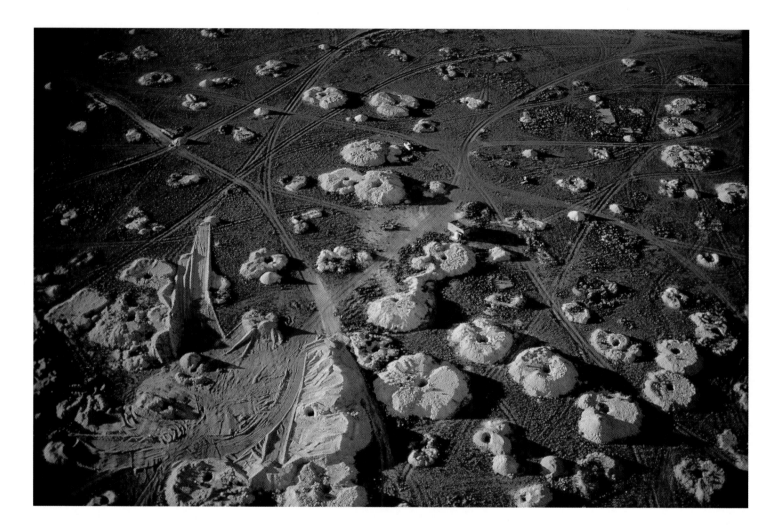

Monuments to ambition: 250,000 entrances to mine shafts dot the landscape around the opal-mining town of Coober Pedy, in South Australia's arid outback. Since opals were discovered in 1915, thousands of fortune hunters have flocked here, pick in hand, to try their luck. The law allows each prospector a 165-foot-square claim, effectively shutting out big mining companies.

Like most residents of the opal mining community of White Cliffs, in
outback New South Wales, 80-year-
old prospector and artist Ivy Kennedy
lives underground to escape savage
115-degree heat on the surface.
Insulated by the chalky earth, her
home stays at 72 degrees year-round.
An illuminated aquarium takes the
place of a wished-for skylight.

Evening rush hour is light on the main street of Rutherglen, a farming village in the cool highlands of northern Victoria. The scene of a rollicking gold rush in 1862, the historic town is now known for its century-old vineyards and fine wines.

Following pages: Clear skies above White Cliffs have a silver lining. With an average of more than 300 sun-drenched days a year, the town was a natural site for the world's first experimental solar power station. Built in 1981, the array of 14 dishes, each a little more than 16 feet in diameter, generates a total of about 42 kilowatts of electricity an hour and is monitored by a video link to a control center in Melbourne.

CHAPTER THREE

The Golden West

There's a rough track near Marble Bar, a hot and lonely mining town in Western Australia's remote northwest, that winds back to the very dawn of time on Earth: Vestiges of a 3.52-billion-year-old landscape miraculously have survived eons of wind and rain. The geologists who found this basalt and chert formation in 1995 were stunned to discover it also had remnants of a soil profile, from which scientists can hope to learn more about the Earth's primordial climate. Nearby are the fossilized remains of the planet's earliest known life-forms, single cell algae known as stromatolites, which date back more than 3.5 billion years. The photosynthetic activity of these bacteria converted the ancient atmosphere of carbon dioxide and nitrogen to the oxygen-rich atmosphere that allowed higher, more complex life-forms to evolve. Incredibly, these same primitive organisms can be found living and prospering today in Hamelin Pool, on Western Australia's harsh and desolate central coast.

To journey along the coast of Western Australia, from the craggy, iron-rich ranges of the Pilbara in the northwest to the aloof, wildflower-covered Stirling Range some 1,500 miles to the south, is to confront the incredible age and remarkable continuity of the continent. Time here is measured in the billions of years. Zircon crystals found in the West Australian bush have been dated as far back as 4.3 billion years—the oldest things yet found on the planet. A little farther south still, in the Cambrian sandstones of Murchison Gorge, in Kalbarri National Park, are a series of tracks some 420 million years old that tell the story of the earliest and perhaps the most remarkable of journeys. Paleontologists believe these scuttle marks in the ancient sands represent the earliest known occasion when life emerged from the water to take its first hesitant steps on land. In studying them, scientists have redrafted their notions of early terrestrial life. Until scientists realized the significance of the Kalbarri tracks in 1995, they had assumed that the first organisms to emerge were herbivores. The creatures scuttling around Kalbarri's ancient pools and dunes, however, were meat-eaters that explored the edges of the water and picked out smaller, algae-eating organisms. And what nightmarish creatures they were: amphibious scorpions that grew up to six feet long and centipedes that were even longer. In 1994 paleontologists probing these fertile fossil beds discovered a six-inch-long cockroachlike amphibian—since named *Kalbarria*—that may be the ancestor of all insects.

Much, much later—around 65 million years ago—at this western edge of Australia the continent broke away from the super landmass known as Gondwana and went walkabout across the widening Indian Ocean. This was the defining event in Australia's natural history. Australia's ancient flora and fauna evolved along their own lines. Branches on the evolutionary tree that withered every place else—primitive orders like marsupials and monotremes—thrived here and helped create the prehistoric-looking landscapes that unnerved early European visitors but captivate artists and tourists today.

Perhaps the most vibrant expression of Western Australia's geological uniqueness is put on display across the southwest each spring, when the wildflowers bloom and the plains, desert scrub, and woodlands burst into color. Lilies, banksias, feather flowers, red and yellow kangaroo paws, grevillea, parrot bush, flowering gums, native foxgloves, flame peas—more than 12,000 named species and another 2,000 unnamed ones. The vast majority of these plants have evolved here, in Western Australia's splendid isolation, and they are found nowhere else on Earth.

To a newcomer traveling along the long and sparsely-populated northwest coast, the scenery isn't much to write home about—aching voids of spinifex and miles of low, flat, charmless scrub sweltering in the heat. There are no hints of gentle greenery, no lush rain forests, and no idyllic palm-fringed beaches as there are in Australia's fertile east. Here the outback simply comes to an abrupt end where the Indian Ocean begins.

Certainly the early Dutch navigators were underwhelmed when they made unexpected landfalls here on their way to Java. Dirk Hartog was the first, sailing his ship *Eendracht* into what became known as Shark Bay on October 25, 1616, and landing on the island that now bears his name. He left a pewter plate to commemorate the occasion and hurried on his way.

Over the decades other Dutch navigators found their way here, riding the fast westerlies from the Cape of Good Hope and overshooting the point at which they should have veered north to Java. Occasionally their miscalculations had tragic results. The coast is strewn with the remains of 17th- and 18th-century ships that came to grief on its unexpected shoals and islands. Others sailed along it, charting its ragged indentations, landing occasionally and shuddering at its primitive, godless bush. After describing a miserable day hiking through the waterless scrub where Perth is today, Mandrop Torst, on an expedition in 1696, wrote gloomily in his journal: "We could see our ships clearly from here and wished a thousand times to be back on board." English buccaneer William Dampier, who visited the northwest in 1687, 1688, and again in 1699, was similarly unimpressed, describing a land of poor rocky soil, scrubby trees that bore no fruit, and flies in plague proportions. The Aborigines who lived here, he wrote, "are the miserablest People in the world."

For the profit-seeking Dutch, who sailed to the unknown Great South Land hoping for gold, jewels, silk, spices, and rare woods, the prospects here were beyond bleak. But of course their 17th-century imaginations could never have dreamed that beneath this unprepossessing scrub and treacherously shallow seas lay almost unimag-

inable wealth. Western Australia is one of the world's richest mineral zones—a treasure trove of gold, uranium, diamonds, iron, bauxite, and zinc. Beneath the turquoise waters of the Indian Ocean are some of the world's biggest reserves of natural gas—billions, perhaps even trillions, of cubic feet of gas, while the seabed along the northwest coast was littered with pearl-bearing oysters. Today, Western Australia contributes a stunning 45 percent of the total value of Australia's mineral production. And for more than a century this promising region, from the Pilbara to the sprawling goldfields around Kalgoorlie, has been known as the Golden West.

It wasn't until late in the 19th century that a swag of hard-bitten adventurers, prospectors, and fortune-seekers began to crack the secret wealth hidden in these ancient rocks. A gold strike near Marble Bar in 1890 brought thousands to this flinty, searingly hot valley about a hundred miles inland from Port Hedland. Gold was only one of the minerals locked in the Precambrian rocks here: Tin, manganese, copper, tantalite, long strands of asbestos—more than 70 minerals in all—were here. The "marble" formation in the normally dry Coongan River that gave the town its name is actually a brilliant hunk of jasper.

Although people still work manganese and tin claims here, and mining companies are coming back to the area after a lapse of a few decades, the town of 300 is best known for being the hottest place in Australia. "One hundred and twenty-five degrees all the week and 128 on Sundays is Marble Bar's proud boast," wrote adventurer and journalist Ernestine Hill when she passed through here in the 1930s. While temperatures have never officially hit those extremes, Marble Bar has achieved immortality in the *Guinness Book of World Records*. In a heat wave during the summer of 1923-24, the mercury topped 100 degrees for 160 consecutive days. Today, Marble Bar's main competition for this dubious distinction is the former copper-mining town of Whim Creek, about 125 empty, mostly waterless miles to the west. I killed a summer afternoon once in the Whim Creek Hotel when it was 112 inside the pub. The temperature outside in the sun and glaring vastness of blistered rock was anybody's guess.

The miners in lonely towns such as Whim Creek, Marble Bar, and Nullagine were only scratching the surface here, however. The primitive stromatolites that created those ancient fossils in the hills outside Marble Bar, and which still live in the turquoise waters of Hamelin Pool, were thriving in what geologists refer to as the Hamersley Basin about 2.5 billion years ago. The oxygen they released through photosynthesis combined with the ferrous oxide in seawater to create ferric oxide.

Over many millions of years thick beds of this iron-rich material were deposited on the seafloor and later, after a period of mountain building, became the incredibly rich iron deposits of the Hamersley Range. The deposits were discovered in the 1960s, and almost overnight Australia became one of the world's largest exporters of iron ore. Huge mines near the Pilbara towns of Newman, Paraburdoo, and Tom Price turn out 120 million tons of ore ever year.

On the outskirts of Port Hedland, I have watched as one of the frequent ore trains rumbled past, coming from the Mount Newman mine, 265 miles away. The ground shook. I tried to count the cars, but they passed into a throbbing blur. These are among the longest trains in the world, more than a mile from the front engine to the caboose. And each car is piled high with dense black hematite ore that is more than 60 percent pure iron. It is on its way to the town's enormous loading facilities, where some of the world's biggest ore carriers wait in the shimmering heat and humidity of the Indian Ocean.

A sleepy country town until its makeover by the mining companies in the 1960s, Port Hedland now is a jumble of giant industrial sites, high-tension electrical lines, freight yards, loading docks, ore stockpiles, and blinding white dunes of salt (another local industry) awaiting export. Port Hedland isn't cute, but then it doesn't pretend to be: People come here to make money. Port Hedland, Karratha, and Dampier exude a sort of gold rush atmosphere, with plenty of high-paying jobs going around for riggers, fitters, carpenters, plumbers, electricians—"sparkies" in the local vernacular—and almost anyone with a strong back. The luckiest or best qualified land jobs with one of the huge mining projects, or with the multibillion-dollar North West Shelf Natural Gas Project at Karratha, with its generous overtime pay, benefits, and subsidized company housing. Others work for the myriad of contractors that have sprung up to service the big projects or start businesses of their own. It is tough up here. The atmosphere is macho

and hard-drinking: A last bastion of unrepentant, unreconstructed Aussie blokedom, with crowded, boisterous pubs and a fishing boat in almost every driveway. It's lonely, too, judging by one of the classified ads I read in a local paper. "Hey all you bikers and Harley Riders," began the ad of a Perth-based working girl who called herself Shagsie. "Meet me at Geckos!"

While the coast may be bleak, the Hamersley Range comprises some of the most magnificent mountains in Australia. Wild and craggy, the mountains rise from golden plains of spinifex and glow rust red in the desert twilight. They are celebrated in a series of splendid national parks. Karijini National Park is set in the Hamersley, around a massive two-billion-year-old weathered formation more than 160 miles long, cut by dramatic gorges banded in shades of mauve, blue, gray, and red and dominated by the 4,000-foot massif of Mount Bruce, the second highest mountain in Western Australia. Millstream-Chichester National Park is a five-million-acre tract of hauntingly empty claypan flats, rolling expanses of spinifex, and craggy, sediment-capped basalt ranges. Beautifully gnarled coolabah trees shade the normally dry watercourses, and in the spring the desert can be carpeted with wildflowers. Ancient gorges along the Fortescue River, with their lush ferns and rushes, form year-round pools in the dry season and are noisy with birds.

The gorges form some of the most beautiful oases in Australia, lush with water lilies, paperbark trees, and Millstream palms that are found nowhere else. Afghan camel drivers used to put in here to rest and water their animals (and themselves) on their endless rounds of supplying the outlying stations and mining camps and carrying loads of ore and wool to market. At some of these springs, such as Python Pool, the drivers planted date palms, which have flourished over the years. The luxuriance of the palm fronds and the invitingly clear pools of water form a stark counterpoint to some of the most inhospitable terrain on the planet.

"A bad Rocky land, without trees, about as high as Dover in England," wrote François Pelsaert of the *Batavia* about the cliff-lined shoreline on the central West Australian coast when he landed in 1629. But he was in a bad temper at the time, with his ship having run aground (on his watch, no less) on a submerged reef near the Houtman Abrolhos Islands. It was an inauspicious introduction to Australia, but for Captain Pelsaert's unlucky companions things were shortly to get much worse. Since there was little food or water to be found (at least to non-Aboriginal eyes) in this breathlessly hot, alien land, Pelsaert decided to take a few men and risk an open boat journey to Java to summon help for the 250 survivors. As soon as he left, the crew, which had been on the verge of mutiny even before the shipwreck, ran amok, murdering, raping, and torturing their fellow castaways. The rest fled into the bush, built a fort, and prayed for rescue. The mutineers had planned to seize any rescue ship that came and embark on careers of piracy. Instead, three months later, Pelsaert—whose career with the Dutch East India Company was in tatters after carelessly losing the ship—returned to find only 125 survivors. He captured the mutineers and meted out savage justice.

The 800-mile stretch of windswept coast between Karratha and Perth has hardly changed since those forlorn castaways watched Pelsaert's open boat disappear over the horizon. Geraldton and Carnarvon are the only two towns of any size, and the North West Coastal Highway (which, in fact, is rarely in sight of the coast) is nearly as lonely and desolate as the road crossing Australia's legendary Nullarbor Plain. I have cycled along this empty stretch of highway in high summer, battling temperatures of more than 110 degrees and powerful, roasting head winds almost every inch of the way. Those ceaseless winds were the same ones that had propelled so many Dutch ships onto this coast three centuries before.

One of the best known was the *Zuytdorp,* wrecked in 1712 near the mouth of the Murchison River, where the *Batavia*'s mutineers had been castaway 83 years earlier. A few years later the *Fortuyne* and the *Aagtekerke* disappeared on their way to Java, presumably foundering on these abandoned shores. In 1727 the *Zeewijk,* carrying ten chests laden with East India Company treasure, ran aground on the Houtman Albrohos, the same reef islands that claimed the *Batavia.* The 88 survivors spent nearly a year on the coast. They eventually built a small sloop, the *Sloepie,* from ship timbers and mangroves and sailed to Java, delivering the recovered treasure. Timbers and artifacts from the *Batavia, Zuytdorp,* and *Zeewijk* can be seen today at the maritime museum in Geraldton.

The history of the area isn't entirely a litany of tragedy. A number of curious 17th- and 18th-century navigators sailed safely along the silent coast, charting its inlets and naming its features. Dutch explorer Willem de Vlamingh landed on Dirk Hartog Island in 1696 and, finding Hartog's pewter plate from 1616, left one of his own. William Dampier came to this same spot in 1699 and, impressed by the sharks he saw, named the broad inlet Sharks Bay. But neither the Dutch nor the English could think of a use for this barren strand and never troubled themselves to claim it. That honor went to the French.

In 1772 the *Gros Ventre,* a tiny, 16-gun ship under the command of François Alesno Conte de Saint-Allouarn anchored at Dirk Hartog Island and put a landing party ashore. The men climbed a hill, raised the tricolor flag, and buried a bottle with a couple of French coins in it to mark the occasion. After burying one of their colleagues who had died of scurvy at sea, they sailed away. France's colonial authorities, however, never followed up this far-flung claim by establishing a settlement here, and the Conte de Saint-Allouarn's bottle of coins was forgotten.

None of these hardened, fortune-hunting sailors or their political masters in Paris, London, or Amsterdam could have dreamed that one day this barren coast would be treasured simply for its unspoiled isolation—that their countrymen would one day pay handsomely to come here and snorkel in its waters. The bland facade of the North West Cape, a scrubby peninsula about 220 miles north of Shark Bay, was seen and dismissed by Dutch mariners as early as 1616. The ethereal beauty of these places lies—literally—below the surface. Beneath the warm shallow seas off the North West Cape, for example, lies jewel-like Ningaloo Reef, a fantasia of brilliant corals and sponges more than 160 miles long. As spectacular as Queensland's Great Barrier Reef, the more readily accessible Ningaloo is only a hundred yards from shore in some places. Here, in spots like Coral Bay, it is possible for a fit snorkeler to make a unique journey: A short swim from harsh outback scrub into a cool, blue underwater dreamscape inhabited by 180 varieties of coral and hundreds of species of fish.

At various times of the year Ningaloo Reef becomes the playground of dugongs, sea turtles, dolphins, humpback whales, and whale sharks. World's largest fish, these gentle plankton-eating giants congregate in these waters in the autumn, drawing divers from all over the world.

Shark Bay, on the World Heritage list, is another powerful tourist drawing card. As the name suggests, the bay teems with marine life thanks to thick sea grass beds that provide food and shelter to huge schools of fish, dugongs, and sea snakes. But it is for its gregarious dolphin population that Shark Bay is most famous. For more than 30 years dolphins have swum into the shallows near the town of Monkey Mia to play with humans, accept fish from them, and offer them gifts of fish.

For many years it was simply a game between marine biologists and the dolphins, but by 1985, when the road to Monkey Mia was finally paved, easy access and a rare opportunity to interact with wild dolphins brought thousands of tourists. Shark Bay also has 70-mile-long Shell Beach, one of the few beaches in the world that is made entirely of non-fossilized shells: billions upon billions of tiny coquina bivalves in beds up to 40 feet thick.

A hundred miles farther south, Kalbarri National Park's spectacular sandstone gorges and the Murchison River are among Western Australia's most popular parks, particularly in the spring. Then the wildflowers come into bloom, and the park becomes a kaleidoscope of grevilleas, banksias, melaleucas, leschenaultias, and sedges.

Stories of the Conte de Saint-Allouarn's claiming this region for France—by now only a matter of historical curiosity—had been circulating since a historian had come across a reference to it in some musty 18th-century archives in Paris after World War I. There was never any proof of the claim, and in fact some of the Conte de Saint-Allouarn's contemporaries in Paris doubted that he'd even set foot in Australia. But in December 1997 archaeologists digging on a hilltop on Dirk Hartog Island made an intriguing find: Two silver French coins, dating from the early 1770s, and a weathered 18th-century wine bottle.

Whatever the Conte de Saint-Allouarn did or didn't do on Dirk Hartog Island, French navigators continued to explore the coast. Aware that the French might establish a base in Western Australia, in 1826 the governor of New South Wales set up a penal colony on King George Sound, where the town of Albany is today. The flag was raised, and the new settlement was christened Frederick's Town, after the Duke of York and Albany. The pleasant seaport on the cool, breezy southwest corner of the continent quickly became a regular port of call for French and American whalers and is known today for its fishing fleet.

English authorities were still nervous about French intentions, however, and when an ambitious English Navy post captain named James Stirling approached them with the idealistic notion of starting a colony of free settlers along the Swan River, they accepted the idea. Nobody knew if the settlement would be viable or not. At the colonial office nobody really cared so long as a new English presence was going to be established on the coast, particularly since private investors were footing the bill. The eager colonists went off, in the words of one contemporary, "without any greater preparation than if they had gone out on a holiday excursion in the woods." In the autumn of 1829, they landed on the coast in a torrential rain and established the town of Fremantle, where the Swan River meets the sea. A few months later some of the party relocated about nine miles upstream, and on August 12, 1829, they proclaimed the town of Perth.

After grandiose speeches and musketry salutes, the pilgrims were left to confront a few harsh realities: They were surrounded by marshland humming with mosquitoes and sand fleas, as far from civilization as any place could be, and nobody else wanted to join them. Why migrate here when, if you wanted to go to the colonies, you could always go to New South Wales? Sydney was a prosperous young city, land was freely available and, better still, free convict labor was available to work it. Consequently Perth attracted few migrants.

For the next 20 years it languished, a dismal shantytown, until in 1850 its leaders relented and began to import convicts to do the grunt work of building public edifices, bridges, and roads. At last Perth began to take shape, and in 1856 it was proclaimed a city. Even so, remoteness and lack of interest made Perth the poor relation to the rest of Australia until 1887. Then a boy near Halls Creek, in the remote Kimberley region on the northwest frontier, picked up a stone to fling at a crow and noticed it was laced with gold. Word of the find spread like wildfire, triggering the first of a fantastic sequence of gold, silver, tin, copper, and manganese strikes. Western Australia has hardly looked back.

Perth today is a sun-splashed city of a million with a glittering skyline along the Swan River, a new-money brashness, and a reputation for being Australia's answer to Dallas. Most of the big money here comes from the west's vast mineral wealth—iron, oil, gold, natural gas, and diamonds—and, like Texas, Perth carries itself with a big-hatted frontier swagger. Back in the rollicking 1980s, it was home to Australia's highest-flying corporate buccaneers, a clique of ruthless, fabulously wealthy self-made entrepreneurs. The nouveau riche excesses—gleaming yachts, private jets, and priceless French impressionists on boardroom walls—of these Gatsbyesque figures defined a jazzy new era for the rest of Australia.

No one personified it better than Alan Bond. A sign-painter turned millionaire property developer and swash-buckling yachtsman, Bond tweaked the old-money noses of the New York Yacht Club in 1983 and took the America's Cup back to Australia in a stunning upset that made him a national hero. But Bond was only one of a coterie of Perth businessmen who became household names and whose faces shone from glossy celebrity magazines. As the decade of junk bonds and conspicuous consumption took shape, the Golden West took on the glow of a magic strike-it-rich place where anything could happen—and frequently did.

Like the gold rush prospectors, pearling masters, and Afghan cameleers who shaped so much of Western Australia's frontier myths, Perth's high-rolling entrepreneurs have largely passed into oblivion—or minimum security prisons. The music stopped after the October 1987 world stock market crash, when public adulation was replaced by the harder scrutiny of a royal commission, police investigations, and deliberating juries. Details of insider deals, art fraud, rigged horse races, and millions of dollars vanishing in the snap of bejeweled fingers alternately fascinated, amused, and outraged the rest of Australia. It still tends to view Western Australia as a world apart.

Even in these days of jet travel and instant communications, Western Australia is seriously remote. Perth is often said to be the loneliest city in the world. Its nearest similar-size neighbor, Adelaide, is 1,300 air miles away, and to get there you have to cross the vast treeless, water-less void known as the Nullarbor Plain. The flight from Sydney takes five hours and, until the airlines started using long-haul Boeing 767s, westbound planes battling head winds often had to make unscheduled fuel stops in Adelaide before tackling the Nullarbor. But it is traveling overland that really brings home the immense distance between Perth and the rest of the world.

Every Monday and Thursday at 2:55 p.m. the *Indian Pacific* pulls out of Sydney's grand, domed Central Railway Station to begin one of the world's great train journeys: across the Australian outback 2,703 miles to Perth. The trip takes 65 hours and crosses some of the most barren and lifeless landscapes on the planet, where temperatures often soar to 120 degrees. One stretch of track, laid across the waterless heart of the Nullarbor Plain, is billed as the world's longest straightaway—310 miles of dead straight rail from a lonely siding called Ooldea, where a few railway maintenance workers live, to a slight bend at another siding called Nurina.

The origin of this trans-Australian rail link goes back to the late 19th century. It was offered as an inducement for the reluctant Western Australia to join the other colonies in forming a united Australian nation. Construction started from the South Australian town of Port Augusta in 1914. While there were no major engineering obstacles to laying a thousand miles of track across the Nullarbor Plain, the project was a logistical nightmare, the Edwardian era's version of building a space station. Since there was nothing in this void to sustain life, everything—food, water, shelter for thousands of workers and pack animals—had to be hauled out into the desert. Portable communities were set up, their butchers, bakers, banks, and post offices on rolling stock ready to be shifted farther along newly laid line as the track stretched deeper into the hostile wastes. Fresh provisions were sent out from Port Augusta every two weeks.

For some 60 years these isolated communities were serviced by the legendary Tea and Sugar Train, a weekly supply line from Port Augusta that brought everything from fresh water to Santa Claus. Airplanes now supply the few remaining settlements.

After the long journey across the continent, Perth appears on the horizon like the Emerald City of Oz. The sudden surge of wealth from Western Australia's huge iron, diamond, and natural gas discoveries in the 1960s and 1970s almost completely transformed the city center. Gone are old buildings, replaced by modern glass-and-steel office towers and sunlit shopping precincts that give the city a fresh youthfulness not found even in other Australian cities, young as they are by world standards. Perth suburbs are a sprawl of 1950s-style Californian bungalows, their swimming pools, television aerials, palms, and jacaranda trees all projecting the same sunny, egalitarian optimism.

Nine miles southwest, where the Swan River meets the Indian Ocean, is the historic seaport of Fremantle, one of the world's best preserved 19th-century maritime cities. Once a working-class domain of Italian fishermen and Irish longshoremen, its fading colonial facades tastefully smartened up for Australia's unsuccessful defense of the America's Cup yachting trophy in 1987, Fremantle remains a raffishly fashionable enclave for Perth's arty set, café society, and professionals escaping both the city and the suburbs. Although it is very close to Perth, Fremantle has strongly retained its distinct identity. About a dozen miles beyond its dazzling white beach, a short ferry ride away, is Rottnest Island—one of Perth's traditional playgrounds for divers, sailors, and beach-lovers.

Fremantle is a sports-mad city that rejoices in its hot dry Mediterranean climate. On weekends its beaches are crowded with bronzing Aussies, the Swan River is bright with yachts, and the parks become playing fields for scores of informal cricket or football matches. The suburban air is fragrant with the smoke of countless barbecues. Even so, in Perth you never lose the sense of being on the edge of the frontier. The flocks of parrots swooping down the streets, and the possums, small kangaroos, and snakes in the parklands are subtle reminders of the vast expanse of bush that stretches thousands of miles beyond the city.

South of Perth the coast becomes cooler and rainier. A big surf washes the shores, and a hinterland rolls deep in the shade of some of the world's tallest timber—towering karri trees, a type of eucalypt that can reach up to 300 feet high. This is some of the prettiest, greenest country in Western Australia, with narrow country lanes, sparkling beaches, farmlands, and orchards. Over the past 35 years this extreme southwesterly outcrop on the continent has been discovered by successive waves of hippies, surfers, wealthy yuppies looking for weekend retreats, artists,

wine-makers, and urban refugees. They give these farming communities a relaxed, offbeat flavor.

Yallingup, about 125 miles southwest of Perth, has been a honeymoon retreat for wealthy couples since the turn of the century, but it was the surfing boom of the 1960s that put it on the map. The reliably huge waves that pound the sands here have made it the traditional location for the Australia surfing competitions and a mecca for globetrotting, summer-seeking surfers. Breaking waves are a lifestyle and a class leveler along this stretch of coast. Go to any of the surf beaches from Yallingup south to Cape Leeuwin, and in the parking lots you'll see an odd mix of gleaming, late-model BMWs and battered Kombi vans out of the sixties. Their owners are all out in the 15-foot waves.

Some of the finest scenery here is underground, in a labyrinth of limestone caves—more than a hundred in all. Many are relatively unexplored. A few, such as Mammoth Cave, Lake Cave, and Jewel Cave, with its delicate crystals, have become major tourist drawing cards.

Back on the surface, the limestone bedrock challenges wine grapes to do their best. More than 40 vineyards—Leeuwin Estate, Cape Mentelle, and Cullen, among other Australian top labels—are centered around the farming community of Margaret River, which is rapidly gaining a following among connoisseurs.

Cape Leeuwin marks the extreme southwest corner of the continent, where the forces of the Indian Ocean and Southern Ocean meet. The Dutch ship *Leeuwin* (Lioness) was blown here in 1622. Never before had a Dutch ship ventured this far south on the Australian coast. Almost two centuries later, in 1801, Matthew Flinders used the cape as the marker for his circumnavigation of the continent, naming the storm-lashed point of land after the Dutch ship.

Western Australia's southern coast is shrouded by solemn forests of jarrah and karri trees and indented by scores of bays and inlets. The timber town of Pemberton claims the tallest karri tree ever felled in the district, a 338-foot-tall giant. Visitors with a good head for heights can climb up 153 rungs that spiral up the massive trunk of the Gloucester Tree to a viewing platform nearly 200 feet high. Closer to the coast, where rainfall is heaviest, Walpole-Nornalup National Park boasts a magnificent stand of tingle trees known as the Valley of the Giants.

Mingled among them are rich stands of casuarina trees, flowering banksias, wild orchids, and felt-like wildflowers called kangaroo paws.

Each spring much of Western Australia becomes a garden of flowers, more than 12,000 species in all. Most of these are unique to Western Australia. Visitors are drawn here from around the world. From October to December flowers seem to be everywhere—even in downtown Perth as Kings Park riots with color. But no place is more richly or colorfully carpeted than the southwest. Perhaps the most spectacular displays are in the Stirling Range, a ragged chain of mountains about 250 miles southeast of Perth. Some of the exposed summits, which are often shrouded with mist, rise more than 3,000 feet above the surrounding coastal plains. Like lofty islands, surrounded by farmland instead of sea, these slopes support their own unique ecology. There are more than a thousand species of wildflowers up here, some of which, like darwinias, dryandras, and Stirling banksias, are found nowhere else. Beyond these ranges the land flattens out and opens up toward the goldfields, the Nullarbor Plain, and the wild, cliff-lined coast of the Great Australian Bight.

The early string of gold strikes in the Kimberley and Pilbara that helped turn Western Australia's fortunes in the late 1880s were merely flashes in the pan compared with the stunning Coolgardie and Kalgoorlie finds in the 1890s. Gold fever struck in September 1892, when two prospectors, Arthur Bayley and William Ford, rode into the mining town of Southern Cross with almost 35 pounds of gold nuggets they had picked up near a water hole. Thousands stampeded to the area, some on camels. Others walked the final 150 miles across arid plains from the railhead at Southern Cross, sometimes pushing wheelbarrows. Tent cities sprang up. And as more prospectors spread out, scouring the ground, more pulse-quickening discoveries were made nearby—at Norseman, Kambalda, Kanowna, and Kookynie. But it was a lucky Irishman named Paddy Hannan who found the mother of all mother lodes in 1893—an unbelievably rich quartz vein running through Mount Charlotte. Reputedly, Hannan was chasing an errant horse at the time. A century later his find remains one of the world's richest gold-bearing areas, and Kalgoorlie, the boisterous town that sprang up around it, is synonymous with wealth and opportunity. Since those first heady days, a staggering 1,300 tons of gold have come out of Kalgoorlie's fabled Golden Mile. More than 800,000 ounces—about 25 tons, or 350 million dollars worth of gold—is still produced here each year.

By 1902 more than 30,000 people were living in Kalgoorlie, making it slightly larger than it is today. The town had 93 pubs and 8 breweries, and its railway line was the busiest in the state. To keep the rapidly growing gold town alive on this waterless waste, a 345-mile-long pipeline was built in 1903 to bring in water from a reservoir near Perth.

Kalgoorlie's streetscapes are pure Australian gold rush: An exuberant hodgepodge of Edwardian, Moorish, and Victorian styles done in stone, brick, and corrugated iron, and embellished with verandas, balconies, gables, and towers. The town, which amalgamated with nearby Boulder in 1989, still has a frontier flair. It is famous—or infamous—for its topless barmaids (known as "skimpys"), its hard-drinking macho atmosphere, and its boisterous games of two-up, a uniquely outback Australian gambling game in which punters bet on the toss of two coins. For many Australians the vast West Australia goldfields represent a place of opportunity, whether for high-paying jobs in the mines, or for the outrageous good fortune of the husband and wife prospectors who found a 97-ounce nugget in nearby Coolgardie.

Fittingly, these goldfield settlements are the first towns of any size westbound travelers see after crossing the long empty wastes of the Nullarbor Plain. They set the tone for the Golden West. For people leaving it, heading east on the Eyre Highway out of Norseman, a foreboding sign warns that along this harsh stretch of the southern shore there will be few places to get water for the next 800 miles.

Following pages: *A traveler trails a plume of dust near the abandoned asbestos-mining town of Wittenoom, in Western Australia's Hamersley Range. Health fears forced the closing of the mine in 1966.*

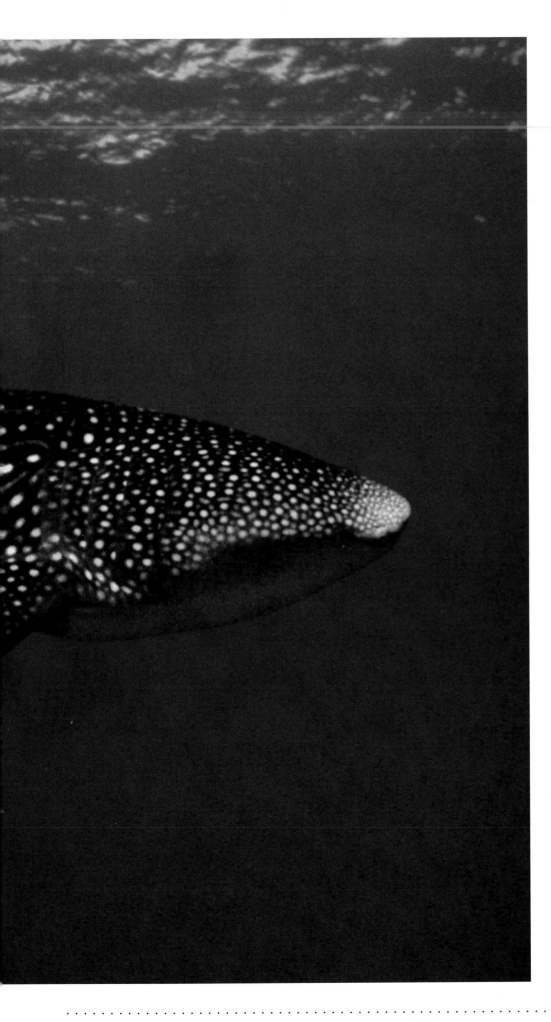

Drifting past a diver, a 35-foot-long whale shark patrols the placid waters of Western Australia's Ningaloo Reef. World's largest fish, whale sharks pose no threat to most reef creatures. The shy fish feed on plankton.

"An upside down snowstorm," divers often say, describing the magical nights in March when corals along Ningaloo Reef release their eggs and sperm. Spawning on the Southern Hemisphere's coral reefs occurs each autumn, usually after the full moon. Carried along by the tides, the fertilized eggs will attach themselves to the skeletal remains of dead corals and begin a new colony.

Discovered in 1989 and unique to the shallows of Hamelin Pool, a species of jellyfish known as Phyllorhiza peronlesueuri *floats above a bed of 4,000-year-old stromatolites, a form of blue-green algae. Tucked in a recess in Western Australia's Shark Bay, Hamelin Pool's sheltered, sunny, and ultra-saline waters make it ideal sanctuary.*

Calm indigo waters, gleaming sands, and a seabed littered with pearl oysters give the Lacepede Islands the look of a paradise, but this lonely archipelago on Western Australia's ragged northwest coast is prey to the capricious winds and treacherous tides of summer monsoons. A tropical cyclone in April 1935 caught the pearling fleet unaware, sinking 21 boats and claiming 140 lives. Divers say copper diving helmets of the dead still roll along the bottom of the sea.

Following pages: Ancient gorges of the Pilbara region plunge into sandstones dating back more than two billion years. Dotted with waterfalls and secluded pools, these deep, palm-lined chasms are havens for birds, kangaroos, and reptiles.

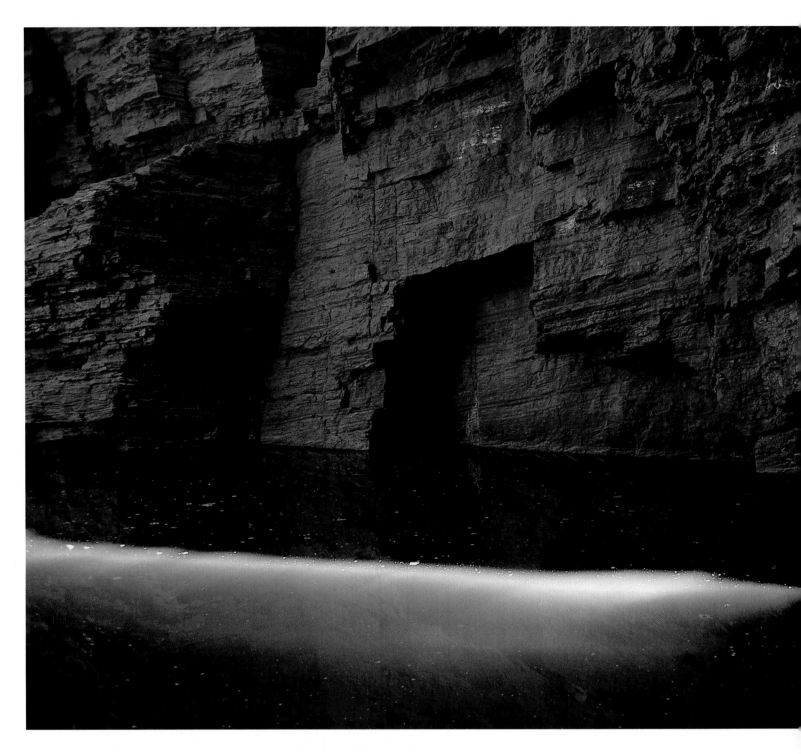

Shaft of sun illuminates a dark pool and sandstone face in Karijini National Park. Eons of runoff from torrential rains have scoured dramatic gorges in the park, part of Western Australia's Pilbara region. Many of the gorges have year-round pools in the dry season.

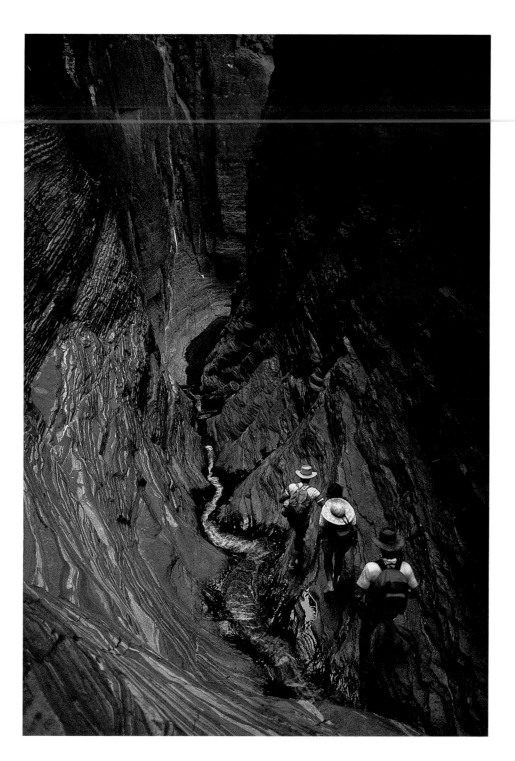

Hiking into history, tour guide Dave Doust of Wittenoom leads a group on a precipitous walk into a gorge in Karijini National Park. The gorges of the Pilbara, eroded by ancient storms, plummet into bedrock walls that are among the oldest exposed rocks on Earth.

Following pages: *Two centuries of shifting dunes have exposed thousands of golden limestone knobs that give the Pinnacles Desert its name. Wind, rain, and sand sculpted the pinnacles, creating an eerie landscape of brooding statues, the main attraction of Nambung National Park.*

A brilliant shawl of wildflowers drapes the desert near the mining town of Mount Magnet. Spring rains deck much of Australia's southwest in a dazzling floral display. More than 12,000 species of flowering plants can be found in Western Australia, ranging from giant hardwood trees to tiny underground orchids.

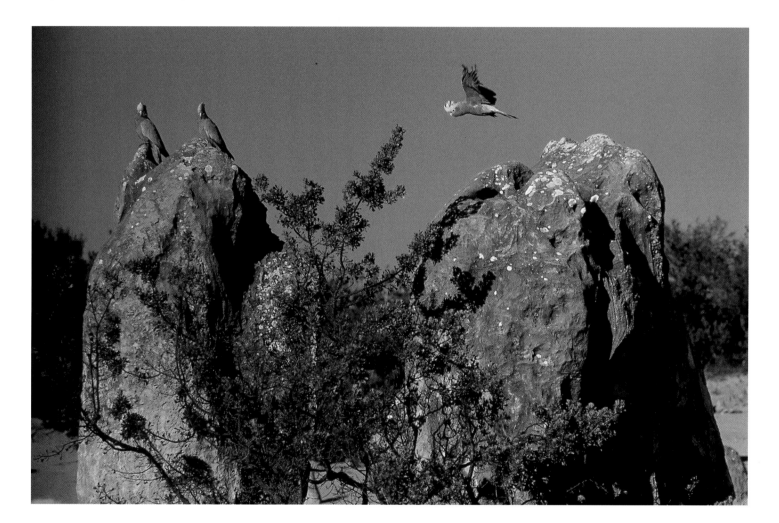

A flash of pink as a galah takes wing adds a spark of color to the muted tones of the bush in Nambung National Park. Pink-and-gray galahs, one of the most common of the 60 species of parrots and cocka- toos found in Australia, often flit along roadsides searching for seeds.

by John Landy

A Unique Flora and Fauna

The first naturalists to record the Australian fauna and flora were intrigued by the unique nature of the plants and animals of the newly found continent. The Europeans who received the first specimen of the duck-billed and web-footed platypus thought it was a fraud or practical joke made of parts of mammals and birds. Joseph Banks, naturalist aboard the *Endeavour* with Capt. James Cook, expressed his surprise on seeing a "kangaru." "To compare it to any European animal would be impossible—its fore legs are extremely short and are of no use to it in walking; its hind legs again are disproportionately long; with these it hops 7 or 8 feet."

Later, Charles Darwin and the eminent botanist J. D. Hooker saw not only the singular nature of much of the Australian biota but also that it had associations with the fauna and flora of other landmasses in the Southern Hemisphere. There were closely similar plants belonging to the family Proteacea growing in southern Australia, Chile, and the Cape Province of South Africa. The large, flightless bird, the ostrich of South Africa, was matched by the rhea of South America and the emu of Australia.

Most theories advanced to explain the origin of plants and animals on the Australian continent assumed that they were invasions from other regions at various times. When the continents were seen as stationary, the most likely means by which these invasions could take place was over land bridges or islands exposed by sea level changes. The acceptance of the theory of plate tectonics, which envisions that continents are resting on plates that move in relationship to each other, opened the way to explaining many of the problems of the evolution and distribution of Australian animals and plants.

Originally Australia was joined with Antarctica, Africa, South America, India, and the smaller landmasses of Madagascar, New Caledonia, and New Zealand in one super continent called Gondwana. Gondwana began to break up 160 million years ago, with Africa separating first. The Australian continental plate, which included Tasmania and the southern portion of New Guinea, began to separate from Antarctica about 55 million years ago. When the Australian continent began its slow drift northward, it was radically different from the land today. The climate was warm and humid; the vegetation of the whole continent was somewhat like a subtropical rain forest. The present flora and fauna, their singular nature and distribution, result from huge changes that took place in the northward drift of an isolated continent. A 45-million-year journey saw a change from a verdant continent to a largely harsh and arid land. While many plants and animals became extinct during this period, others proliferated as the closed forest cover was replaced by grasslands, woodlands, savannas, and deserts. Eucalypts and acacias radiated to become the dominant group of Australian plants, and marsupials occupied the many new environmental niches that became available.

Fifteen million years ago the drifting Australian continent converged with the Sunda Islands Arc plate of southeastern Asia, forming the present island of New Guinea. Bats and rodents, the only two groups of native terrestrial placental mammals in Australia, probably made their entry at this time for southeastern Asia, as did plants of Indo-Malayan origin.

The last 2.4 million years have seen an intensification of the drying process in Australia. The last glacial period peak, some 18,000 years ago, is believed to represent the driest period in the continent's history. Then, 70 percent of the landmass was windblown sand, there was less than 20 percent tree cover, and many ecosystems were reduced and fragmented to refuges in favorable locations in valleys, mountains, and creek beds. The climate began to grow wetter 14,000 years ago, and the plants and animals confined to refuges started to extend outward and repopulate previously more arid territory.

Today, in the better watered regions and in the semiarid areas that border the interior, the eucalypt, or gum tree, dominates the flora, with some 500 species adapted to a great variety of habitats. Eucalypts range from the towering, 300-foot-tall mountain ash, the world's tallest flowering plant; the stunted multitrunked malle gum that dominates the semiarid region and seldom exceed 20 feet in height; and the shapely white-trunked snow gum that occupies the alpine and subalpine regions. Eucalypts are by far the most important group of trees—biologically and economically—in Australia. They dominate the landscape of the better watered regions and are absent from the dry interior except along water courses and at the foot of stony outcrops. The major trees of the outback are the yellow, flowering acacias, or wattles. They are even more prolific than the eucalypts, with more than 600 species. The most widespread is the mulga, famous for its hard, multicolored wood and useful as stock feed for cattle during drought. Vegetation dominated by mulga covers about 20 percent of the continent.

The most authentic relics of the original Gondwanan forests that once clothed the continent are now confined to isolated patches of rain forest. Here, some of the original Gondwanan plant families still flourish. But the progenitors of these plants can be found only as fossils over much of mainland Australia. The temperate rain forest of southeastern Australia, dominated by beech, is also a remnant of Gondwanan forest, though modified more over time than its tropical counterparts.

Australian fauna is unique in its variety of marsupials and the existence of a very ancient group, the egg-laying monotremes represented by the platypus and the echidna. Fossil evidence demonstrates that marsupials existed in Gondwana and that they lived a hundred million years ago in North America and Europe. Today, they survive outside of Australia only in the form of the carnivorous opossums of North and South America. Fossils of a relative of the platypus have been identified recently in southern Argentina, but there are no living monotremes outside Australia and New Guinea. While the present Australian placental mammals, rodents and bats, are traditionally believed to have reached Australia from southeastern Asia long after Australia broke away from Gondwana, recent fossil evidence seems to show that placental mammals, including bats, derived from Gondwana did, in fact, exist earlier.

Scientists still do not know why marsupials succeeded so well in Australia, why monotremes survived, and why the early placental mammals failed to dominate as they did elsewhere in the world. Marsupials have radiated spectacularly in Australia to fill many environmental niches occupied by placental mammals elsewhere in the world. The carnivorous thylacine, or Tasmanian tiger, strongly resembled a wolf, and the tiny marsupial mole that burrows in the sand hills is nearly identical to the placental mole of the African desert. Of the monotremes, the platypus is still quite common in the rivers and creeks of eastern Australia. Due to its shy habits, however, it is

rarely seen. The echidna, or spiny anteater, is common throughout mainland Australia and occupies almost every environmental niche from alpine regions to the driest areas. When alarmed, the echidna burrows downward vertically with amazing speed, soon disappearing from sight. As its common name suggests, it feeds mainly on ants, but also eats termites.

Transverse stripes marked the largest of the carnivorous marsupials, the Tasmanian tiger, or thylacine. The thylacine once roamed across the entire Australian mainland. It became extinct, most probably through competition from the dingo, introduced perhaps 4,000 years ago by Aborigines. Abundant in Tasmania last century, the thylacine was hunted ruthlessly. It was a sheep killer, and the government placed a bounty on its scalp. The last thylacine died in captivity in 1936, and numerous attempts to locate it in the wild have since failed.

Australia's best known herbivorous mammals—and the most famous of its fauna—are the koala, wombat, kangaroo, and wallaby. The koala and the three species of wombats, although quite different in appearance and habits, are related. Both have a pouch for their young that opens to the rear, as well as a very shortened tail. The koala rarely leaves its perch in eucalypts, resting in a fork of the tree when not feeding. The larger, powerfully built wombat lives underground and emerges at night to feed on grasses. The koala is widely distributed across eastern and southeastern Australia. Koalas find sufficient moisture in the leaves of the eucalypts that are their sole diet. Hunted for its fur last century and early this century, the koala is now protected. The aging population of koalas, their susceptibility to disease, and their low birth rate have contributed to what scientists think is a general decline of the species. Kangaroos and wallabies are the largest and most readily seen of Australian marsupials. There is no precise definition of wallaby or kangaroo. Animals weighing more than 44 pounds tend to be called kangaroos, and those of lesser weight, wallabies. The largest kangaroo is the red, which dominates the inland. The male may reach seven feet and weigh 187 pounds.

The hopping gait of kangaroos and wallabies is unique among large mammals. The only other animals that share this motion are small hopping mice, and it is thought that kangaroos and wallabies may have evolved from quite small ancestors. The bipedal bounding movement of the kangaroo and the wallaby, achieved by the balancing effect of a large and heavy tail, is marginally more efficient at high speeds than the quadrupedal gait of placental animals, but it has some obvious disadvantages at slow speeds. Kangaroos and wallabies use their tail as a prop when standing and as a lever to awkwardly lift their hind legs forward when moving slowly as they graze. The animals cannot move backwards easily.

The bird fauna of Australia is very rich and diverse, with some 700 species compared to 750 in all of North America. Australia has the world's most varied groups of parrots, which include cockatoos, a large number of bright-colored seed-eating parrots, and specialized nectar feeders, the lorikeets. Of all Australian birds the lyrebird is perhaps the most striking and unusual. The male's lyre-shaped plumage, dancing routine, and extraordinary mimicry make the bird stand out. Possessed of a singular song of its own, the male lyrebird intersperses that call with the mimicked songs of numerous birds in its locality. His song, which varies in content of mimicry from place to place, is so intense and clear that it can be heard over long distances in dense scrub and fern gullies.

Other birds unique to Australia and New Guinea include birds of paradise and the bowerbird. The most spectacularly plumaged birds of paradise occur in New Guinea, but representatives of the bowerbird are more evenly distributed. These birds build a bower, which may consist of a platform and an avenue of upright sticks, where courting and mating usually take place. The male adorns his bower with various objects, with scant concern as to their origin, to attract a female. Often the objects are of one color. The satin bowerbird, which favors blue, collects things as diverse as berries, feathers, bits of paper, cloth, and glass.

Scientists once thought that the majority of Australian bird families were related to Asian birds that had migrated to Australia through Indonesia in the distant past. Recent studies using DNA technology, however, suggest that the birds are mostly of ancient Australian stock and have evolved in isolation over long periods. That they resemble Asian birds is a function of adopting similar habits in similar environments.

The soils of Australia are the poorest and shallowest of all continents, the result of millions of years of continuous weathering. There has been no widespread replenishment of soil from the Earth's interior resulting from volcanic activity. Nor has there been a cultivating effect from huge ice sheets as there was in much of North America during the Ice Age. Paradoxically, the extremely infertile soils of the sand plains of southwestern Australia

have proved to be the most species diverse botanical region on the continent. Isolated from eastern Australia by the arid Nullarbor Plain, less disrupted by very dry glacial phases, and with a more consistent pattern of winter rainfall, the sand plains have spawned an extraordinary number of plant species. To date more than 10,000 have been identified, with 70 percent of them endemic to the region. No one genus or species has become dominant. The sand plains are especially rich in highly colored flowering plants such as banksias, hakeas, and grevilleas. Carnivorous plants, particularly sundews, thrive because of their ability to augment the very low levels of nitrogen in the soil with insects they catch.

A feature of this flora, and, in fact, much of the flora of Australia, is the manifestation of scleromorphy—a condition whereby the plant is often reduced in size and the leaves may be reduced to spikes or thorns. At first scleromorphy was thought to be a response to aridity and a means of reducing transpiration under increasingly dry conditions. It is now believed to be an adaptation to the extraordinary low levels of soil nutrients, particularly phosphorus and nitrogen, so characteristic of the vast majority of Australian soils.

Fire has played a critical role in the evolution of Australian flora, and Australian plants generally are particularly well adapted to respond to fire. Eucalypts, for example, grow thick, protective bark, and almost immediately after a fire send out sprouts from buds on the tree trunks or from enlarged woody roots. Other eucalypt species produce great numbers of seeds at the time of a fire that readily root in the ashes. Volatile oils in the foliage of eucalypts actually encourage fire, as does the accumulation of shed bark and leaves that builds up in the understory.

Recovery from fire can be surprisingly rapid. In February 1983 the Ash Wednesday Fire in southeastern Australia killed 70 people and destroyed hundreds of thousands of hectares of bushland and farmland. The heathlands near Anglesea, 60 miles southwest of Melbourne, were devastated, reduced to blackened stumps and white sand. Yet, in the space of three years, all but one of the more than 600 native plants that occurred in the heathlands were again flourishing. That missing plant, the rare elbow orchid, was located a few years later. Even more startling, wrinkled buttons, a plant considered extinct for more than 60 years, was rediscovered.

Like fire, the unpredictability of the weather greatly

influences agriculture in Australia and must have had a profound effect on the direction of evolution of life on the continent. In addition to anticipated seasonal fluctuations in temperature and rainfall is a meteorological phenomenon, the El Niño Southern Oscillation, or ENSO for short. Its onset is accompanied by drought on the Australian continent, particularly the eastern half. In the last 200 years Australian farmers have adjusted to this unpredictable element by conserving water and fodder, by growing plants that are drought resistant, and by stocking their properties conservatively. Long before the farmers, the Aborigines developed a nomadic system of life that allowed for the inevitable but uncertain onset and duration of drought. Like the people, Australian plants and animals have evolved so as to be able to survive this uncertain aspect of their environment.

The reproductive pattern of the female red kangaroo, for example, is closely adapted to the precarious inland habitat. Shortly before the joey in her pouch is ready to leave, a reserve dormant egg, or blastocyst, in the female begins to develop. As soon as the joey leaves the pouch, or if it dies, a newly born kangaroo makes its way to the pouch. The milk secreted from the teat to which the newly born kangaroo attaches itself is quite different from that which the joey outside the pouch continues to suckle. Soon after giving birth, the female mates. In drought conditions, however, she does not. Instead, she produces one more young from the dormant egg.

As soon as the drought breaks, the female's estrus cycle resumes, and in several months she will be associated with three stages of development: A quiescent blastocyst, a tiny kangaroo in her pouch, and a joey at her feet. In prolonged droughts, female red kangaroos, which normally begin breeding before the age of 20 months, may not breed for 3 years or more. The onset of rain, accompanied by the growth of fresh vegetation, induces an immediate response, and the animals begin breeding.

In response to climatic uncertainty an unusually high number of Australian birds have adopted a nomadic lifestyle. This applies particularly to those birds that exploit the dry inland, where the erratic nature of rainfall is accentuated and where there are frequently long periods of total drought. The budgerigar moves in large flocks to new sources of seed as soon as they become available after rain and begins breeding. Pelicans, ducks, and cormorants, normally inhabitants of the better watered coastal areas, seek out newly formed lakes and running creeks after rain.

Plants of the interior can withstand the effects of desiccation and respond quickly to the onset of rain by flowering and setting seed. These adaptations allow them to survive prolonged drought. Ephemerals, mainly of the daisy family, spring to life after heavy rain and provide a breathtaking kaleidoscope of color across the dry land. Perhaps surprisingly, succulents are not a prominent feature of the drier areas of Australia. Though able to grow in conditions of very low moisture, succulents are not adapted to the erratic rainfall pattern.

The evolution of Australian flora and fauna is a story of remarkable adaptations over 50 million years to an increasingly arid and impoverished landmass. The plants and animals of Australia developed on a continent isolated for millions of years. When explorers arrived more than 200 years ago, they found organisms new and totally different from those they knew.

The coming of Europeans has greatly increased the pressure on many of the continents' plants and animals. Forests have been cleared, grassland and heathland habitats have disappeared under crops and pastures, and salted areas have increased. Many plants and animals, such as the thylacine and the paradise parrot, have become extinct, and some 5 percent of plants are extinct, endangered, or vulnerable.

In the last 20 years there has been a gradual public awakening to the importance and the fragility of the Australian environment. With the rising land-care movement, the creation of more national parks, and government-supported programs of tree planting and habitat preservation on private land, the future looks somewhat brighter for Australia's plants and animals—flora and fauna delightfully different from those anywhere else in the world.

Following pages: *Dust veils sheep on a station near Gascoyne Junction, in Western Australia. The nearby Gascoyne River often runs dry for months at a time, but the water table below the sandy surface provides a steady source of water. When it does rain, the Gascoyne can flood spectacularly, occasionally inundating the Ten Mile Bridge near Carnarvon, some 40 miles downstream.*

Sheep await the shearer's comb in a holding pen on Bidgemia Station, in the Gascoyne River region. Shearing usually takes place around October or November, with each sheep producing several pounds of thick fleece. An experienced shearer can expect to clip more than 200 animals a day.

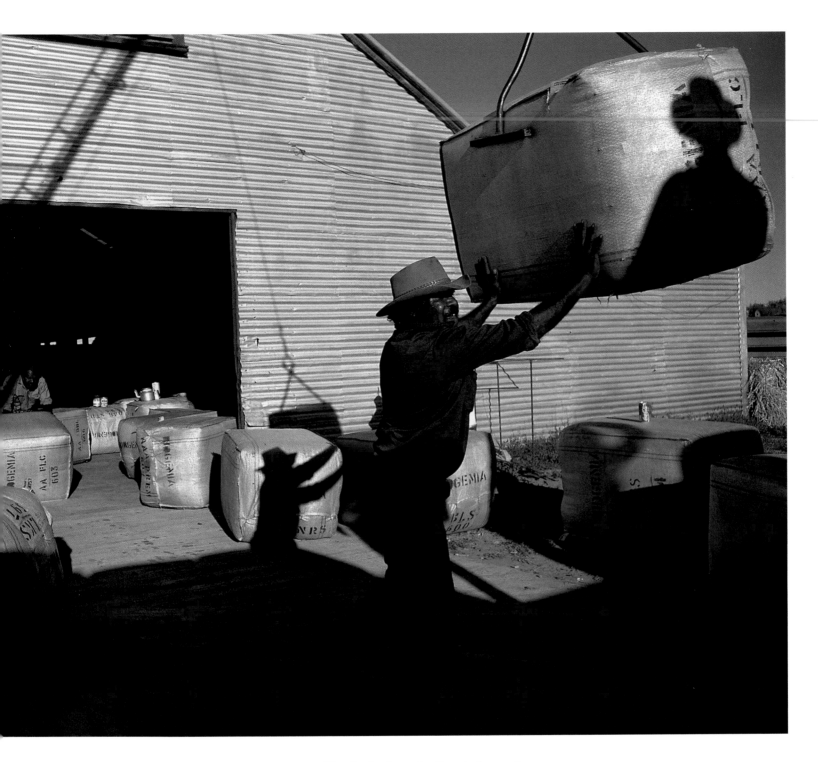

Harsh shadows trail a stockman in
the rugged Gascoyne River country
as he guides a 400-pound bale of
wool onto a truck bound for market.
Although Australia's economy no
longer "rides the sheep's back"
as it did a century ago, wool from
the nation's 120 million sheep
makes up 2.6 percent of the country's
total exports.

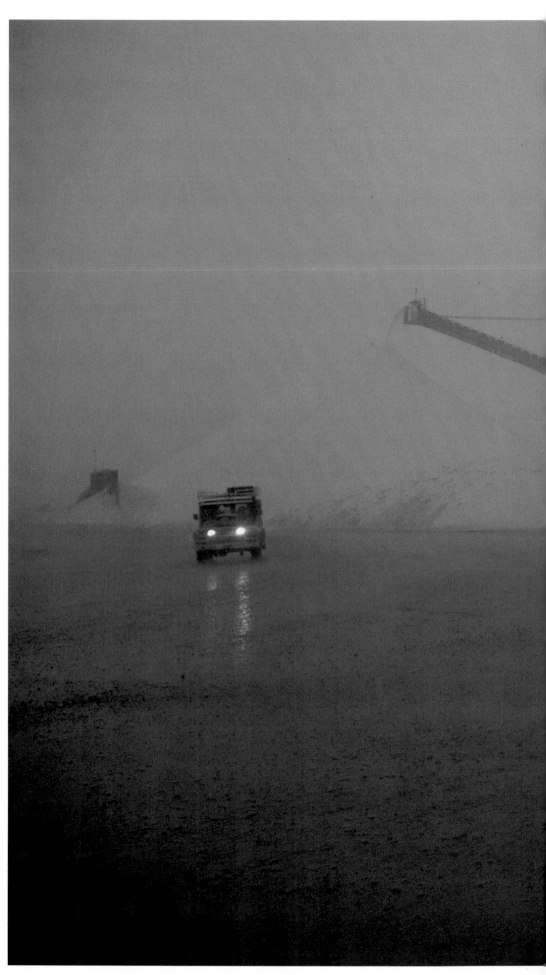

Like snowdrifts in wintry twilight, massive dunes of salt await shipment in the steamy town of Port Hedland, on Australia's stark Indian Ocean coast. More than two million tons are exported from this busy port each year, a mineral wealth celebrated in the Pilbara's Fe-NaCl-NG Festival. The tongue-twisting name comes from the chemical symbols for the northwest's main exports: iron, salt, and liquid natural gas.

*The shattered windshield of his
trusty Holden taped to hold it
together and protect it from further
damage, a long-haul driver checks
the glass before taking off. Rocks and
pebbles kicked up by road trains on
unpaved outback highways play
havoc with cars on the routes.*

Next landfall: the African coast. Christmas lights lend cheer to Cape Leeuwin lighthouse caretaker Kevin Rose's lonely vigil over the southwest tip of Australia, where an area of the Indian Ocean known locally as the Southern Ocean churns. Presiding over one of Australia's busiest shipping routes, the lighthouse has a million-candlepower beam that can be seen for nearly 30 miles.

A surfer rides a wave off the coast of Margaret River, where beaches sport nicknames such as "Suicides," "Boneyards," and "Guillotine." Since the 1960s the area's powerful beach and reef breaks have been drawing surfers from around the world and have been the site of Australian surfing championships.

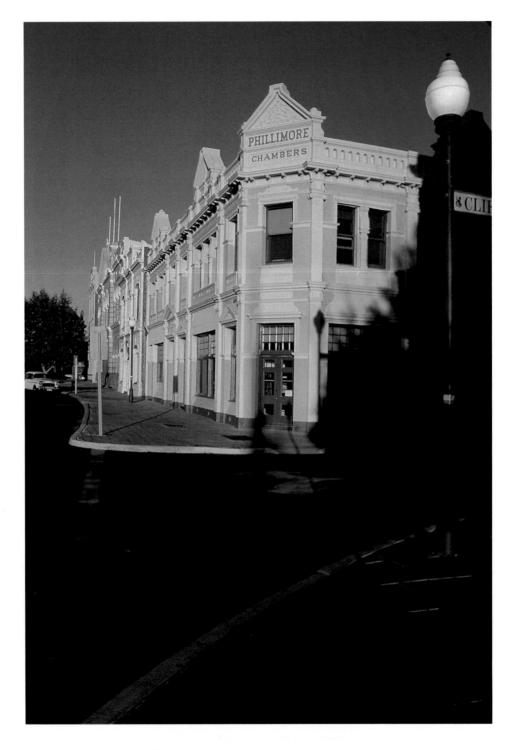

Fremantle flourished on the back of Western Australia's gold rushes in the 1890s, when so many thousands of prospectors passed through the port that authorities had to enact traffic laws governing camel trains on its streets. Nearly a century later Fremantle's Victorian architecture got a makeover when the city hosted the 1987 America's Cup Challenge.

Many hands make light work: Rowers coordinate the launch of a dragon boat on the Swan River in preparation for a Chinese New Year regatta. On weekends Perth hits its stride: Fine weather and a watery setting bring out thousands of surfers, sailors, and sunbathers. In this sports-mad, fiercely egalitarian city, more than 80 percent of river frontage is public parkland.

Following pages: The lights of the world's loneliest city shimmer to life as the last of the sun's rays recede over the Indian Ocean. Separated by 2,000 miles of desert and mountains from Australia's eastern cities, Perth evokes a frontier feeling—a sense that the bush is never far away— that belies its modernistic skyline and air of prosperity.

The Southern Shores

CHAPTER FOUR

"We reached the cliffs, which fell perpendicularly into the sea and, although grand in the extreme, were terrible to gaze from…we all ran back, quite terror stricken by the terrible view," wrote explorer John Forrest, who led a party along the rim of the Great Australian Bight in 1870. I could understand how he felt. Cycling across the lonely Nullarbor Plain on the Eyre Highway a few years ago, I turned onto a dirt track and rode up to that precipice myself. There I found myself gripped by the incredible windswept loneliness these cliffs inspire. A solemn hush and then, far below, I heard the hollow, timeless boom of the breakers as the southern Indian Ocean beat at Australia's rampartlike southern rim.

These southern shores are where the cold, violent waters of the Roaring Forties collide with the extreme harshness of Australia's outback. From the Indian Ocean south of the continent, an area known locally as the Southern Ocean, winds and waves lash at the coast. Like pebbles on a beach, the lonely islands of the Archipelago of the Recherche are scattered south of the town of Esperance. I have savored this southern coast from the sheer cliffs at the edge of the Nullarbor Plain more than 1,600 miles to the aching desolation of the Coorong, a strand of sandbanks and brackish lagoons along South Australia's southeastern flank. The southern shores can be terrifyingly moody and fickle, particularly along the broken edge of the Nullarbor Plain.

Only two days earlier, back at the old telegraph town of Eucla, I had been pinned down by 120-degree heat and seemingly ceaseless northerly winds that had roared out of the Great Victoria Desert for nearly a week.

Then, suddenly the weather turned. A raw southerly gale blew in from the Antarctic, and I found myself huddled, shivering, behind a clump of saltbush as a cold rain began to fall. I agreed with what South Australian explorer Richard Maurice wrote about traveling the Nullarbor more than a century ago: "Any man who would travel this country for pleasure would go to hell for a pastime."

Indeed. Few places are more barren and hostile than this 77,200-square-mile limestone plateau, an ancient seabed that was lifted out of the water about 15 million years ago. It is one of the world's largest karst systems: The massive limestone bed is riddled with about 200 labyrinthine caverns, many of which, like the famed Cocklebiddy Caves, are filled with water. Ironically, some of the world's most challenging underwater caves are here in this haunting desert, and cave-diving records have been set here.

The surface of the plateau, though, is seemingly dead flat, lacking trees and surface water, baked by the sun, scoured by the winds, and girt by towering cliffs and dunes on its broken southern edge. It is almost uninhabited. Although a few groups lived there, even the Aborigines largely avoided it. The region was given its Aboriginal sounding name by Edmund Delisser, a South Australian surveyor, in 1865. He corrupted the Latin for "no trees"—*nullus arbor*—into Nullarbor.

I was cycling along the Eyre Highway, the lonely road that follows the tracks of explorer Edward Eyre, who in 1841 became the first European to cross the Nullarbor Plain. His was a nightmarish expedition, the party tormented by heat, thirst, and roasting winds. Only Eyre and his Aboriginal guide, Wylie, survived the crossing, stag-

166

gering into the West Australia port of Albany months after having been given up for dead. Eyre described the Nullarbor as "a hideous anomaly, a blot on the face of nature, the sort of place one gets into in bad dreams." In the 1870s the telegraph line between Adelaide and Perth was built along this cliff-lined coast. Camel trains and Afghan camel drivers kept the lonely outposts supplied. A series of rough stock tracks allowed the first automobile crossing in 1912. As recently as the early 1960s, word that a family car had made it across the Nullarbor was sufficiently newsworthy to make the Perth newspapers.

Today's paved highway, occasional roadside water tanks, and a handful of lonely roadhouses make the crossing far easier, but it is still an adventure. The heat wave that had pinned me down for several days at Eucla had melted the bitumen on the road, forced roadhouses to stop pumping fuel (it was evaporating too fast), and made many of the huge road trains pull off and wait for cooler night temperatures.

But it is the stunning line of cliffs and windswept dunes along the Nullarbor's coast that most readily seize the imagination and the photographer's lens. Like sturdy ramparts against the storminess of the ocean, they seem to capture perfectly a sense of Australia's incredible isolation, insularity, and uniqueness. The sweeping arc of the Great Australian Bight stretches from West Point, on the southern tip of South Australia's Eyre Peninsula, to Cape Pasley, in Western Australia. The distance is about 700 miles as the tern flies, but much farther if you hug the line of towering cliffs and golden dunes. The fierce winds and currents of the Roaring Forties swirl in powerful eddies in the bight. Its stormy waters teem with fish and dolphins and are a favored breeding habitat of whales. At least 17 species of these marine mammals have been spotted in the bight—including endangered blue whales, southern right whales, and humpbacks, as well as sperm whales. Fur seals and rare Australian sea lions frequently bask on the rocks at the foot of the cliffs.

Far less cuddly creatures lurk here as well. These waters are the haunts of some of the world's biggest white pointer sharks. The largest ever caught on hook and line—a 2,664-pound monster—was taken in 1959 off the coast of the South Australian port of Ceduna. When Steven Spielberg wanted live shark footage for his 1975 horror classic, *Jaws,* he sent a film crew to Port Lincoln, a fishing village near the eastern tip of the Great Australian Bight. Today, in an ironic twist, people come to Port Lincoln and pay handsomely for the privilege of swimming with these magnificent apex predators—in a suitably strengthened safety cage, of course.

For all their fearsomeness, sharks are misunderstood creatures and play a vital role in the ocean's food chain. That chain rarely includes people. Since 1788, when records of these things started being kept, about 200 Australians across the nation have been killed by sharks—an infinitesimal number considering the millions who head for the beach each weekend. Honeybees kill more Aussies than sharks do. In 1997, with shark numbers declining, an enlightened Australia became one of the few places in the world to place these so-called man-eaters on a protected species list.

In truth, the only "man-eating shark" a visitor is likely to see on an Australian beach is just that—a bronzed Aussie devouring a serving of fish and chips. This classic beach fare typically consists of fillets of harmless school or gummy sharks fried and traditionally served wrapped in newspaper. One of the richest commercial fisheries in Australia for school and gummy sharks is the Great Australian Bight. These same waters have healthy stocks of tuna, crayfishes, pilchards, oysters, snappers,the delectable King George whiting, and lucrative abalones. These prized shellfish are so highly sought after by well-heeled Japanese gourmands, and the catch quotas are so tightly controlled, that a commercial abalone license is regarded as virtually a ticket to print money. One diver told me that the going rate to purchase an abalone license is a million dollars—but even then only if you can find anyone willing to sell.

The first Europeans known to have charted Australia's southern shores were Dutch merchantmen aboard the Java-bound East India Company ship *Gulden Zeepaard,* which detoured along the coast in 1627. Another 175 years passed before English navigator Matthew Flinders continued the job, probing the islands, bays, and gulfs of southern Australia, and naming the continent's vast indentation "the great bight or gulph of New Holland."

Just east of this "great bight," on the evening of March 21, 1802, Flinders came upon a long dark island a few miles off the mainland coat. "Neither smokes nor other marks of inhabitants had as yet been perceived upon the southern land, although we had passed along seventy miles of its coast," Flinders wrote in his journal. "It was too late to go on shore this evening; but every glass in the ship was pointed there to see what could be discovered. Several black lumps, like rocks, were pretended to have been seen in motion by some of the young gentlemen, which caused the force of their imaginations to be much admired."

The next morning Flinders led a landing party ashore, where the men found large numbers of seals and kangaroos. They killed about 30 kangaroos to replenish their ship's stores, and his delighted crew feasted on fresh meat for the first time in four months. "In gratitude for so seasonable a supply," wrote Flinders, "I named this southern land Kangaroo Island."

Almost 100 miles long and 35 miles across at its widest, Kangaroo Island is Australia's third largest island (after Tasmania and the Northern Territory's Melville Island). It was a low coastal range on mainland Australia until 10,000 years ago, when rising sea levels at the end of the last ice age flooded the lowlands and turned the hilltops into an island. At the time Flinders arrived, the island was uninhabited, although archaeologists have since found evidence that Aborigines lived here thousands of years ago.

Left in seclusion, the island's flora and fauna followed slightly different evolutionary paths than their mainland cousins. Its kangaroos have distinctively dark, sooty coats; some of its birds, such as the crimson rosella, have unique color variations; and there are around 40 species of wildflowers here that are found nowhere else. Until humans arrived, the island was also home to a now-extinct species of dwarf emu. Since the wildlife on Kangaroo Island had never before encountered human beings, the animals had little fear of the newcomers, and Flinders and his crew marveled at their tameness. It surprises visitors even today. At Flinders Chase National Park, along the island's wild and beautiful western tip, fences around the Rocky River picnic area protect tourists from having their lunches swiped by cheeky kangaroos.

It wasn't long before hunters instilled fear in the island's fur seals. In 1803 a rough gang of sealers—

escaped convicts and the riffraff of passing Yankee whalers—set up a camp on the north shore of the island. There they fashioned a 35-ton schooner, the *Independence,* out of local materials and went into the sealing business, slaughtering the helpless creatures by the thousands. They also raided Aborigine camps on the mainland coast, kidnapping the women and stealing food supplies. By 1827 this unsanctioned settlement on Kangaroo had acquired such an evil reputation that authorities in Sydney sent a military expedition to the island and brought most of its inhabitants back to the city in chains. An attempt to establish an official colony at Reeves Point in 1836 failed for lack of fresh water. During the next century, however, the island slowly became settled, although by World War II it was still so sparsely populated that the government offered free land to any returned veteran who would settle there. About 200 took up the offer.

Today, the rural island is a popular weekend getaway for fishermen and tourists seeking a glimpse of Australia's wildlife in the wild. Most take the ferry from Cape Jervis across the Backstairs Strait to Penneshaw, on the eastern half of the island. The crossing takes only an hour, but the journey is like stepping back in time to an uncomplicated Australia of quiet farm towns, dirt roads, and old-fashioned general stores. Historic lighthouses and dramatic rocky coastlines that have claimed more than 50 ships since the first wreck was recorded in 1847 add to the island's sense of insularity. About one-third of the island has been set aside as national parks or conservation areas, home to thriving populations of seals, sea lions, fairy penguins, kangaroos, echidnas, wallabies, and more than 250 species of birds. Since the 1920s Kangaroo Island has served as a latter-day ark. Wildlife authorities have transplanted at-risk species such as the platypus to the safety of this secluded island wilderness.

Some of these newcomers have made themselves a little too much at home. By 1923 koalas were already being squeezed out of their mainland habitats by the rapidly expanding suburbs on Australia's east coast, and it was decided to introduce 18 breeding pairs of koalas to Flinders Chase National Park.

The koalas prospered beyond anyone's imagination. For them this was an island paradise. No diseases or predators such as dingoes or foxes threatened them here.

Instead there was an abundance of blue and manna gums along the river systems—favorite food for koalas, whose finicky digestive tracts can handle the leaves of only 20 or so of Australia's 700 varieties of eucalypts. Now the island's 5,000 koalas outnumber the human population, and their unbridled appetites are devastating the island's stately 300-year-old gum trees. It is a problem that can be hard for an outsider to take seriously at times.

A few years ago I walked along the Cygnet River under the mischievous gaze of a dozen or so koalas, listening to a farmer gripe about the depredation to his land. An image popped into my head of Santa Claus complaining about his elves, and I started to laugh. The farmer glanced sharply at me for a second, then he too began to chuckle. "That's just the problem," he said. "They're too damn cute." So cute that when politically naive wildlife officials suggested culling 2,000 or so in 1995, a worldwide furor erupted. Today, an elaborate—and costly—fertility control and relocation program is in place to bring koala numbers into check.

South Australia's first permanent European settlers arrived on the H.M.S. *Buffalo* late in 1836, landed on a sheltered beach on the Gulf St. Vincent, and, under a gnarled gum tree on December 28, proclaimed the new colony of South Australia. It was founded as a utopian ideal, the brainchild of Edward Gibbon Wakefield, an English Quaker and libertarian. There would be no convicts sent here; only decent, hardworking settlers who brought capital and the Protestant work ethic would be welcome.

Wakefield believed that much of the problems in the Australian colonies stemmed from the fact that land was being given away free to anyone who came. Far better, he argued, to sell the land at a nominal rate, say a pound an acre, thereby attracting the sort of migrants who either had capital to invest, or who would work as paid laborers for those who did, thereby getting the colony's economy off the ground. Wakefield's book *The New British Province of South Australia* attracted a lot of attention when it was published in 1834, and a few wealthy backers came together to form the South Australian Company.

The old gum tree where the utopian colony was proclaimed is still standing, surrounded now by the beachside suburb of Glenelg. This breezy, sun-drenched town recalls an old-fashioned English seaside resort with its long jetty, grand old hotels along the waterfront, beachy amusements, and Jetty Road, which is lined with cafés, ice cream shops, and fish and chips joints. South Australia's capital city, Adelaide, is about five miles inland. A much-loved vintage 1929 tram makes regular trips between Victoria Square, in the city, and Glenelg. It is only a 30-minute ride, but 60 years ago that was far enough for Glenelg to be considered a holiday destination. One hundred and sixty years ago, when the site for Adelaide was selected, it was far enough from the sea to spark a bitter debate.

The site was chosen by a British Army engineer, Colonel William Light, who had been sent ahead of the colonists to select and survey land for a township. He had originally been told to situate the town near the mouth of the Murray River. There were hopes in London that the great river might prove to be an Australian Mississippi, a 2,000-mile inland waterway that could be the perfect highway for bringing wool from the outback stations to waiting clipper ships that would whisk it to London. A seaport built near its mouth might well become an antipodean New Orleans.

But Light was a soldier, not a sailor, and when he saw the silty mouth of the Murray, with its treacherous sandbars and currents, he decided it wasn't reliable enough for navigation. With a shipload of expectant settlers already on their way, he didn't have much time to waste. So he made an executive decision and situated Adelaide on a gentle plain several miles inland from the Gulf St. Vincent and at the foot of a line of hills that provided a magnificent backdrop. A genius of a town planner, Light had been strongly influenced by the early Roman cities he had seen on visits to Italy. His design for Adelaide was elegant in its simplicity. He set out the city on a Roman grid pattern exactly one imperial mile square, with broad boulevards, gardens, and landscaped town squares. He then surrounded it with about 2,000 acres of parklands. Its main axis was King William Street, the widest main street of any Australian capital city, and one so brilliantly conceived that even today, with

Adelaide's population topping one million, serious traffic congestion is virtually unknown.

Nevertheless, when John Hindmarsh, an old navy man and the colony's first governor, learned that Adelaide was to be situated inland, he was furious. An angry debate sprang up between the two men and their supporters. In 1839 Light confided to his journal: "The reasons that led me to fix Adelaide where it is I do not expect to be generally understood or calmly judged of at present. My enemies, however, by disputing their validity in every particular, have done me the good service of fixing the whole of the responsibility upon me. I am perfectly willing to bear it and I leave it to posterity and not to them, whether I am entitled to praise or to blame."

Posterity has come down squarely on Light's side. In what must be the ultimate I-told-you-so, his journal entry is inscribed beneath a bronze statue of him in North Adelaide. Adelaide is perhaps Australia's most charming and best preserved capital city, with its elegant Victorian architecture, its old-fashioned cricket oval (said by cricket aficionados to be the prettiest in the world), its magnificent neo-Gothic St. Peter's Cathedral, and its stately mansions. Known as "the city of churches" and with a reputation for primness, Adelaide also regards itself as Australia's culture and fine arts capital, and its arts festival is the biggest and most elaborate in the nation. The city is an epicure's paradise. Favored by a hot, sunny Mediterranean climate and surrounded by world-class vineyards, olive groves, and orchards, Adelaide is famed for its markets, fine restaurants, and buzzing café scene. Some of Australia's most prestigious wine-making regions—the Barossa Valley, the Clare Valley, McLaren Vale, and Coonawarra—are easy drives from the city. If all that sounds a little snobbish, well, Adelaide is known for that too. This was the only Australian state that was never a penal colony, a matter of quiet pride among South Australians ever since.

Perth's founders, of course, had similar lofty ambitions for their colony, only to see it stagnate on a forgotten corner of the continent for 60 years until the fabulous gold strikes at distant Coolgardie and Kalgoorlie could get it on its economic feet. South Australia was luckier. The ancient Precambrian rocks that contain so much of Australia's mineral wealth lie only 60 miles north of Adelaide.

In 1842 a fabulously rich deposit of blue and green copper ores was discovered near the farm town of Kapunda. This was followed in 1845 by another rich copper strike, 50 miles farther north in Burra. These were Australia's first big mineral discoveries, and the news triggered a stampede of immigrants. Thousands of Cornish and Welsh miners flocked to the suddenly booming new colony. More lucrative copper strikes were made on the Yorke Peninsula in 1859 and 1860.

While Western Australia—which by then had begrudgingly started importing convict laborers—languished, South Australia had become known around the world as the "Copper Kingdom." Adelaide was already a wealthy city of wide streets and gracious Victorian buildings, its open opportunities attracting the interest of the second sons of England's landed gentry.

Geography was kind to South Australia in other ways, too. Here Spencer Gulf cuts a deep indentation into the continent. The gulf was a boon to explorers who were seeking to open up the interior in the belief that an inland sea and fertile plains waited just over the horizon. There was no such sea, of course, but the many expeditions that set forth from Adelaide opened vast tracts of arid grazing land and launched some of Australia's wealthiest pastoral dynasties.

It was from the copper town of Kapunda that Sir Sidney Kidman, Australia's greatest cattle baron, ran his vast empire. At his peak, in the early years of the 20th century, Kidman controlled a chain of cattle stations that stretched from outback South Australia across the continent to Queensland's Gulf of Carpentaria: Estimates of its size range from 49,000 to 65,000 square miles. Kidman was the biggest of South Australia's barons, but by no means the only one. Many of the elegant mansions in and around Adelaide were built on the state's enormous grazing wealth.

South Australia's explorers opened up more than just new grazing land. The meticulous maps and journals of John MacDouall Stuart, who successfully crossed the continent in 1861, led to Adelaide's becoming the southern terminus of the Overland Telegraph from Darwin in 1872. The telegraph, which linked the South Australian capital to London via connections across Asia and Europe, cost £479,000 to build but brought in a cool £1,000,000 its first year in operation. Later, news on the wire that Europe was experiencing a wheat shortage gave South Australian growers an inside run for Australia's first wheat exports. The engineers and surveyors who built the railway line north to Alice Springs also relied on Stuart's notes.

Hard on the heels of the explorers came settlers with sheep, cattle, wheat—and grapevines. Forty miles north of Adelaide is the Barossa Valley, named by Colonel Light for the Barrosa, a ridge in Spain where he had fought a battle in the Peninsular War in 1811. Drive into the valley today along the quiet road through Seppeltsfield that is lined with stately Canary Island date palms and vineyards, and you get a feel for the valley's hot, dry Mediterranean flavor. This is Australia's premier wine district, and it looks the part.

The Barossa Valley was settled in the late 1830s. George Fife Angas, a wealthy founder and director of the South Australian Company, claimed an enormous tract of land through here. In a happy blend of philanthropy and real estate development, Angas helped several hundred struggling Prussian and Silesian refugees migrate to the Barossa Valley. Devout Lutherans, they had been suffering religious persecution in their homelands. One of their leaders, pastor August Ludwig Christian Kavel, was convinced that his flock could enjoy religious freedom in South Australia and approached Angas for help. Angas, who admired the doughty work ethic of the Prussians, was intrigued by their plight and agreed to fund their immigration to Australia. The refugees came and prospered, bringing with them their wine-making skills. The first vines were planted by a Silesian named Johann Gramp at Jacob's Creek, near Rowland Flat.

One hundred and fifty years later, the Barossa Valley probably is the closest thing Australia has to a distinct cultural province. The landscape is dotted with picturesque Lutheran churches. They are attended by families with names such as Doering, Lehmann, Hoezenroeder, and Henschke, who have lived in the valley for five and six generations. Some of the older residents still speak a form of Australianized German known as Barossa-Deutsche. Village bakeries offer assortments of apple strudel, *honigkuchen* (honey biscuits), and *quarkkuchen* (cheesecake). Butchers smoke their own meats—bratwursts, *mettwursts, blutwursts,* and *leberwursts*—according to family recipes passed down for generations.

But it is for fine wine that the Barossa is most famous. The appropriately bottle-shaped valley is carpeted with more than 20,000 acres of grapevines. Jacob's Creek, where it all began, is one of Australia's most popular labels: Orlando Winery exports more than two million cases of it each year. The valley is home to internationally acclaimed and award-winning wineries such as Peter Lehmann, Henschke, and Penfold. Penfold's flagship label, Grange Hermitage, is routinely ranked among the finest reds in the world. In 1999 the influential *Wine Spectator* magazine included the '55 Grange in its "Dream Case" as one of the greatest wines of the 20th century. Another local maker, Seppelt, famous for its fortified wines, is the only winery in the world to have an unbroken line of vintage ports dating back to 1878.

North of the Barossa the landscape opens to bronze wheat fields and rolling expanses of arid pastureland that helped build some of Australia's finest merino studs. A century ago vast chunks of it were held by wealthy pastoralists who lived in grand storybook homesteads such as Analby, near Kapunda; Bungaree; and Wolta Wolta. Possibly the grandest of these mansions is Martindale Hall, a magnificent Georgian edifice built in 1879 near Mintaro by the son of an early grazier who had made a fortune. Local legend has it that he built the stately pile to impress an eligible English lady he hoped to marry. No expense was spared. Artisans, rare timbers, and stone were imported from Europe; the grounds were stocked with quail for gentlemanly hunting; and an elegant cricket oval was built on the landscaped grounds at which the English cricket team came and played. Despite his efforts, the lady married someone else. Her failed suitor seemed to take his loss well. He married another and lived on in grand style, throwing lavish parties and gambling on horse races until he eventually squandered his fortune. Martindale Hall passed into the hands of a sober Adelaide banking family. Today, it is on the register of the National Estate.

The town of Clare was named by an Irishman, Edward Gleeson, after his home in Ireland, but it was a group of Austrian Jesuits who put the area on the map. They arrived in 1851, established a monastery at a place they called Sevenhill after the hills of Rome, and began planting vines. The idea was to make sacramental wine, but as demand grew for their product, they expanded into fortified wines and, since the 1950s, into dry table wines as well. Other wineries were established over the years, slowly at first, and then in a rush over the past decade as Australia's wine industry blossomed. About 30 wineries are nestled in the Clare Valley today—including Sevenhill Cellars, where wine is still produced by the Jesuit brothers at the imposing monastery.

With the exception of Clare, most of the towns through the Barossa were railroad towns, built in the heady age of steam when railroads were stretching out from Adelaide toward the Flinders Ranges to bring in the area's vast wealth of copper, wheat, and wool. Peterborough, nestled in the southern Flinders Ranges, used to be a bustling railhead with three different gauges of track running through it—narrow, standard, and broad—depending on whether the line was heading northeast to Broken Hill, northwest to Port Augusta, or south to Adelaide. Passengers had to detrain here while the wheel assemblies were changed on the rail carriages to accommodate the different gauge tracks.

Nearby Terowie claims that it was during one such interlude, in 1942, that Gen. Douglas MacArthur, southbound from Darwin to Melbourne, conducted his first press conference after fleeing the Philippines and made his now-famous vow: "I shall return." It was an ephemeral moment of glory for the town and is immortalized in a plaque on the station wall. In the decades after the war the towns went into a long, genteel decline when the tracks were standardized and the *Ghan* to Alice Springs was rerouted through Port Pirie, a lead-smelting port on the Spencer Gulf.

Farther north toward the Flinders Ranges the climate becomes drier, and the landscape is dotted with the crumbling ruins of stone cottages and abandoned farm buildings—a legacy of the ambitious and the greedy who attempted to farm the outer limits of South Australia's fertile southeast.

After a severe drought in the 1860s, South Australia's surveyor-general, George Woodroffe Goyder, studied the colony's soils and rainfall areas. The result was Goyder's Line, a line of demarcation that indicated the extent of useful farmland in the colony. A run of gentle seasons and pent-up demand for more land inspired further settlement, however. In the 1870s a wheat rush drew settlers ever farther north until there were even wheat fields being planted in the craggy deserts of the Flinders Ranges.

Few reckoned on the fickleness of the South Australian outback, which might be kind and rainy for a few seasons, and then savagely hot and dry for a decade. Drought, disillusionment, isolation, and the hostility of local Aborigines forced most of the settlers off the land. The ruins of long-abandoned homesteads and small towns are scattered across the landscape. Isolated communities such as Hawker, which started out as thriving wheat-growing towns, are now jumping-off places for tourists venturing north into some of Australia's most dramatic landscapes.

The Flinders Ranges were named for English navigator Matthew Flinders. They are the nubs of mountains that were pushed up 600 million years, reduced by 540 million years of wind and rain, then uplifted and whittled away again. The ancient rocks on the western side of the mountains, in a place called the Edicarra Hills, contain some of the earliest known fossils of multicellular life: Sea stars, trilobites, worms, corals, and anemones that dwelled on the seafloor 650 million years ago.

Human history here dates back more than 30,000 years. The mountains were home to the Adnyamathanha people (their name means "hill dwellers") and were a major stopover on the Aborigines' north-south trading routes. Rock shelters here are decorated with rock carvings and paintings, the best known of which is Sacred

Canyon, with its 20,000-year-old art galleries.

The 230,000-acre Flinders Ranges National Park is prized for its dramatic beauty: Serrated mountain tops, deeply carved gorges, and desert basins carpeted with brilliant red, pink, yellow, mauve, and white wildflowers after the spring rains. Its hidden rock pools, massive gnarled trees along the creeks, and the fine, clear, fragile quality of the light have drawn artists and photographers from all over Australia. Among the best known was Sir Hans Heysen, who painted many of his outback land-scapes here. Heysen first came to the Flinders Ranges in 1926 and returned many times to try to capture the subtle moods and shifting hues in this ancient land. It was his paintings, more than anything else, that brought these dramatic and remote ranges into the public's eye. At the heart of the park, and its most sensational feature, is Wilpena Pound, an immense amphitheater walled in by sheer cliffs of purplish red quartzite. The name "Wilpena" comes from an Aboriginal phrase meaning "fingers of a cupped hand."

Access to the pound is on foot—either through the narrow walled canyon of Wilpena Creek in the south, or through the twisting Edeowie Gorge in the north. In the early years of the century the floor of Wilpena Pound was leased to pastoralists who used it to run sheep and cattle, as well as for growing wheat. Due to a local cli-mate anomaly, the interior of Wilpena Pound gets more rain than the surrounding areas, creating a sort of oasis with dense pine forests on its inner slopes, rolling grass-lands, and wildflowers. Floods washed out the main access track in the early 1900s, and the stations in the pound were abandoned. Since 1920 the area has been protected, first as a forest reserve and since 1972 as a national park. Today, it is noisy with flocks of galahs, rosellas, budgerigars and wedge-tailed eagles. There are vast numbers of red kangaroos and possums here, as well as rare yellow-footed rock wallabies. Soaring above the lowlands, St. Marys Peak forms the highest rampart overlooking Wilpena Pound. From the summit, at almost 4,000 feet, hypnotic suites of the reds, mauves, browns, and grays of desert ranges stretch deep into the timeless outback.

South Australia is reputedly the driest state in the driest inhabited continent, with much of its 380,000 square miles taken up by the Nullarbor Plain and the vast salt pans and stony desert that stretch for hundreds of miles across its north. Only the lower southeast of the state is fertile, and that thanks to the presence of the Murray River. At 1,565 miles long—more than 2,000 miles if you include its major tributary, the Darling River—the Murray is by far Australia's largest river. The Murray-Darling watershed covers one-seventh of the continent. Although it is a merely a trickle compared with the Mississippi or the Amazon, on this sunburned land the Murray is a life-giving miracle. Its waters support most of Australia's orchards and vineyards, irrigate vast cotton fields in outback Queensland and New South Wales, and even wash rice fields in parts of New South Wales. Much of Australia's finest grazing land and wheat and barley fields, and its best wool-producing areas, are in the Murray watershed.

But no state relies on the river more than South Australia, where long pipelines cross the country to bring drinking and irrigation water to rural communities on the Eyre Peninsula, the Flinders Ranges, the Barossa Valley—even the city of Adelaide itself. During a dry summer Adelaide's one million residents obtain more than 90 per-cent of their drinking water from the Murray. The river starts high in Victoria's alpine country, forms the Victoria-New South Wales border for much of its length, then joins forces with the Darling River near the outback New South Wales town of Wentworth. The Murray enters South Australia a few miles above the town of Renmark.

South Australia may have only the lower 400 miles of the Murray River, but it has the lion's share of the river's grandeur. Here the Murray winds through deep gorges of honey-colored sandstone, creates shimmering lagoons raucous with bird life, and flows beside banks shaded by massive red gums more than 300 years old. Seen from the air, the river, with its handsome trees and willowy banks, seems an alien intruder as it wends its way across miles of hot, empty mallee scrub. But its waters have turned once-dusty towns such as Loxton, Barmera, and Kingston into oases of palm trees, fruit and nut orchards, and lush vineyards. This remarkable transformation was the genius of two Canadian brothers, George and William Chaffey, who were invited to Australia in 1887 by the government of Victoria.

The Chaffeys had earlier established a successful irrigation project in California, and it was hoped they could do the same with Australia's Murray River. The brothers settled on nearly 250,000 acres near Mildura in northeast Victoria. Handing over such a large plot of land to "Yankee adventurers" created a political storm, and the project was put on hold. While they were waiting for a response from the government of Victoria, the Chaffeys asked the government of South Australia if it would be interested in the project. The answer was yes, and the Chaffeys agreed to set up an irrigation colony near Renmark. By this time the Victorians had reconsidered, and the Chaffeys oversaw both irrigation projects.

Over the next couple of years thousands of acres of scrubland were cleared, miles of irrigation channels were dug, and special water pumps were designed to transport millions of gallons of water from the Murray River to parched outback soil. The town of Renmark was laid out on a grid. To lure migrants, a handsome folio-size prospectus was printed and distributed around England. I had a look at one of those books. It was handed to me by a man whose family had come over in the early days. Its crimson cover was embellished with gold lettering, and its pages were illustrated with drawings of orchards and vineyards heavy with ripe fruit that looked remarkably like English estate gardens.

The truth was a little different. This was still outback scrub, with its hot, dust-laden winds and flat, cheerless stretches of stunted mallee. Summer temperatures out here can hit 120 degrees, and the glare can be blinding. Not surprisingly the middle-class English migrants who had bought into the project were aghast when they stepped off the steamboat.

To add to their woes, Australia was suffering a severe economic depression in the 1890s. There were also floods, droughts, and soil salinity problems, to say nothing of the transportation difficulties in getting their produce to distant markets. Many migrants walked off their land. The Chaffeys went bankrupt. Local governments and farmers bought the project and ran it as a trust, and

today the region is a cornucopia of citrus, wine and table grapes, stone fruits, nuts, wheat, and wool. More irrigation schemes were set up in Berri, Barmera, and Waikerie, a former dust bowl that is now the center of Australia's biggest citrus-producing district.

One of the best ways to get a feel for the impact the river has on the landscape is to see it from the air. The town of Waikerie—an Aboriginal name meaning "everything that flies" because of the area's profusion of bird life—has been a magnet for glider pilots since the first local club was formed in 1937. It has been the site of national and international championships, with the lightweight craft riding the area's strong thermals into the clear South Australian sky. Far below, the Murray River now winds its way through fruit orchards and vineyards—land that once was a cliff-lined vein of flat, harsh mallee scrub.

In the 1850s South Australian authorities hoped the Murray would prove to be another Mississippi, a lucrative waterway that could bring wool clips down from outback Queensland and New South Wales to warehouses in Port Adelaide. So keen were they that a £2,000 reward was offered to each of the first two people to take an iron-hulled steamboat up the river from Goolwa as far as its juncture with the Darling.

It was a very generous offer, and soon there was an even bigger incentive: Huge gold strikes had been made in Victoria, the river ran reasonably close to some of the goldfields, and an entrepreneurial boat owner could make a fortune hauling prospectors and supplies to and from the diggings.

A South Australian flour miller named William Randell, in the river town of Mannum, decided it was time to expand into the shipping business—carrying flour to the diggings—even though he had never seen a steamboat before and claimed later he was unaware of the bounty. He had the local blacksmith knock together a crude boiler out of quarter-inch iron, put it on a semi-open 50-foot boat he named the *Mary Ann* (after his mother), and set out to make his fortune. As soon as the steam pressure was raised in his jerry-built boiler, it swelled up like a football, prompting the *Mary Ann*'s terrified engineer to run for the bush. Afterward the backyard mechanics wrapped chains around the boiler to keep it in shape, then set off again up the river, the boiler swelling and breathing like a concertina. Randell never got the reward—his ship didn't meet the government's specifications—but he started an era.

Within a few years there were dozens of steamboats plying this shallow outback river, and not just for the quick gains of bringing prospectors, food, and supplies to the goldfields. Now station owners could get their wool clip to market in a matter of weeks instead of holding it for a year or two until a team could be spared for a six-month overland trek. And with the cash they could buy new supplies, saddles, boots, books, plates, crockery—whatever the city offered—and have it sent up by steamer. For the first time they could expect to get their flour fresh and clean and white, straight from the Adelaide mills, instead of stale and gritty with dust after a long wagon trek. Living standards and property values along the river routes skyrocketed.

Like the Mississippi River, the Murray had its glory days of brawling riverfront towns that housed gamblers, prospectors, saloon keepers, and colorful steamboat captains. The journey to transport wool to market was an adventurous relay. Camel trains carried wool bales from remote stations to dusty outback river towns far upstream of the Murray's confluence with the Darling. Here, in places like Bourke and Wilcannia, the wool was loaded onto shallow-drafted steamboats for the long trek downstream. From one of South Australia's bustling inland ports, such as Morgan or Mannum, or from the seaside town of Goolwa, bales of cotton were transported by oxcart or rail to the wharves of Port Adelaide.

It was too lucrative a business to let the South Australians have it to themselves. In 1864 the Victorian government built a railroad to the bustling inland river port of Echuca to intercept some of the river traffic. By 1878 a railroad line stretched from Port Adelaide to the river town of Morgan, on a sharp bend in the river about a hundred miles northeast of the city.

Robbed of their traffic, the once-bustling river ports of Mannum, Murray Bridge, and Goolwa, on the mouth of the river, withered like grapes on a vine. By the mid-1930s trucks and trains had taken over from the steamboats completely.

It is only about an hour's drive south of Adelaide now to the seaside resort of Goolwa. And every weekend the Main South Road is lively with holiday-makers. Goolwa never came near the grand New Orleans-scale aspirations held for it last century. A series of shipwrecks along this treacherous coast and the fickleness of the Murray, which often stops flowing in drought years, eventually killed that hope.

It was refreshing sea breezes, a shoreline teeming with cockles, and growing middle and upper classes in Adelaide that made Goolwa's fortunes. Homesick English migrants began coming to the town around the turn of the century to unwind by the sea and dig cockles, just as they used to back home in Brighton, Bognor Regis, or Blackpool. By the 1920s the train between Victor Harbor and Goolwa was so heavily used by holiday-makers that railway timetables officially referred to it as the "Cockle Train." Today, a restored steam train still makes the run for tourists. Property values are booming.

In the winter months the cliffs between Victor Harbor and Goolwa are thronged with visitors surveying the southern right whales that migrate here to breed. Beyond Goolwa, where the Murray River sluggishly empties into the sea, are the hauntingly beautiful coastal dunes, marshes, and lagoons of the Coorong, from the Aboriginal word meaning "long neck of water."

Here the southern shores end as they began, in silence and loneliness, looking out onto the cold and empty waters of the Southern Ocean.

Following pages: *Lit by dawn, the Nullarbor Plain ends abruptly at limestone walls that plunge 300 feet into the treacherous waters of the Great Australian Bight. Loud in the desert silence, the hollow boom of the surf and the haunting cries of cormorants and sea lions echo along Australia's lonely and forbidding southern coast.*

In a maneuver that would do a sheep dog proud, a shark musters salmon into shallows near the base of Western Australia's Baxter Cliffs, on the west end of the Great Australian Bight. In winter these waters, among Australia's richest fisheries, are a breeding ground for endangered southern right whales.

A leafy sea dragon flutters through cold, clear waters off the South Australia coast. The ragged membranes that give it a bizarre appearance serve as camouflage in the dense seaweed of the creature's habitat.

Lured by a slick of tuna entrails, a great white shark breaks the surface near South Australia's aptly named Dangerous Reef. Some of the largest sharks ever caught have been pulled from these waters. Here, Steven Spielberg filmed his live shark footage for the movie Jaws. Today, Australian law protects these magnificent predators.

Following pages: From a rocky perch on Dangerous Reef, black-faced cormorants scan the sea for tides and currents that signal a plentiful catch of fish. Gulls share the space and salvage any meals or leftover morsels.

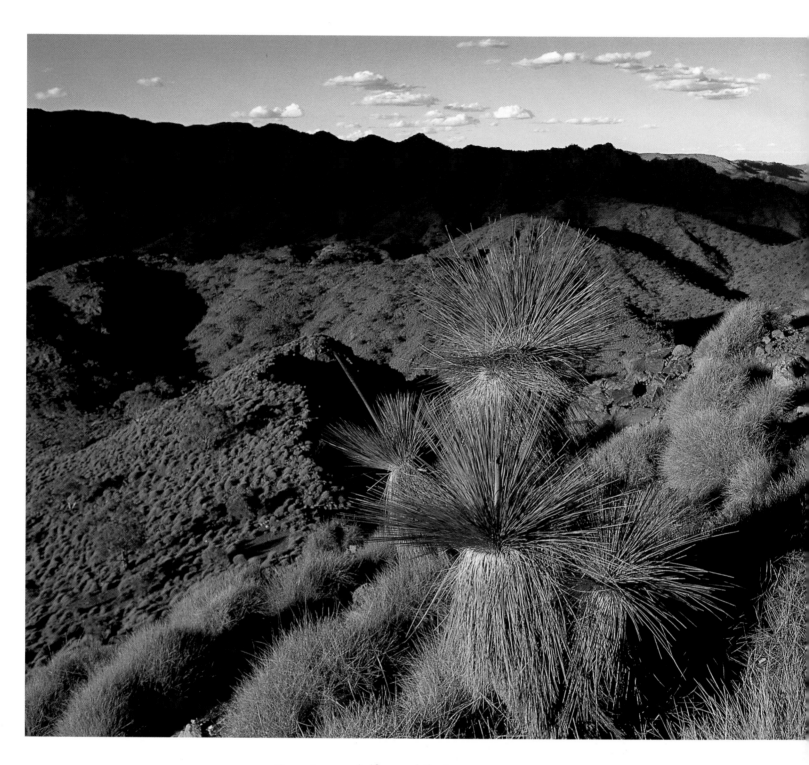

Grass trees, spinifex, and the bronze
glow of an outback sunset spill down
the rocky flanks of South Australia's
remote Gammon Ranges, a last stony
bastion before the great sweep of the
country's central deserts begins to the
north. The ancient reddish outcrops
in these mountains contain more
than 50 minerals, including copper,
iron, uranium, and radium.

Once avidly hunted for its ornamental pelt, the yellow-footed rock wallaby has bounded back from the endangered list. The beautiful marsupial is found only in rock formations in the Flinders Ranges and in isolated pockets of the nearby Gawler Range. The animal's unusually long tail helps it keep its balance in the precarious terrain it favors.

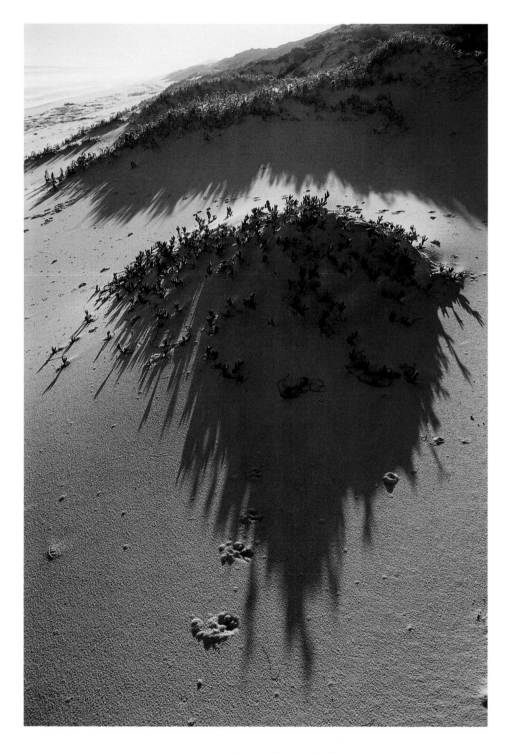

Tender green shoots of coastal pigface belie this dune plant's toughness. It flourishes in the sands of Western Australia's Nuytsland Nature Reserve, a protected strip of coastline on the Great Australian Bight.

Like snowy Christmas ornaments, little corellas adorn the branches of a cypress pine. A type of parrot, these nomadic, arid-country birds live on a boom-and-bust cycle. In good years thousands flock around the outback; in times of drought their numbers swiftly decline.

Following pages: *Stately silver trunks of river red gums, largest trees in the Flinders Ranges, inspired Australian landscape artist Hans Heysen. Old-timers called these trees widow-makers because of their tendency to shed limbs unexpectedly in times of drought, sometimes killing luckless swagmen camped underneath them.*

Using its neck like a graceful periscope, a snake-necked tortoise gently breaks the glassy surface of Piccaninnie Ponds, a labyrinth of deep freshwater sinkholes on the South Australia-Victoria border. The ponds were formed when rain dissolved limestone and filled underground aquifers. The treacherous, crystal-clear waters attract divers from all over Australia.

Water means life in the outback, and
spring-fed creeks in the Flinders
Ranges have made these desert
mountains unusually rich in bird
life, including four subspecies of
rainbow-hued mallee ringneck
parrots. Alert and intelligent, these
birds have readily adapted to
changes in their environment,
quickly discovering a use for a water
pipe at Wilpena Pound.

Mouth agape, a skink hisses to ward off enemies. That sound and the reptile's defiant attitude serve as its only weapons against the hostile outback environment. Typically fat and slow-moving, these gentle lizards eat flowers, berries, and dead insects. Although they live alone, they are monogamous, seeking out the same partner each year.

Rounding one of the few bends in the line from Port Augusta, the Tea and Sugar Train rolls west across the Nullarbor Plain. Until it stopped running several years ago, the "T&S" took supplies and water to railway maintenance workers and rabbit-shooters who lived in isolated camps and siding along the line.

Following pages: *Soon after sunrise dabs of greenery stand out against red hills at Arkaroola in the North Flinders Ranges; from the air trails pinpoint an isolated research station. Human history, represented in rock paintings and carvings, dates back 30,000 years in this land of sharp-toothed peaks, carved gorges, and desert basins.*

Warped by time, the windows of the abandoned general store in Walloway, South Australia, frame plains once replete with wheat fields. The town's old schoolhouse has been restored as a weekend retreat. Faced with droughts and other hardships of life in rural Australia, many residents have fled to the cities.

Riesling grapevines planted in the 1970s edge a fence in the Clare Valley of South Australia; a house abandoned some 20 years ago now serves as a storehouse. Austrian Jesuits who arrived in 1851 established a monastery and vineyard in the area. Today, some 30 wineries exist in the valley.

Following pages: *Mirroring muted clouds, Lake Hillier spills across Middle Island in the lonely Archipelago of the Recherche; algae paints the water pink. Now a nature reserve, the scattering of a hundred granite islands off the coast of Western Australia near Esperance once lured hordes of sealers.*

CHAPTER FIVE

Tasmania:
The Other Australia

For nearly two weeks we steamed through the emptiest quarter of the southern Indian Ocean, in heavy gales and mountainous seas, through the fearsome latitudes the old mariners knew as the Furious Fifties and the Roaring Forties. We were traveling from Australia's lonely station at Mawson, in east Antarctica, toward Tasmania. The island appeared like an apparition out of the rainy mists after breakfast one morning. Forbidding rocky spires jutted from the waves; craggy cliffs and promontories lined the coast; and behind them lay mountains cloaked in dense primeval rain forests.

I was on the bridge, awed by the spectacle and nursing a cup of mint tea to settle my stomach against the hideous lurching of the round-hulled icebreaker as she battled the waves. Over the radio came somber updates about the battered yachts attempting the Sydney to Hobart race. The same storm that made our 3,600-ton icebreaker bob like a cork was throwing those boats about unmercifully, breaking masts, tearing sails, and sending much of the fleet scurrying to shelter. In conditions such as this only a few skippers could or would risk crossing the wind-whipped waters of Bass Strait, which separates Tasmania from mainland Australia.

No place could have seemed wilder or more inaccessible than Tasmania on that stormy morning late in December 1993, and nothing could have captured its essence better than that first glimpse of its primal southwest coast. Tasmania is a place to approach by sea, as the awed Dutch explorers did in 1642, as England's doomed convicts glimpsed it nearly 161 years later, and as I was fortunate enough to do that morning. The island exudes a moody, gothic atmosphere that suggests its dark past.

Tasmania is about the size of Ireland, but far wilder and more forbidding, buffeted by Roaring Forties gales and storms blowing up from the Antarctic. It was sculpted by glaciers during the last ice age, then cut off from the Australian mainland about 11,000 years ago by rising sea levels as the world's ice sheets melted. The Aborigines who had walked here in the Dreamtime, the island's unique plants and animals—its Huon pines, Tasmanian tigers and Tasmanian devils—were sealed off like a time capsule, virtually undisturbed until 1803. Insularity has defined Tasmania ever since.

"It is different from the hot Australian mainland; it has a different weather and a different soul, knowing as it does the sharp breath of the south, facing the Antarctic," wrote Tasmanian-born novelist Christopher Koch in his 1958 book, *The Boys in the Island*:

No wars, no disturbances have ever reached the island: no horrors at all, since the last convict transport made the long run from England, when the island's dreaded name was Van Diemen's Land, in that bad, smelly old century of rum and the lash....

It has two small cities, Hobart, the capital, in the south, and Launceston, in the north. At their centres are the solid, ornate stone buildings of Georgian and Victorian England; in the suburbs, small swarms of twentieth century bungalows, with galvanised iron roofs and neat front lawns, spread to the edges of the country. There are prosperous farming districts and occasional little townships; and the rest is bush, its metallic green tides ebbing and flowing mile upon mile across the hills and gullies.

And the bush is silent. There is a silence in the island, outside the towns, which the prosperous life of today cannot break: the silence of a land outside history, almost outside time.

Dutch explorer Abel Tasman was the first European known to have sighted the island, in 1642, naming the unexpected landmass Van Diemen's Land after one of his superiors at the Dutch East India Company. Tasman had been sent to find and map a new Pacific trade route, but his reports—of storms and treacherous coasts, black natives roving the beaches, and smoke from campfires rising deep in the forest—did little to enthuse the profit-minded burghers in Amsterdam and Java. They sent Tasman on another expedition to the area in 1644, and he did discover what would become New Zealand. His search for a new Pacific trading route brought little results, however. The burghers lost interest, and Van Diemen's Land resumed its slumbers.

For the next century or so Europeans left the island pretty much alone, but then ships started coming relatively thick and fast. The island's early colonial history reads like a veritable *Who's Who* of Oceania's great 18th-century navigators: James Cook, William Bligh, Matthew Flinders, Bruni D'Entrecasteaux, and Nicholas Baudin, not to mention a host of French and Yankee whalers and sealers. British settlement dates from 1803, when a group of soldiers and convicts under the command of Lt. John Bowen established a settlement near the site of present-day Hobart. The British came partly to take possession of the island ahead of the French—who were starting to show interest in Australia—and partly to establish a place of ultimate banishment for the worst and most violent felons, men for whom even Botany Bay was too gentle a punishment.

In that aim they certainly succeeded. Over the next 50 years Van Diemen's Land became synonymous with cruelty, barbarism, and jackboot discipline, vying with the nightmarish Norfolk Island as the nearest thing to hell on Earth. To some that notoriety was a point of pride. "Prisoners upon trial declared that they would rather suffer death than be sent back to Macquarie Harbour [site of one of the most brutal of Tasmania's prison camps, founded in 1821]," wrote one of its early governors, William Sorell, in a letter urging ever greater discipline and the hardest

possible toil for the convicts. "It is the feeling I am most anxious to be kept alive."

So evil was Van Diemen's Land's reputation that after transportation ceased in 1853, authorities were obliged to change its name to Tasmania to try to make the island a little more palatable to the free settlers they were trying to attract. They succeeded to a point, but few places are more hostage to their stormy past.

Reminders of that history are everywhere. Hobart is a city of 200,000, with a strong maritime flavor and deep colonial roots. It shows its best face to those who arrive by water, sailing up the Derwent River, 12 miles from its mouth to a historic waterfront that still retains much of its early character, reflecting the days when Hobart was a brawling port of call for the world's whaling fleets. Now it is famous as a boisterous haven for the fleet of yachts at the finish of the annual Sydney to Hobart Yacht Race, one of the world's premier blue-water races. It traditionally starts from Sydney on Boxing Day, December 26, and concludes with a huge New Year's Eve party in Hobart The rest of the city is arranged around its seaport.

Hobart's suburbs are tiered on the steep slopes overlooking this superb deepwater harbor. Dominating the city is the 4,000-foot summit of Mount Wellington. "Just enough of a mountain to give excitement to ladies and gentlemen in middle life," according to English novelist and traveler Anthony Trollope. He was being a little churlish. The view from the summit is spectacular.

Hobart's seafaring atmosphere, cool climate, and bright, timber-framed cottages and old terrace houses give the city a European flavor, particularly in winter, when the summit of Mount Wellington is mantled with snow. Hobart has hung onto its early colonial architecture much more tightly than Sydney has. The high concentration of elegant Georgian and Victorian buildings, typically built of honey-colored sandstone by convicts, makes it feel older and more Old World than any other Australian city. The large and gracious stone warehouses on Salamanca Place, which were Hobart's commercial focus in whaling days, have retained their bustle, this time as shops, restaurants, and art galleries. Narrow stone steps behind them lead into a warren of cottages and lanes in Battery Point, once a working class enclave, and now a fashionable address for urban professionals.

A seaward-looking city of yachts and ships, Hobart largely ignores the wild Tasmanian bush that surrounds it. "It is a city, but only just," wrote Christopher Koch, in *The Boys in the Island*. "The fragrant foreign breath of the country can move in summer down Elizabeth Street, catching at the people on the pavements of midday. The country's yellow grass reaches stray fingers into the suburbs; and standing in almost any street, you can glance up and see the near rusty-green and farther dream-blue ranges, their tree-serrated tops poignant against the sky; a reminder of farness.

So the island has two horizons, two barriers against the world: there are the ranges of hills, and there is the coast; in the north and east, green-laced beaches, facing the world; and in the south, black primeval capes of rock: final walls facing the Antarctic, pitted and rowelled by the wild southern storms of winter."

One such wall extends south on a spit of land about 60 miles south and east of Hobart. Separated from the rest of the island by a narrow neck of land, lies the haunting peninsula on which the hellish Port Arthur penal colony was established in 1830. Although other of Van Diemen's Land's brutal prison camps—including Sarah Island, in Macquarie Harbour—were arguably even worse places to be sent, no colony captured the imagination or inspired dread like Port Arthur. Its end-of-the-world setting may have had a lot to do with it.

Arriving by highway, it seems surprisingly beautiful. Gentle, green pastures and crumbling, ivy-covered ruins of a Gothic-style church give it an elegiac quality. For the prisoners, who saw it for the first time from the sea, Port Arthur, with its bleak and forbidding ramparts of dolerite and dark seas filled with deadly currents and sharks, must have seemed like the portals of hell. It was supposed to be forbidding. Its founder, Lieutenant Governor George Arthur, had left standing orders: "The most unceasing labour is to be exacted from the convicts, and the most harassing vigilance over them is to be observed."

Under the strict discipline of the commandant, Charles O'Hara Booth, the convicts worked long hours, in total silence and often in heavy irons, while constantly under the threat of the lash or solitary confinement in one of the dank punishment cells. No infraction went unpunished. Escape was almost impossible. The sea was too dangerous, and, as with the mythical gates of hell, a line of vicious dogs guarded the isthmus that led to the main part of the island. For many the only release was the one-way trip to the Isle of the Dead, where more than a thousand convicts were buried in communal graves.

More exquisite levels of torment were still to come. Between its completion in 1852 and 1877 Port Arthur was the site of the Model Prison, devised along the lines of England's Pentonville Prison, where prisoners were subjected to almost complete sensory deprivation. Recalcitrants were confined in dank cubicles 23 hours a day, unable to see, hear, or speak. During their solitary hour of exercise, they shuffled in irons around the prison yard—hooded, so that they were unable even to draw comfort from the soft green hills. Many went insane. Even by Victorian standards of justice, the goings-on at Port Arthur were considered grotesque, and the outcry after the 1874 publication of Marcus Clarke's highly popular novel, *For the Term of His Natural Life*, which detailed existence here, helped in the decision to shut the place down three years later.

Locals shunned the site long after it was shut down, changing its name to Carnarvon and hoping to forget its brutal past. When fires swept through the old buildings in the 1890s, many hoped the flames would erase what memory could not. "It is our Paestum and our Dachau rolled into one," wrote Robert Hughes in *The Fatal Shore*. "Far more than Macquarie Harbor or even Norfolk Island, Port Arthur has always dominated the popular historical imagination in Australia as *the* emblem of the miseries of transportation, 'the Hell on Earth.'" Over the past century morbid fascination and the gentle melancholy of its rather English landscape have made Port Arthur one of Tasmania's biggest tourist drawing cards. Thousands come here of a weekend to walk among the ruins.

Sadly, Port Arthur's tragic history hadn't ended with the closure of the penal colony. On a beautiful Sunday afternoon in April of 1996 a troubled loner named Martin Bryant chose these haunting ruins for one of the world's worst mass murders, killing 35 sightseers and wounding dozens more. The Broad Arrow Café, where the killing spree began, has been gutted and a monument erected to his victims. Bryant himself is serving a life sentence—without possibility of parole—in a Hobart prison.

Brutal though its prison camps were, the bloodiest and most chilling chapters of Tasmania's troubled history were written in the bush, with the calculated extermination of the island's Aborigines. Trouble between the races started only a few days after the first settlers arrived, with a mass murder of Aborigines camped near Hobart Town in 1804. Things only grew worse after that. Because food was so scarce in the early days of Hobart Town, some of the convicts—miscreants who were considered too rough and violent even for Botany Bay—were given shotguns and sent out to the bush to shoot kangaroos. With so many weapons in such dubious hands, Van Diemen's Land soon developed a culture of guns and senseless violence unlike any place else in the colonies. Many of these convict-hunters vanished in the dripping wilderness, setting themselves up as bandits, robbing and harassing white and black alike, even sinking to cannibalism on occasion. Others shot Aborigines for sport.

The Aborigines fought back, ambushing settlers, spearing shepherds, and attacking lonely outposts. Life on this gloomy island spun into a sickening vortex of uncontrollable killing. Although he recognized that the aggression had all come from the whites, Governor Arthur declared martial law in 1828, permitting soldiers or settlers to shoot on sight any Aborigines found in settled areas. Two years later he announced his final solution: Round up the Aborigines and send them into the dense forests of Tasmania's rugged northeast.

To this end the infamous Black Line was formed, with more than 2,000 soldiers and settlers beating the bush as though they were driving pheasants. For seven weeks they worked their way through the bush, from the central highlands down toward the Tasman Peninsula, where they hoped to round up the captive Aborigines for shipment. Most of the Aborigines slipped through the line, but the drive fragmented their clans, forced them away from their traditional lands, and broke their spirit.

A well-meaning philanthropist named George Robinson drove in the final nail when he managed to convince the remaining Aborigines that their best hope was to move to a sanctuary on remote Flinders Island, in Bass Strait. There they would be safe, clothed and fed and brought to Christ. By 1834 the last of Tasmania's Aborigines had been removed to Flinders Island, where new diseases, a strange diet, and grief whittled their numbers. In 1835 fewer than 150 Tasmanian Aborigines remained, out of an original island-wide population estimated at up to 7,000. A decade later there were 47. Toward the end, these few survivors were allowed to move to Bruny Island, about 20 miles southwest of Hobart. The last of Tasmania's full-blooded Aborigines, a woman named Truganini, a native of Bruny Island, died in 1876. Her skeleton was a curio in the Tasmanian Museum until 1947. Finally, it was cremated, and her ashes were scattered over the D'Entrecasteaux Channel in 1976.

Today, the D'Entrecasteaux Channel is popular with yachtsmen, while Bruny Island and the nearby Huon Valley, only an hour or so south of Hobart, are pleasant with neat orchards, cider mills, and English-style cottages. Driving past these miles of apple orchards and manicured farmland it is easy to think of Tasmania as an island with a split personality—bloody history and country churchyard settings. Long-established farms and prosperous villages that look a part of Kent or Sussex lie only a few miles away from primeval rain forests and jagged mountain peaks. This is a state that has produced some of Australia's most radical environmental crusaders as well as world-champion axmen, 300-pound fairground showstoppers who can chop through a 20-inch log in less than a minute. Tasmania seems equally proud of both types. On the Midland Highway, an old coach road that stretches through the center of the island between Hobart and Launceston, Tasmania present its English face.

This is the Tasmania of stately Georgian manors with hawthorn hedges and sturdy oaks, of traditional hunts and dry-fly anglers wading into sparkling streams and lakes. Trout were introduced to Tasmania by amateur naturalists in 1859 to provide gentlemanly recreation. They quickly spread through many of its waterways. Now the island is famous for its trophy-size brown and rainbow trout, and places like Lake Crescent, in the central part of the state, draw anglers from all over the world.

The towns along this drive, such as Oatlands, Ross, and Campbell Town, have a poetically English feel, with their stone cottages, leafy European trees, and gracious old pubs. The bridge at Richmond, a detour about 15 miles northeast of Hobart, is the oldest in Australia and one of its most beautiful. St. John's Roman Catholic Church rises in the background and flocks of ducks paddle in the gentle Coal River.

But Tasmania's brutal history is never far away. This elegant four-span bridge was built by convicts in the early 1820s. In chains and under constant threat of the lash, they were forced to haul quarried stone to the site in handcarts. The bridge is said to be haunted by the ghost of a particularly brutal overseer who was murdered by the convicts. The paradox of this picturesque setting and its violent past calls to mind Mark Twain's comment on the island's history when he visited Tasmania in 1895: "It was all out of keeping with the place, a sort of bringing of heaven and hell together."

The village of Ross, about halfway between Hobart and Launceston along the Midland Highway, has another, and even more picturesque convict-built sandstone bridge. It spans the Macquarie River. Designed by colonial architect John Lee Archer, it was completed in 1836. Daniel Herbert, the convict stonemason who carved the 186 magnificent Celtic symbols and animals that decorate the bridge, received a free pardon for his magnificent work. Governor George Arthur presumably was unaware of Herbert's equally talented carving of a rat wearing a judge's crown and wig that adorns the keystones beneath the bridge! Ross, an important coach stop in the old days, is a quiet period piece today. Sheep graze in the old churchyard, and gracious elm trees line the main street. Ross is at the heart of one of Australia's finest wool districts, famed for superfine fleeces that can literally be worth their weight in gold.

Immense pastoral wealth created some grand mansions in the midlands, such as Clarendon, near Evandale. A magnificent home that is considered to be one of Australia's finest examples of Georgian architecture, it was built for the wealthy wool-grower James Cox in 1838 and is now owned by Australia's National Trust.

Farther north is Launceston, Tasmania's second city and the third oldest city in Australia, founded in 1805. Nestled in the valley where the North and South Esk Rivers join to form the Tamar River, the industrial city of 67,000 grew on the back of woolen mills and the mining wealth of Tasmania's 19th-century mining boom. Far more provincial than Hobart, Launceston is a city of landscaped gardens, Victorian architecture, and quaint, Dickensian establishments such as the Old Umbrella Shop on George Street. The gracious Kings Bridge, built in 1867, spans the South Esk River, near Cataract Gorge, which has been drawing sightseers for more than a century.

In the same gentle, Old World vein, Tasmania's eastern coast, with its fresh, mild climate, is a run of pleasant surfing beaches, sheltered inlets, and scenic fishing villages. Freycinet National Park, declared in 1916 on the peninsula of the same name, is a beautiful blend of eucalypt forests, rolling hills of pink granite, and sparkling white beaches. It is famed for its walking tracks. One of the best tracks leads to Wineglass Bay, which harbors a swimming beach of pure quartzite sand. This secluded spot was once the site of a royal "picnic," when Queen Elizabeth's yacht *Britannia* anchored here while the monarch was on a state visit. Farther south is Maria Island National Park, with its sandstone cliffs, forests, and the remains of a penal colony built in 1825.

It is on the west coast and in the forbidding mountains rising in the central part of the state that Tasmania shows its darker, brooding side. The west takes the full brunt of the violent gale-driven seas so feared by old mariners. Jagged mountains in the interior of the island rise to cool alpine heights. More than a mile high, they are buffeted by these same sub-Antarctic gales. The land between rocky coast and alpine summit is riven by deep gorges and cloaked in virgin rain forests.

Until the winding road from Hobart to Queenstown was completed in 1932, the only access to Tasmania's west coast was by sea, through the treacherous sandbars and riptides of the dangerously narrow Hell's Gates to Macquarie Harbour. A penal colony was established here in 1821 on Sarah Island, which soon became one of England's most feared gulags—arguably even worse than Port Arthur. Instead of constant mental torment, Sarah Island's convicts were subject to a brutal regime of working long, backbreaking hours, sometimes in chains and often in cold, pouring rain, felling timber, working in saw pits, and building boats and ships. There were many deaths—and few escapes. Those who did break out found themselves lost in primeval swamps and leech-infested rain forests. Some of the most desperate resorted to cannibalism, killing and eating their fellow escapees when food ran out. These horror stories only enhanced Van Diemen's Land's unsavory reputation.

Despite the hardships along this coast, with its 80-inch annual rainfall, a succession of gold, silver, lead, copper, and tin strikes drew thousands of fortune seekers into these forests in the 1880s and 1890s. Towns like Queenstown, Zeehan, and Strahan sprang up. Sawmillers came to reap fortunes from the ancient stands of Huon pines that grew here. The slow-growing Huon pine—unique to Tasmania—was much sought after by shipbuilders for its supple grain and its rot-resistant qualities, while cabinetmakers prized the malleable wood for its lovely golden sheen and subtle fragrance. Rushing streams fed by constant rainfall seemed to promise abundant free energy for running mills and making electricity.

So much potential wealth and so much fragile pristine beauty in such a small island has meant Tasmanians have had to do a lot of soul-searching—and squabbling—over how to manage their resources. On one hand are loggers, miners, and energy workers who want more jobs; on the other are environmentalists who want to preserve what is one of the world's last pristine wilderness areas. Bitter battles over hydroelectric projects, wood-chipping plants, and smelters have shaped politics in this state for the past 30 years.

Tasmania has set aside more of its territory for national parks and wilderness areas—about 30 percent—than any other Australian state. One of the best known areas is the 398,000-acre Cradle Mountain–Lake St. Clair National Park, in the central part of the state, with its ancient dripping forests of pandanus, beech, and Tasmanian myrtle; jagged mountain peaks stretching more than 5,000 feet high; and a jewel-like glacier lake at its heart.

The untouched beauty of the area so captivated an Austrian naturalist named Gustav Weindorfer that he and his wife, Kate, moved to the foot of Cradle Mountain in 1912 and spent the next decade lobbying for the magnifi-

cent area to be made a national park. Today, their chalet, rebuilt from local pine, sits near the northern terminus of Australia's most famous hiking trail, the 50-mile-long Overland Track. The Overland is not a walk for the faint-hearted or ill prepared. It entails a week's hard trekking across remote moorlands, often swept by sudden cold storms, around Mount Ossa, Tasmania's highest peak, and through dense marshy forests to the southern tip of Lake St. Clair.

Merging with this vast area on the east is 128,000-acre Walls of Jerusalem National Park, where a spectacular line of jagged dolerite peaks have created an immense amphitheater, locking away vast, ancient forests, marshland, and scores of tiny glacial lakes. The unbroken wilderness extends still farther south, melding into 1.1-million-acre Franklin-Gordon Wild Rivers National Park, and beyond that the immense Southwest National Park and the Southwest Conservation Area. The two total more than 1.6 million acres of untouched wilderness .

Few places anywhere are like western Tasmania, with its treacherous coast, leech-infested marshes of button grass, and silent, impenetrable rain forests rising to forbidding alpine peaks almost a mile high. These strongholds, which make up the Tasmanian Wilderness World Heritage Area, are some of the world's last great tracts of virgin temperate rain forests, home to Huon pines some 2,000 years old and towering stands of swamp gums, the world's tallest species of hardwood. Two centuries of European settlement have left these gloomy shores virtually untouched. Abel Tasman, who sailed along the southwest coast in 1642, would still recognize it. I recall reading, I think in a novel by George Eliot, "there should always be some unknown regions preserved as hunting grounds for the poetic imagination." Perhaps no place better fits the bill than this storm-tossed island, frozen in time.

Following pages: *Moody, tempestuous, parts of it even marked on early charts as Transylvania, the storm-tossed coast of Tasmania gave pause to sailors and struck fear into the hearts of convicts who were banished here as the ultimate punishment.*

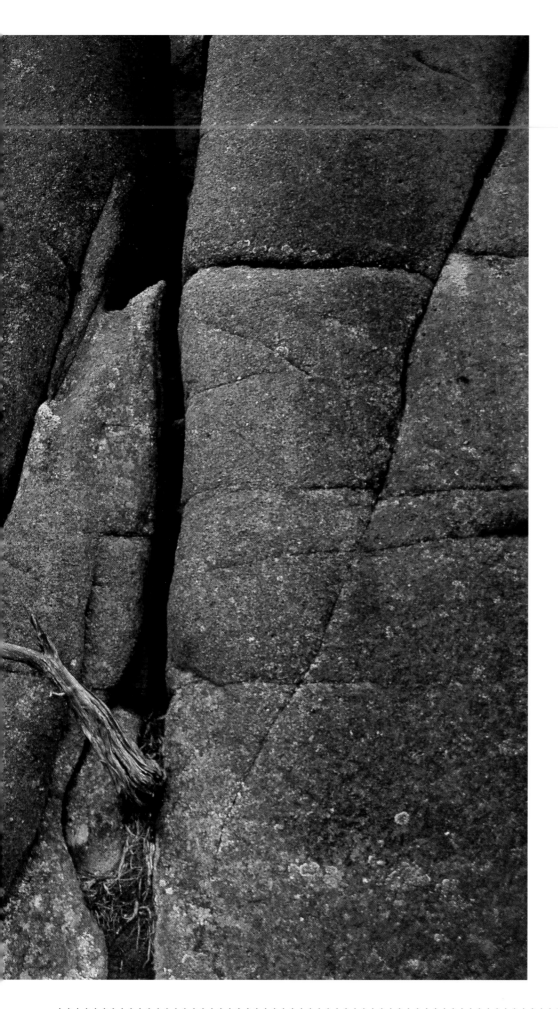

Clinging to life, a tree softens a sheer granite face in the Hazards, a dramatic range of 2,000-foot-high mountains that dominates the Freycinet Peninsula, on Tasmania's eastern coast. The rugged peninsula, with its cliffs, wildflower-dotted coastal heaths, and shimmering quartzite sand beaches, was declared a park in 1916. Nearly one-third of Tasmania has been set aside as parks or reserves.

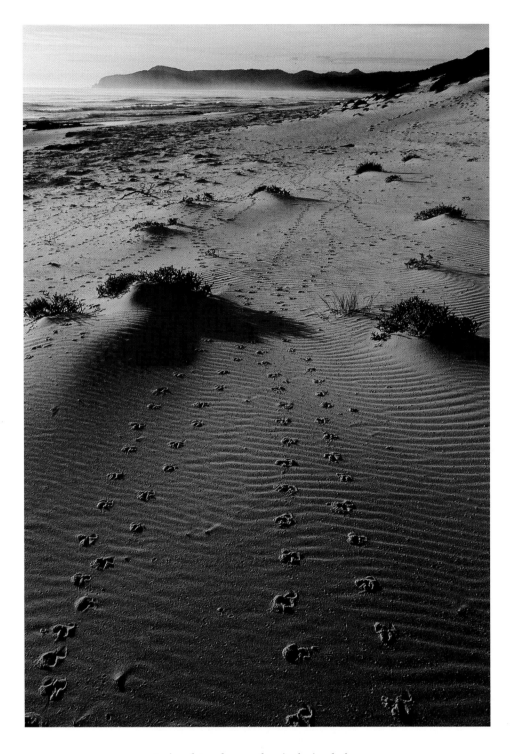

Animal tracks mark wind-rippled
sands on the Freycinet Peninsula.
For thousands of years the penin-
sula's dunes and beaches were a
favorite food-gathering place for
Aborigines, who came here to
collect shellfish.

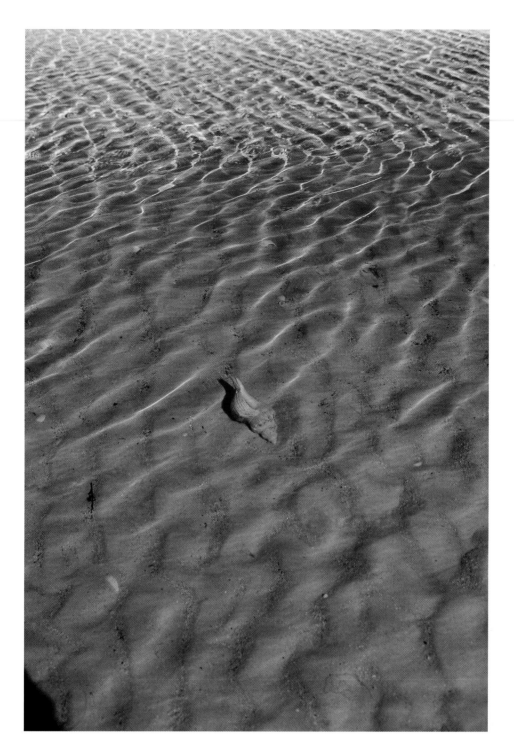

Shallows stained with tannin from nearby tea trees gleam copper at Freycinet National Park's Hazards Beach. Shell middens left behind attest to the area's bounty and serve as a mute reminder of a people exterminated by settlers, armed convicts, and disease. The last full-blooded Tasmanian Aborigine died in 1876.

Following pages: Silvery threads of Russell Falls provide a 120-foot-high backdrop to a magical valley of ferns, sassafras, and 250 year-old gums in Mount Field National Park, about 50 miles west of Hobart. First seen by Europeans in 1856, Russell Falls was proclaimed a reserve in 1885. Tasmania's last known thylacine, or Tasmanian tiger, was trapped in this region in the 1930s.

Bathed in mists, the austere profile of Cradle Mountain dominates Lake Dove, in Cradle Mountain–Lake St. Clair National Park. Dove was formed more than 20,000 years ago when glacial moraine dammed a deep valley.

Waldheim—*German for "forest home"—was built in 1912 by Austrian conservationist Gustav Weindorfer, who devoted his life to preserving the Cradle Mountain area. "Everyone should know about it and come and enjoy it," he once said—and they do. The 50-mile-long Overland Track, Australia's most popular walking trail, winds through the World Heritage site park near Weindorfer's chalet.*

Bright with blossoms, an English-style garden lends a touch of the old country to meadows and farmlands along the Derwent River Valley northwest of Hobart. Much of Australia's hops are grown near here, and the area's quaint old oasts, rows of poplars, and colonial architecture evoke England's Kent.

Following pages: *Straight lines of vines climb a curving hillside in the Tamar River Valley near George Town, on Tasmania's north coast. One of the earliest parts of Tasmania settled by Europeans, the fertile area is now the hub of Tasmania's flourishing wine industry.*

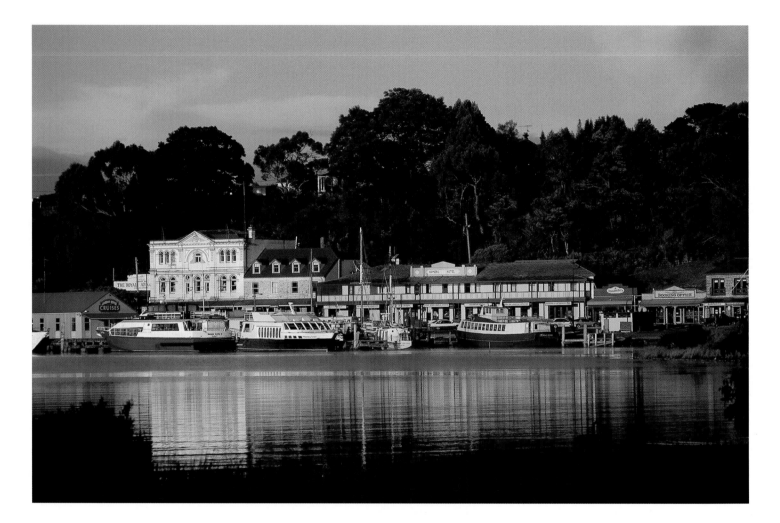

*Treacherous sandbars and riptides
of an inlet known as Hell's Gate
guard the seaport of Strahan,the
only town on Tasmania's wild and
dangerous west coast. The area's first
settlers were convicts and guards
of the brutal Macquarie Harbour
penal colony. The Union Steamship
Building and the Customs House are
tangible reminders of Strahan's
glory days during the mining booms
of the 1890s.*

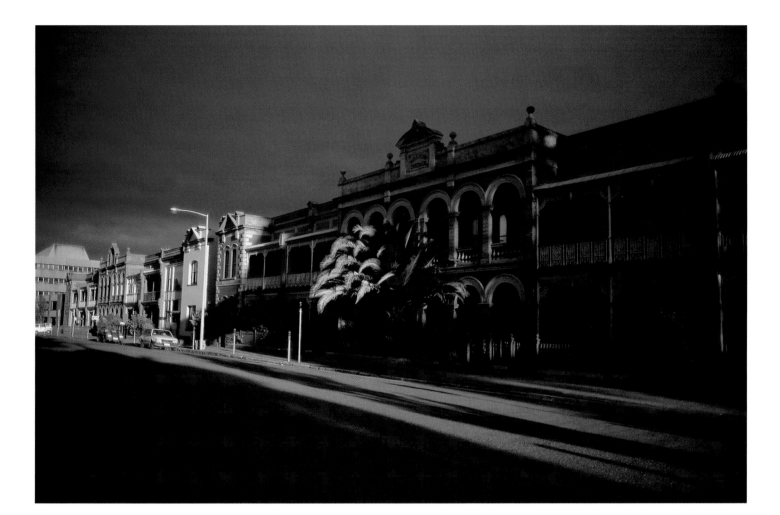

Elegant Georgian and Victorian façades line Cameron Street in Launceston, Australia's third oldest city after Sydney and Hobart. Settled in 1805, Launceston was an important industrial center by the 1880s. Known as the "city of gardens" for its many parks, reserves, and fountains, it is nestled in the hills where two rivers meet.

Following pages: *Like a troubled dream, Port Arthur's eerie ruins and brutal past have haunted Tasmania's memories since the penitentiary closed in 1877. Known throughout the empire as a living hell, the prison housed more than 12,000 convicts who endured hard labor and merciless discipline on this rocky peninsula guarded by a line of fierce dogs. A fire in 1897 destroyed many of the buildings; the legacy remains.*

The Heritage Coast

The extreme southeastern coast has been the cradle of Australia's most enduring myths and icons: Convicts clanking ashore in irons at Sydney Cove in 1788, the brawling Victorian goldfields of the 1850s, colorful bushrangers such as Ned Kelly, and Banjo Paterson's legendary horseman, "the man from Snowy River." This is the home of the Sydney Opera House, the Harbour Bridge, and Australian Rules football. Melbourne and Sydney, Australia's two biggest cities, are here, and between these jealous rivals lies the carefully planned capital city of Canberra. This area, often called the Heritage Coast, is the prettiest corner of Australia in a gentle, European sense—green and well watered. In the winter snow mantles the mile-high plains of the alpine country.

The region begins near the old whaling port of Warrnambool, on Victoria's dramatic coastline west of Melbourne, and stretches almost 700 miles through rain forests and towering stands of mountain ash, the freshness of the Snowy Mountains and the Great Dividing Range, and ends in the magnificence of Sydney Harbour.

No stretch of scenery is more beautiful or dramatic than that along the Great Ocean Road, a stunning drive that winds along Victoria's cliff-lined coast for 200 miles between Warrnambool and the beachside resort town of Torquay. A public works project begun in 1918 to honor soldiers who fought in World War I, it provided work for the unemployed during the Great Depression and was completed in 1932. I cycled along it over a few days in autumn. At first a cool breeze and a few odd showers blew in off the troubled waters of Bass Strait. Then the sun broke through, bringing a sparkling seaside freshness.

The road is hilly, twisting, and narrow as it hugs the beaches and cliffs that guard this stretch of coast. Then it veers inland through dripping rain forests of the Otway Ranges before rejoining the coast near the weekend resort towns of Lorne, Anglesea, and Torquay.

The road's grandest moments are along the hauntingly beautiful rocky sentinels known as the Twelve Apostles. These weathered remnants of an ancient cliff line east of Port Campbell have become symbols of the wild grandeur, fierce gales, and pounding surf of what 19th-century mariners knew as the Shipwreck Coast.

More than a thousand ships have come to grief here. The earliest may have been a 16th-century Portuguese caravel, one of a small flotilla under the command of Cristovão de Mendonça, which some scholars believe made a secret reconnaissance of the Great Southern Land at a time when arch rival Spain was claiming much of the Pacific. That voyage, if it occurred, would be the first known exploration of Australia by Europeans. A reference to the flotilla having sailed south from Java in 1522 and a series of French maps that seem to suggest a working knowledge of Australia's southern coast are the only hints of such a journey. Mendonça's journals were believed lost in the Lisbon earthquake in 1755. In 1836, however, the hull of a strange old vessel, supposedly built of mahogany, was found in the dunes near Warrnambool. No contemporary ship was known to have been lost in these parts, and local Aborigines said the wreck had always been there. This curio remained visible in the sands until a huge storm in 1880 obliterated the site, and the origin of the "Mahogany Ship" remains one of Australia's most enduring historical mysteries.

One of the most famous shipwrecks here was the iron clipper *Loch Ard*, which ran aground off Mutton Bird Island on a foggy night in 1878. Of 54 people on board, only 2 survived—an 18-year-old sailor named Tom Pearce and 18-year-old Eva Carmichael. The tragedy moved the country, and for a time sentimentalists hoped the young survivors might marry. But the wealthier Eva Carmichael went to live with relatives in Ireland, while Pearce returned to the sea, where he was to survive two more shipwrecks in his career.

The story of the ports and bays along the southeastern coast is mostly one of whalers and sealers seeking refuge from Bass Strait's dangerous seas, fishing trawlers, historic lighthouses, and timber-fellers dragging logs to the beaches for shipment to market. But there is a genteel touch, too. Since the 1860s wealthy pastoralists in Victoria's prime sheep-grazing country around Hamilton and well-heeled gentry from Melbourne and Geelong have been coming to these breezy seaside villages for summer holidays. The advent of the automobile and the Great Ocean Road opened the area to all and sundry, and today towns such as Anglesea and Torquay are thriving resorts, thronged with visitors from Melbourne on long-weekend holidays. The booming surf cursed by last century's mariners is today's blessing, giving this stretch of coast some of Australia's finest surfing beaches. The Bells Easter Classic, held near Torquay, has been one of the top events on the world's professional surfing circuit since 1961.

Melbourne and the maritime city of Geelong got their starts on the back of a shady real estate deal. Although Matthew Flinders had sailed into Port Phillip Bay in 1802, and there had been a short-lived attempt to establish a penal colony here in 1804, the magnificent bay was unappreciated by Europeans until an entrepreneur from Van Diemen's Land named John Batman set eyes on it in 1835. He liked what he saw. "I went on shore to look at the land, which appeared beautiful, and with scarcely any timber on. On my landing I found hills of a most superior description—beyond my most sanguine expectations," he wrote. "The land was excellent and very rich—and light black soil, covered with kangaroo grass two feet high, and as thick as it could stand. Good hay could be made and in any quantity. The trees were not more than six to an acre, and those small she-

oak and wattle. I never saw anything equal to the land in my life...." In what was arguably the best real estate bargain since Peter Minuit bought Manhattan for $24 worth of trade goods, Batman acquired 600,000 acres of land around Port Phillip Bay from three Aboriginal chieftains for shirts, scissors, and 50 pounds of flour.

Batman's transaction was technically illegal, despite his attending to niceties such as drawing up triplicates of the deeds of title, since the colonial office back in London did not permit independent speculation in what they regarded as crown land. Although unhappy about it, the bureaucrats let the deal stand, and two years later the town of Melbourne was laid out on a flat plain near the head of the bay, where the Yarra River flows into the sea.

The idea behind the new settlement—which was named Victoria after Britain's monarch—was that it could help service the prosperous and rapidly expanding pastoral and grazing interests in the southern part of Australia. Many of Melbourne's first settlers were gentleman farmers who built elegant homes in town from which they could vicariously manage their vast holdings in the hinterland. With money enough to have their choice of land, most of these wealthy pastoralists built on the gently rolling south bank of the Yarra River, which tends to be green and pretty. They established a trend. Over generations, the Yarra has become the defining social and economic boundary in this class-conscious city. Most of the city's prosperous middle- and upper-class suburbs—places such as South Yarra, Toorak, and Prahran—have grown on the fertile banks south of the Yarra and along the southeast flank of Port Phillip Bay. The hotter, flatter, and drier land to the north and west is generally given over to heavy industry. Fueled by huge offshore oil and gas reserves in Bass Strait and rich coal deposits in the nearby La Trobe Valley, Victoria became Australia's industrial heartland—replete with aluminum smelters, auto factories, and petrochemical plants.

Melbourne may have been founded on pastoral interests, but a string of fabulous gold discoveries around the colony in the 1850s changed everything, quickly turning the fledgling settlement into Australia's richest and biggest city, its streets lined with imposing Victorian architecture. The heady brew of gold and commerce made Melbourne Australia's banking and financial hub and home to most of the nation's largest corporations, a title it now grudgingly shares with Sydney. But there are important differences between these two money capitals. Melbourne is proudly disdainful of Sydney's nouveau riche brashness. As a former New England Yankee, I've always felt more at home in Melbourne, with its Bostonian airs. This is an intensely clubby city where imponderables like family bloodlines and old school ties—notably Geelong Grammar, the alma mater of prime ministers and business luminaries such as Rupert Murdoch—matter more than income.

Perhaps not surprisingly, given such old world shadows, Melbourne is Australia's most European-feeling city, with tree-lined streets, landscaped parks, and magnificent fin de siècle architecture. Green-and-gold trolley cars clanging along the busy city streets; fairy lights in the plane trees at the exclusive Paris End of the city, near the theaters, State House of Parliament, and the grand old Windsor Hotel; and elegant bridges across the Yarra accent this European flavor. So does Melbourne's cosmopolitan population. Vast numbers of immigrants from all over Europe, particularly Greece and Italy, came here in the years after the Second World War. The world's largest population of Greeks, after Athens, is reputedly found here, while Lygon Street is famous for its cavalcade of Italian restaurants, pastry shops, cafés and *gelateria*. Since the early 1980s the largest number of the city's immigrants have been Asians. Little Bourke and Victoria Streets, with their jumble of Chinese apothecaries, Vietnamese grocers, and dim sum restaurants, throb with the vibrancy of an Asian market. Crowded footpaths are bright with fruit stalls; butcher-shop windows are festooned with ducks, chicken feet, and pig carcasses; and the air is redolent with cooking oil and scorched spices.

Melbourne is home to some of Australia's most enduring and defining traditions, classics such as the Melbourne Cup. On the first Tuesday of every November since 1861 the entire nation has come to a halt to watch the running of this horse race at the Flemington Racecourse. The first official international test match between the English and Australian cricket teams was played in 1877 at the Melbourne Cricket Ground. And it was here that Australian Rules football was invented. Those who believe that Australian institutions must be young can note that the Melbourne football club—formed in 1858—is older than any organized club in Europe. Melburnians have always been sports mad. Perhaps one of the reasons they could afford the time for such indulgences was that Sydney and Melbourne were the first places to adopt the eight-hour workday. By the 1890s football matches in Melbourne were drawing crowds in the tens of thousands—by far the largest in the world.

It was in the rustic villages along the Yarra Valley, on the outskirts of Melbourne, that Australia began to see itself through uniquely Australian eyes. In the late 1880s a clique of nationalistic Melbourne artists led by Tom Roberts, Arthur Streeton, Frederick McCubbin, and Charles Conder began taking their easels out to the countryside to paint the Australian landscape as it really was—hot, bright, and glary, with gnarled gum trees and sun-browned grasses. Their masterpieces owed nothing to traditionally pretty English scenes. Far from gentling their images, these Heidelberg School artists, so-called after one of the Yarra Valley villages where they frequently painted, ventured into the blinding afternoon sunlight and celebrated the heat and dust and antipodean weirdness of their native land. Charles Conder's masterpiece "A Holiday at Mentone" depicts archly Victorian holiday-makers unwinding in the purplish heat of one of Melbourne's beachside suburbs. When I look at it, I can feel the breathlessness of the afternoon and the sweat running down the gentleman's collar as he eyes the girl in a beach chair reading a book. An unashamedly Australian lifestyle was taking shape. Tom Robert's 1890 "Shearing the Rams," celebrating the working-class camaraderie in the shearing shed, is an Australian icon.

Melbourne was built on gold—some of the richest finds the world has ever known. An hour's drive north through rolling farmlands lies the town of Ballarat, in the heart of Victoria's fabled gold diggings. With a population of about 65,000, it is Australia's biggest inland city. Its grand, tree-lined streets with Italianate buildings, landscaped gardens, and classical statuary made of rare marble hint at the prodigious wealth that came out of the ground here. In the early days of 1852 armed caravans brought more than half a ton of gold each *week* from gold-rich Ballarat and Bendigo to the bank vaults of Melbourne.

The catalyst for Victoria's astonishing gold strikes was the discovery of gold near Bathurst, New South Wales, by Edward Hargraves in February 1851. Word that gold had been found triggered a stampede to the Bathurst fields, which by then had been named Orphir by Hargraves. Small wonder—one nugget alone yielded 1,272 ounces—almost 80 pounds—of gold. Irritated at losing their workers to the New South Wales goldfields, Victorian businesses put up a reward in May 1851 for the person who could find gold in *their* colony.

They didn't have long to wait. On July 5, 1851, gold was reported at Clunes, about a hundred miles northwest of Melbourne. In August gold was found near the town of Buninyong. The next month a digger stumbled onto the spectacular Ballarat goldfields. More strikes came, thick and fast, until it seemed as though all of Victoria's creek beds must be sparkling with nuggets and gold dust. At Ararat and Beaufort, Castlemaine, Creswick, and Maldon—gold seemed to be everywhere for the taking. Still more fabulous strikes were reported along the Ovens River, in the northeastern part of the colony.

Word of the bonanzas spread around the world, sparking one of the world's great gold rushes and changing the face of Victoria forever. In Melbourne shops and businesses were closed: Every able-bodied man had grabbed tools and raced for the diggings. Ships, deserted by their captains and crews, crowded the harbor. Fortune hunters flocked to Melbourne from all over the world: More than 90,000 immigrants a year landed here in the headiest days of the gold rush. Victoria's population jumped 400 percent between 1851 and 1854. By 1861 more than half a million people lived in upstart Melbourne, and it had supplanted Sydney as Australia's biggest city. Gold lured the first mass influx of Asian immigrants to Australia. Thousands of Chinese rushed to the diggings in New South Wales and Victoria. To them Bendigo was known as "Golden Mountain." When a xenophobic Victorian government tried to curtail this influx with a £10 levy on Asian migrants, the Chinese disembarked in South Australia and made their own way to the goldfields.

If Melbourne seemed like a ghost town at the height of the boom, there were riotous times at the muddy shanty settlements near the diggings. Saloons and brothels ran round-the-clock; struck-it-rich prospectors slurped champagne and showered dance-hall girls with nuggets. The most colorful entertainer was the hot-blooded Lola Montez, an exotic dancer and adventuress whose scandalous, globe-trotting career had already taken her from the court of King Ludwig I of Bavaria to the brawling California goldfields by the time she reached Victoria in 1855. Her notorious spider dance was a hot favorite with the miners, although it drew a censorious editorial in the *Ballarat Times*. In one of the town's most celebrated incidents, Montez sought out the paper's editor, Henry Seekamp, and gave him a sound thrashing with her whip—another performance that delighted the miners.

The goldfield towns reached their pinnacle of opulence and style in the 1880s. Their wide, gracious streets were lined with grandly proportioned mansions—gaudy, ornate, and nouveau riche—in rich combinations of classical, Gothic, Victorian, and Italianate styles. In Ballarat the Academy of Music, built in 1875 and embellished with a domed ceiling and opulent tiered balconies, billed acts like Victoria-born Nelly Armstrong, who would become international opera diva Dame Nelly Melba. In Castlemaine the town markets were built of stone along classical lines and topped with a statue of Ceres, the Roman goddess of the harvest. Maldon, its main street lined with deep verandas and bluestone pavements, was declared Victoria's first "notable town" by the National Trust in 1965. Most of these towns faded after the gold finally petered out in the first half of the 20th century, but they are finding their niche today as living museums, their peaceful antique streetscapes popular with tourists. Sovereign Hill, a re-creation of life in Ballarat's wild gold rush days, is one of the state's biggest drawing cards.

In 1854 Ballarat was the site of the Eureka Stockade Uprising, Australia's landmark political rebellion. The rebellion was the nearest thing the six colonies had to a civil war. And in the years since, the Eureka uprising and the rebels' flag it produced have been potent symbols of Australia's fiercely independent spirit.

The Eureka incident was brought about by a stiff fee on prospecting—30 shillings a month, or a full day's boomtown wages for a carpenter. The levy was payable whether a digger discovered gold or not, and anyone found without this license was subject to prosecution—or worse, since the revenue agents deputized to collect the fees and inspect the licenses were little more than thugs and tough ex-cons.

The Victorian government's rationale for the hated license was to discourage workers from quitting their jobs and running off to the diggings, where most were unlikely to find anything but trouble. Also, the hordes of foreigners coming into Australia would probably take away what gold they found, and officials saw in them a good opportunity for revenue raising. And, while nobody in those jackpot days quite dared to raise the point that under long-standing British law all minerals automatically belonged to the crown, a license did guarantee that the crown got at least a piece of the action.

Whatever the bureaucrats' logic, the miners' resentment is easy to understand. Digging for gold in a deep, wet mine shaft was dirty, frustrating, exhausting, and dangerous, but it seemed to be the little guy's best chance of cracking a fortune in Australia. All the best pastoral land in the new country had already been handed out by the hundreds of square miles to the wealthy or well connected. But nuggets of gold were there for the taking. There were no powerful mining interests—yet—to take up major holdings. A typical claim on the Ballarat diggings was 12 feet square—workable by a single digger of any class, creed, or color. And for once fortune actually favored the working class, since they generally had the strongest backs and the most calloused hands—traits far more valuable in a muddy mine than a private school education.

Even so, few struck it rich. Most toiled long hours for little or no reward. They lived amid squalor and disease, took daily risks in the mine shafts, and paid huge markups on everything from flour to shovels. Adding a 30-shilling-a-month license fee seemed grossly unfair. Even more infuriating was the way the law was enforced. A miner had to carry his license on his person at all times or be hauled in front of a magistrate and fined. It didn't matter if the miner was working waist-deep in water. The precious paper license had to be on his person—not back in his tent where it was dry. License checks were mad-

deningly frequent. Smirking enforcers often ordered miners to climb up out of hundred-foot shafts in order to inspect their licenses—and then returned an hour later to summon them up all over again.

By October 1854 the Ballarat diggings were smoldering with resentment. Tensions were raised even higher by the murder of a miner by a local publican who was acquitted, allegedly because he was friendly with the goldfield's corrupt administration. Over the next few weeks the hot-tempered diggers—Irish republicans, German and Italian revolutionaries, freewheeling Americans—began to talk rebellion. To this end a Canadian, Charlie Ross, raised a flag he and his wife had fashioned: the Southern Cross on a blue field. The *Ballarat Times*, edited by the same Henry Seekamp who would soon be horsewhipped by Lola Montez, came out strongly in support of the miners. He urged the end of license fees and that miners be given the right to vote and run for office.

Several hundred miners met under the Southern Cross flag on November 29th. Some burned their licenses and dared authorities to do anything about it. Bullheaded goldfields commissioner Robert Rede promptly obliged, ordering a mass license inspection. Shots were fired, the riot act was read, and some miners were arrested. The miners gathered again a few days later, this time electing an Irishman named Peter Lalor to be their leader and swearing allegiance to their new flag. The poorly armed rabble then retreated behind a hastily built stockade in a strongly Irish section of the Eureka diggings.

After a bit of sober reflection, many of the miners quietly slipped away, unwilling to take up arms against Britain. There were only 150 or so left in the stockade when 400 police and troopers launched a surprise predawn attack on the compound on the morning of December 3, 1854. The battle lasted only a few minutes, but 30 miners and 5 soldiers were killed. Peter Lalor, the leader, escaped, but his left arm had to be amputated a few days later. Most of the rest of the rebels were captured and charged with high treason.

The miners lost the battle at the Eureka Stockade, but they won the war: Melbourne juries refused to convict them. The hated license was abolished, and in its place came the miner's right, which allowed the bearer to fossick for gold for a year for a payment of one pound sterling. Miners were allowed to vote and to run for office. One of those who did was Peter Lalor, who was elected to the Victorian parliament the following year. Today, a new, 2.5-million-dollar Eureka Stockade Centre sits on the site of the encounter, and the original flag is on display in the Ballarat Fine Art Gallery.

Along with Victoria's incredible wealth came outlaws. Highwaymen—or bushrangers as Australians called them—achieved a sort of perverse folk-hero status on the outback frontier, just as they did in America's Wild West. Perhaps they were even more idealized in Australia. After all, it was founded as a penal colony. In a place ruled by the lash, any form of dissent was likely to take on heroic stature among the rank and file. Politics played a role, too. Many of the bushrangers were Irish republicans, some of them children of rebels sent to Australia in chains who saw their crimes as blows for freedom. And in the eyes of the rural poor—who were also, typically, Irish Catholics—bushrangers took on a Robin Hood aura.

Bushrangers existed from the colony's earliest days. Generally, they were escapers, or "bolters" who had fled into the bush and waylaid passersby for money, food, or supplies. Present-day Tasmania became so badly infested with bandits in the early 1800s that the governor declared martial law, fearing they might take over the island. But it wasn't until the gold rush days, when there was finally wealth worth stealing rattling along the lonely bush tracks, that the era of the bushranger reached full flower. Highwaymen like Frederick Ward (a.k.a. Captain Thunderbolt), Daniel "Mad" Morgan, and Ben Hall became cult figures. But by 1880 they had faded to footnote status beside the exploits of a 25-year-old from Victoria named Ned Kelly. Australia's most famous bushranger and national hero, he has been the subject of countless movies, ballads, songs, and biographies.

Kelly was born in 1855, the son of an Irish ex-convict and part-time cattle rustler, on a dirt-poor farm in the backwoods of Victoria's northeast. A ruggedly built brawler, Ned's first brush with the law came at the age of 15, when he was brought up on assault charges. Two years later the young hoodlum drew three years of hard labor for horse theft. He was convicted largely on the perjured evidence of a corrupt policeman who apparently wanted to be rid of a troublemaker. Kelly graduated to the big time in 1878.

The story the Kellys told was that Ned and his brother Dan came home one evening to find a police officer paying unwanted attention to their sister, and Ned gave the constable a sound thrashing. The constable claimed Ned pulled a gun and shot at him. Knowing that the policeman's story was likely to stick, Ned and Dan and two of their mates, Joe Byrne and Steve Hart, fled into the bush. An armed posse came after them, supposedly planning to administer summary justice in the bush.

But the Kelly Gang—which had been advised of police movements by sympathetic rural poor—ambushed the troopers at a place called Stringybark Creek and killed three of them. There was no turning back. For the next 19 months the Kelly Gang hid out in the wild Strathbogie Ranges of northeast Victoria, their superb horsemanship and bushcraft making a mockery of their pursuers. The myth about them grew. While the authorities saw him as a murderous ruffian who had to be stopped, Kelly considered himself an Irish political rebel and a champion of the underdog rather than an outlaw. He certainly enjoyed a strong following among the struggling farmers. One crime was especially popular: When Ned robbed the bank at Euroa in December 1878, he built a bonfire in the street and burned all the mortgage documents he could find. On another occasion, he and his gang took over the town of Jerilderie, where Ned dictated a rambling 10,000-word political manifesto that was sent to police in Melbourne.

The end came in June 1880 at the town of Glenrowan, where Kelly and his gang decided to make a stand against a trainload of troopers who were coming into the mountains to track them down. Forewarned, the troopers stopped the train a little way before the town, crept up, and surprised the gang at the Glenrowan Hotel. A furious gunfight erupted and lasted through the night. Kelly was outside the hotel when the gun battle started, and, although badly wounded in the first exchange, he might have escaped. Instead, he donned a clumsy suit of "bulletproof" armor he had made out of plowshares and charged the troopers who had his brother and mates trapped in the burning hotel. He was brought down by a shotgun blast to his legs and captured. The rest of the gang perished. When he was asked by reporters why he hadn't escaped when he had the chance, Kelly supposedly replied: "A man would be a nice sort of dingo to walk out on his mates." It was a response that epitomized the outback code of honor—of mateship, courage, and disdain for authority—that had already made Kelly a hero.

Ned Kelly's court appearance in Melbourne was Victoria's trial of the century. He was found guilty and, despite a petition for mercy bearing more than 60,000 signatures, was hanged at Melbourne Gaol on November 11, 1880.

Fed by his gallant martyrdom, Ned Kelly's aura snowballed to superhero status. In 1906 he was the subject of the world's first feature-length film, which used as a prop Kelly's original armor. *The Story of the Kelly Gang* was so sympathetic to the outlaw that nervous Victorian authorities, fearing it could provoke a popular insurrection, banned it from Kelly's old stomping ground around the Strathbogie Ranges. Kelly is still a national hero. The gallows on which he was hanged, his armor, and a death mask are among the biggest drawing cards at the Old Melbourne Gaol Museum. The town of Glenrowan, about 140 miles northeast of Melbourne on the Hume Highway, commemorates Kelly's last stand with a 20-foot statue of the outlaw in his homemade armor.

Southeast of Glenrowan, and purplish in the distance on a clear day, are the Australian Alps. I climbed the highest of Victoria's mountains, 6,514-foot Mount Bogong, on a blustery autumn day. A biting wind gusted from the south, and the valleys below were thick with clouds and rain. It was a steep and muddy climb. Dense forests dwindled to wind-stunted scrub. The last miles, across ridges of frost-cracked rock toward Mount Bogong's lonely summit, evoked Scotland rather than Australia. Stretching into the swirling mists was a chain of cairns built along the ridge top. The rocks guide hikers along the Australian Alps Walking Track, a 403-mile trek from Valhalla in the south to the outskirts of Canberra.

Australia's highest mountains are more like a series of alpine plateaus than peaks, and, although the highest range is called the Snowy Mountains, they do not have year-round snow. Still, they are unlike anything else in Australia, with their ghost gums, clear cold streams, alpine grasses and lichens, and carpet of wildflowers in the spring.

Aborigines came to these highlands every summer for thousands of years to collect bogong moths. They roasted the nutritious insects, which have a nutty flavor. But it was rich alpine grasses that drew Australian cattlemen here into the high country in the 1860s. One such cattleman was Jack Riley, said to be the inspiration for Banjo Paterson's *The Man From Snowy River,* one of the best loved poems in Australia. The ballad celebrates the legendary horsemanship, recklessness, and love of adventure of the daring cowboys of the mountains.

There was movement at the station, for the word had passed around / That the colt from old Regret had got away, / And had joined the wild bush horses—he was worth a thousand pound, / So all the cracks had gathered to the fray.

They chase the herd, hard and recklessly, mile after mile through the steep and dangerous high country until it finally races down a slope so treacherous that even these hard-riding horsemen pull up. All except one, that is. Without a second's hesitation and with a wild whoop, the man from Snowy River gallops down the slope in hot pursuit. His mates watch in awe as they see him reappear on a distant hillside, still hard on the heels of the herd, trail them, and finally turn them toward home.

And, as Paterson notes in the penultimate line of the ballad, "the Man from Snowy River is a household word today." Indeed, anybody who can recite the entire 104-line ballad from memory has a good chance of being shouted a few beers at any bush pub. Riley himself is less celebrated. He lived and worked along the Victorian side of the mountains, near the rapidly flowing headwaters of the Murray River, for half a century. He died in 1914 and is buried in an unobtrusive cemetery near the town of Corryong, about 200 miles northeast of Melbourne.

The Snowy Mountains are famous for another daring feat—not so much by rugged individualists, but by 100,000 men from some 30 nations working in concert over a period of a quarter of a century. There was no balladeer laureate to record these exploits—Paterson died eight years before the project began—but the Snowy Mountains Scheme was one of the world's greatest and most ambitious engineering projects. It came about in the heady years after the Second World War as a giant public works project to irrigate farm fields and supply hydroelectricity to the rapidly growing cities along Australia's southeast coast. Work began in 1949. Throughout the 1950s and 1960s, dams were built, tunnels were punched through mountains, power stations were constructed, and rivers were diverted. Entire towns were relocated and old sites flooded. The immensely complicated project—which cost 121 lives—wasn't completed until 1974. Perhaps the greatest marvel about the Snowy Mountains Scheme had nothing to do with groundbreaking engineering—and everything to do with the human spirit. Thousands of workers, many of them immigrants from a war-shattered Europe, and at least some of whom had fought on opposite sides of that war, came together in harmony to build a future in the sunny promise of Australia.

On the northern fringe of the Snowy Mountains, in the valley of the Molonglo River, is Canberra—Australia's carefully planned capital.

The early days of a new century, January 1, 1901, marked the birth of a new nation—Australia. After years of politicking and diplomacy, the six Australian colonies had agreed to set aside their competitive squabbling and unite under a federal government. The new nation would still be British of course—with the ruling British monarch as its head of state, the Union Jack on its flag, its laws subject to veto by Britain's parliament, and its court decisions subject to review by the privy council in London. But patriotism for queen and empire was a reliable sentiment in 1901, and few Australians were troubled by this version of nationhood.

The big issue was where to locate the new federal capital. Although arch rivals Sydney and Melbourne could both make compelling cases for earning that distinction, the new constitution cleverly stipulated that the new capital had to be in New South Wales, yet had to be at least a hundred miles from Sydney. While the new capital was being established, the seat of government would be in Melbourne.

For the next seven years a number of towns put their hats in the ring. For a while Wentworth, an outback New South Wales town at the juncture of the Murray and Darling Rivers, was a leading contender. In the end, however, after much wrangling, two royal commissions, and numerous parliamentary inquiries, a site on the grazing lands in the Yass district was chosen. It was diplomatically located between Sydney and Melbourne or, as puckish wits later observed, equally inconvenient to reach from either city. In 1911 New South Wales transferred a thousand square miles to the federal government to form the Australian Capital Territory. The port of Jervis Bay was included as an annex so that the federal government would have a seaport.

A radical young architect from Chicago named Walter Burley Griffin, who had worked with Frank Lloyd Wright, won an international competition to design the new capital. His plan called for a European-style city to be laid out on three main axes that would form what he called a parliamentary triangle, with man-made lakes and minor streets radiating outward in concentric circles. Construction began in 1913, but was interrupted by World War I and continual bickering over Griffin's controversial plans and his appointment to direct the work. Twelve years passed before Griffin's plans were formally adopted—with a few revisions that he detested. By then young Griffin and his wife, who was also an architect, had settled permanently in Australia.

Parliament House opened for business in 1927, but it was 1964 before Griffin's key feature, the lake, was completed and the city actually began to resemble his vision. The final piece of his layout was slotted into place in 1988, when a 660-million-dollar Parliament House was opened on the top of a low grassy hill at the apex of Griffin's original parliamentary triangle.

Like Canberra itself, the new Parliament House was the result of an international design competition. It was won by American architectural firm Mitchell, Giurgola, and Thorpe. To maintain the integrity of the landscape, it is built into the hilltop, and the roof is grassed over. The interior of the monumental building is magnificent. It is a showpiece of colored marble, splendid Australian timbers, marquetry depicting Australia's unique flora, and a magnificent Aboriginal mosaic titled "Meeting Place" by Michael Tjakamarra Nelson. The building houses thousands of Australian paintings, sculptures, and tapestries, as well as one of only four known original copies of the Magna Carta, the document England's King John signed in 1215 that has since become the basis of all British law.

The Australia of today is vastly different from the one that constructed the old Parliament House, now home to the National Portrait Gallery. In the decade since Queen Elizabeth II opened the new parliament building, a centenary move to launch Australia as a republic in 2001 has rapidly gained momentum. Looking to Asia for its future, self-confident, relaxed, and no longer distracted by ties to a distant Europe, Australians are questioning the need to have England's monarch as their head of state. That topic, radical only a few years ago, is today's mainstream debate. No longer do newly inducted Australian citizens swear allegiance to the queen. Her portrait is gone from most public offices, and in November 1999 Australians will go to the polls in a historic referendum to decide their nation's future.

A fast expressway links Canberra with Sydney, 190 miles to the north. To appreciate its magnificent harbor, its coves lined with yachts and mansions; the sail-like Sydney Opera House; and the Harbour Bridge, however, the best way to approach Sydney is by air or water. "The finest harbour in the world, in which a thousand sail of the line may ride with perfect security," crowed Capt. Arthur Phillip, the colony's first governor, when he delivered the first load of convicts to these shores in January 1788.

Despite its beautiful setting, Sydney was a wretched place for its first few years. It teetered on the brink of famine, and most of its population—mainly thieves, pickpockets, and prostitutes from the London slums—toiled in chains and under threat of the lash. "A more wicked, abandoned and irreligious set of people had never been brought together in any part of the world," lamented a later governor, John Hunter, in the 1790s. As Sydney grew, it became a lusty port of call for South Sea whalers. It gained notoriety for its rum trade and a mutiny in 1808 by the breathtakingly corrupt military against the colony's discipline-minded governor, Captain William Bligh of *Bounty* fame.

It was the reform-minded Governor Lachlan Macquarie, arriving in 1810, who set Sydney on the path to becoming the city it is today. After breaking the power of the military junta, which monopolized trade, he estab-

lished the colony's first banks, set up its currency, and embarked on an ambitious public work's program with the aid of a convict architect named Francis Greenway. Greenway designed more than 40 buildings, including some of the colony's finest—St. James Church, the Hyde Park Barracks at Victoria Square, and the Courthouse at Windsor. Roads were laid out, bridges were built, and by the end of Macquarie's ten-year residence, Sydney was a prosperous seaport of more than a thousand buildings.

The oldest part of Sydney, where early convicts set up their first camp, is a warren of narrow streets and stone buildings nestled around the southern end of the Harbour Bridge. Known as "The Rocks," it was once the most squalid, lawless, and dangerous neighborhood in Australia. Brothels, grog shops, seamy lodging houses, and waterfront pubs crammed the narrow streets. Razor gangs, pickpockets, and thugs lurked in its rat-infested alleyways. An outbreak of bubonic plague in the early 1900s forced authorities to step in and raze many of the filthy slums. Still more were leveled in the late 1920s to make way for the Harbour Bridge. A bitter controversy erupted in the 1970s, however, over plans to demolish the rest of Sydney's oldest buildings to make way for skyscrapers. Instead, the seedy neighborhood was lovingly restored and reincarnated as Sydney's most popular tourist precinct, a picturesque enclave of Dickensian cobbled streets and old stone shop fronts that house art galleries, cafés, and fashionable boutiques.

Some of Sydney's emancipated convicts, those who were shrewd enough to see opportunity even when it came disguised in the form of banishment for life, were fast becoming wealthy citizens. By the time he died in 1838, Samuel Terry, an illiterate former convict and stonemason, owned Sydney real estate worth over £250,000 pounds. One of the wealthiest men in the nation, he was known as the Rothschild of Botany Bay. By 1836 a visiting Charles Darwin noted the staggering real estate prices, adding: "The whole population, poor and rich, are bent on acquiring wealth." That was Sydney, just hitting its stride.

Now in its third century, Sydney presents a flamboyant Manhattan-style skyline, stunningly arranged around its spectacular harbor. Two of Australia's most recognized emblems, the Opera House and the Sydney Harbour Bridge, are barely a stone's throw from Circular Quay, the bustling ferry landing where thousands of commuters arrive each morning from waterfront suburbs such as Hunters Hill, Neutral Bay, and Manly.

Sydney is an aggressive, glitzy town, the financial capital of the South Pacific and headquarters to some of Australia's biggest banks, corporations, and stockbrokerages. The city's futures market is one of the world's busiest. It is home to Australia's richest people, its tallest buildings, and its priciest real estate. Sydney's collective obsession with money, glamour, and harbor views has driven the prices of mansions in dress circle locations, such as Point Piper and Vaucluse, to eight-digit heights, while even modest homes with harbor frontage can easily fetch millions. Much as Sydneysiders love their harbor, high real estate prices have forced most of the city's 4 million residents to live well back from the water. Sydney sprawls. Although its population is modest by world standards, the metropolitan area, with 45 local government areas, covers about 900 square miles. Ascend the thousand-foot-high Sydney Tower, and you see the western suburbs spreading outward toward a line of hazy bluish peaks—the Blue Mountains.

In Sydney's early days, those mountains were a formidable barrier to inland expansion, so steep and densely forested that it took early pioneers until 1813 to find a route through them. Today, it takes about two hours by train from Sydney's gracious Central Station to the mountain resort of Katoomba. The train rolls through the sprawl of Sydney's working-class western suburbs and climbs through foothill towns.

The name "Katoomba" may be a corruption of an Aboriginal word meaning "falling water," a comment on the numerous streams that spill over the edge of the spectacular sandstone escarpment and into the thickly forested Jamison and Megalong Valleys hundreds of feet below. Katoomba and the other villages in the mountains sit on the edge of this sandstone escarpment. The view is breathtaking, and often in the early mornings the cliff-lined valleys are blanketed with thick mists. Echo Point,

on the rim of the valley, is famous for its view of the Three Sisters. These stone pillars have come to symbolize the Blue Mountains. According to Aboriginal legends, they are three girls who were turned into stone by their magician father in a frantic bid to protect them as they were being attacked by a fearsome creature known as a bunyip. When the frustrated bunyip turned on the father, he transformed himself into a lyrebird. Unfortunately, in the confusion, he lost his magic wand and was unable to change anybody back.

The Blue Mountains are a part of the Great Dividing Range that runs the length of Australia's eastern seaboard. The mountains got their name from the fine mist of eucalypt oil given off by the dense forests: Billions of fine droplets diffuse the sun's rays, tinting the air, blurring the horizon, and giving the mountains their famous bluish, painted-on appearance. This bracing, eucalypt-tinged air, coupled with the mountains' refreshing climate, was thought to be therapeutic. By the 1870s the mountains were a popular retreat for wealthy invalids and Sydney's well-to-do families, who came here for their summer holidays to escape the city heat and take the air. In the 1920s the mountains were popular with adventurous honeymooners, who risked the narrow roads in their jalopies to visit Jenolan Caves, on the western flank of the mountains. Today, villages retain a quaint, turn-of-the-century atmosphere. The elegant façades of grand hotels and art nouveau guest houses line the streets.

For all the gentility of the Blue Mountains, and the sometimes gentle melancholy of the Heritage Coast, Sydney is a brash, outward-looking city. Its gaze, like that of much of the continent's inhabitants, is fixed on the sunshine of Queensland, and beyond that to the bustling financial markets of Asia and the rest of the world.

Following pages: *Dawn lights morning mist rising from the surface of Lake Catani, in Victoria's Mount Buffalo National Park. Seemingly as old as the hills around it, the lake is actually man-made, created in 1908 to supply water for forest-fire fighting in the high country.*

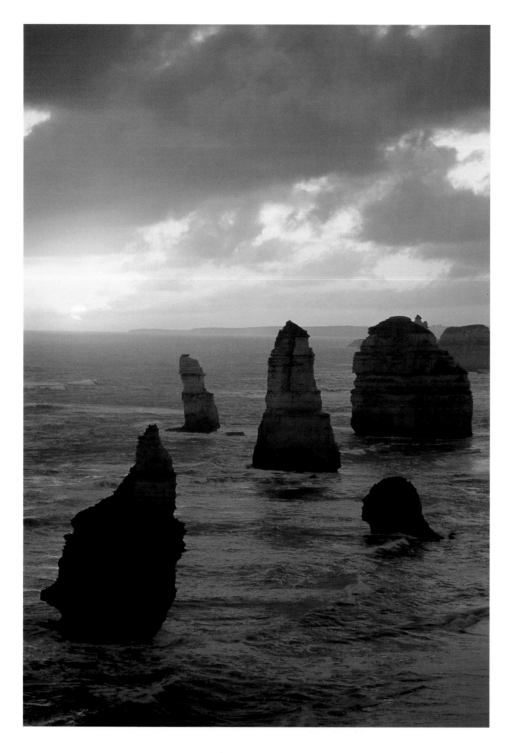

*Remnants of an ancient coastline,
the limestone sea stacks known as the
Twelve Apostles are the most famous
of the rocky promontories, islands,
arches, and blowholes along Victoria's notorious Shipwreck Coast,
where about 1,200 ships and hundreds of lives have been lost.*

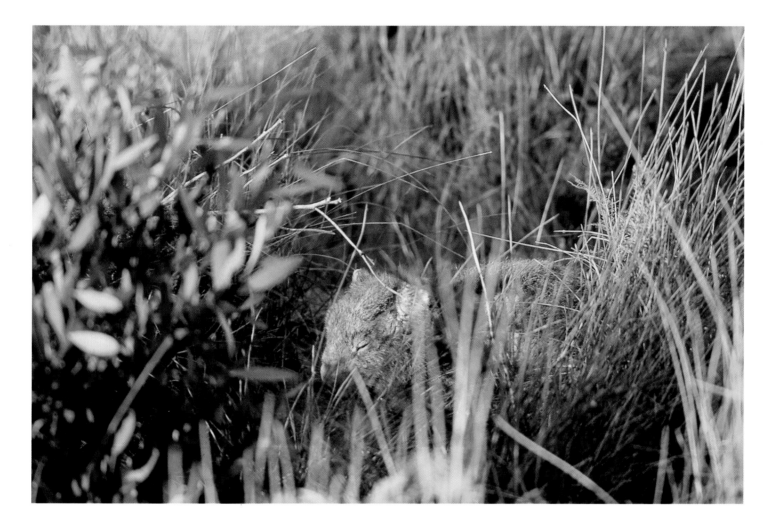

Tall grasses camouflage a wombat in Victoria's Wilsons Promontory National Park, a granite peninsula 125 miles south of Melbourne. Wombats range throughout the southern Australia coast and Tasmania. The roly-poly marsupials sleep most of the day and forage for roots and grasses at night.

Following pages: *Lifeblood of an arid continent, the Murray River wends through Dora Dora Flats, on the Victoria–New South Wales border. Stretching 1,565 miles from its source in the Snowy Mountains to the sea in South Australia, the Murray is Australia's longest and grandest river. Dams and reservoirs harness its waters, which, with the Darling River, support 75 percent of Australia's irrigated farmland.*

Smoothed granite boulders and a glassy pool create a tranquil still life at Whale Rock, in Victoria's Wilsons Promontory National Park. The mountainous and windswept promontory, which juts into Bass Strait, is the southernmost point on mainland Australia.

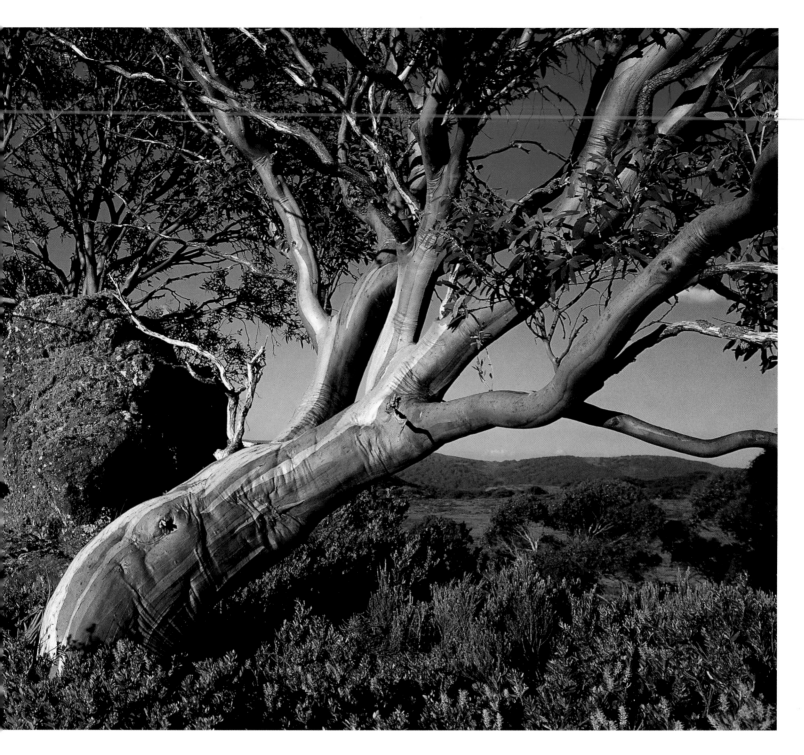

Shaped by the icy winds and blowing snow that can blast the Victorian Alps, snow gums such as these in Alpine National Park can live for nearly 500 years. A waxy film coats their leaves, buds, and flowers, protecting them from the bitter frosts of the high country. As the trees age, their smooth bark changes color from green to dusky pink, adding to their gnarled beauty.

Rushing through the densely forested flanks of the Blue Mountains in New South Wales, Jamison Creek takes a tumble at Weeping Rock on its way to much higher Wentworth Falls. The falls, one of the area's biggest attractions, was named in honor of William Wentworth, one of a trio of explorers who discovered a route through the mountains in 1813.

Cows graze steep pastures in high
country near the Victorian town of
Omeo, west of Alpine National Park.
Since the 1860s cattlemen have
driven their herds on Australia's
alpine plateaus to take advantage
of rich summer grasses. One of them,
a hard-riding cowboy named Jack
Riley, may have inspired Banjo
Paterson's poem The Man from
Snowy River.

by Geoffrey Sherington

A Land of Immigrants

Since its foundation as a British colony in 1788, Australia has been a land of immigrants. The colonial settlement of the Great South Land was inspired in part by the establishment of the United States of America. With the loss of the 13 American Colonies, Britain turned to "the East," seeking new opportunities for trade and a new penal settlement for convicted felons.

The convicts and many of their jailers were reluctant exiles, although many benefited from trade and some helped establish the early Australian wool industry. By the 1820s the prospect of land grants was attracting free settlers to the continent.

The European view of wealth coming from the land contrasted with the view of the indigenous population. Australian Aborigines saw land as a spiritual form to which people belonged. The philosophical gulf between the original Aboriginal peoples and the new settlers remains today, and its legacy is strong in the current discussion and debate over indigenous land rights.

The idea of wealth coming from the land lay behind the mid-19th century colonial gold rushes that transformed Australia in many ways. With the discovery of gold, the Australian continent was now seen as a land of opportunity in ways not previously imagined. Between 1851 and 1871 Australia's population quadrupled—from 437,665 people to 1.7 million. One third of those immigrants had been born in the United Kingdom.

The lure of gold also brought many immigrants from outside Britain. Prior to the strikes, few foreigners came to Australia. Only a small number of the convicts had been born outside Britain, although some had been captured in the Wars of Empire. German immigrants escaping religious persecution had settled in South Australia in the 1830s, but in the 50s and 60s large numbers of emigrants from Europe, Asia, and even North America came to dig in the goldfields of Victoria. For a period the colonial city of Melbourne became almost multilingual, with voices from many lands across the world. Not all the new settlers stayed. Like thousands of the gold seekers to California, many who rushed to Australia were sojourners out to try their luck before returning home.

Many of the gold rush generation did remain, however, particularly in the state of Victoria, which retains its legacy of gold not only in the regional centers of Bendigo and Ballarat but also in the wide, planned streets and colonial buildings of Melbourne. The country's burgeoning population would actually reinforce what had already been a feature before the discovery of gold. From the mid-19th century Australia has been one of the most urbanized societies in the world.

Despite the vast open spaces of the Australian continent, most of the new immigrants settled in the cities along the coast. Sydney had been established as a seaport, and most of the other colonial capital cities had close associations with the ocean. Most of the new arrivals settled in the capital cities such as Melbourne or Sydney. Others left the immigrant ships to try to find work along the coast, leading to the growth of the regional centers of Townsville, Rockhampton, Gladstone, and Bundaberg in Queensland. In Western Australia in the 1890s, it was the lure of gold rather than the promise of land that brought a new population to settle in the mining center of Kalgoorlie and the capital city of Perth.

From the mid-19th century to the mid-20th century, Australian governments tried to attract immigrant settlers with offers of assisted sea passages and land grants. Almost all such schemes of settling new immigrants on the land failed because much of the good land had already been claimed: Settlers of the early 19th century had taken up pastoral leases for sheep. These newcomers displaced the indigenous populations and held out against plans to divide up leases for later new arrivals. Even in the far north of Queensland many of the settlers became rural workers or sheep shearers. The shearers banded together to establish the powerful Australian Workers Union. Its formation led to conflict with the pastoralists and eventually to the formation of the Australian Labor Party as a major political force.

Trade unionism was not the only institution imported from Britain and that took a particular form in Australia. Almost all Australian political and social institutions established in the mid to late 19th century had their origins in the British Isles. Political representation came in the Westminster style, with governments formed on the basis of controlling a majority in parliament. Australian initiatives did sometimes take precedence, with the adult female franchise introduced here in 1902—before it was accepted in Britain. Universities and schools were modeled principally on British forms. Other cultural institutions, including sporting clubs and associations, often followed British examples.

By the late 19th century the dominant group in Australia consisted of English Protestants. With their religious and cultural allies, Australian Scots and Protestants from Northern Ireland, Anglo-Australians made up more than 70 percent of the population. Apart from the German settlers, the Australian-Irish Roman Catholics were the only group representing major ethnic and cultural differences. A separate Catholic school system helped maintain this difference, while the continuing English rule of Ireland left a division between Irish-Australians and those Anglo-Australians who pledged allegiance to the English monarchy.

Ethnic and religious differences were thus basic causes of sectarian animosities arising out of immigration. Forms of assimilation did emerge, however. In contrast to North America, Irish-Australians did not necessarily live alongside one another. Ethnic neighborhoods were not major features of Australian colonial cities.

Moreover, unlike other settler societies in the British Empire, such as Canada or South Africa, language was not a cultural barrier. The Irish-Australian Catholics may have had their own festivals and feast days, but they shared English as a common language with almost all other immigrants. Speaking the same language as most fellow Australians, the Irish used their own ways to express a native Australian identity. While the Roman Catholic Church became part of their cultural expression, the Irish-Australians began to predominate in the Australian Labor Party, which came to represent Australian nationalism.

During the late 19th and early 20th century Irish-Australians and other Australians of British origin united on whom they wished to exclude as future settlers. Chinese immigrants had come as gold diggers in the mid-19th century. Many then settled in goldfield towns or in cities. On grounds of race, and with efforts to protect jobs, there was a rising anti-Chinese feeling. Similarly there was opposition to the employment of Pacific Islanders in the cane fields of north Queensland. As

on the west coast of North America "great white walls" went up to remain in place for almost a century. When the six Australian colonies became a federation in 1801 the first piece of legislation enacted by the new Australian Parliament created the White Australia Policy, which effectively excluded most potential immigrants of non-Caucasian background.

For most of the first half of the 20th century the new Australian federation had a policy of continuing preference for British immigrants. Australia cooperated with Britain in "Empire Settlement," which had its heyday in the 1920s.

Various schemes brought families as well as boy and girl settlers and even child migrants. In valiant efforts to become Australian farmers ,the Empire Settlers cleared the jarrah forests of southwest Western Australia and struggled in the mallee district of northwest Victoria. Other British immigrants of these years came from British cities and settled in Australian cities or regional centers, bringing much needed industrial skills for a changing Australian economy.

Even in the era of Empire Settlement the pattern of Australian immigration was changing. Since the 19th-century seafaring sojourners from the coast of Italy and the Greek islands of the Aegean had been arriving in small numbers. The decision of the United States in 1921 to restrict its flow of immigrants led some from these Mediterranean regions to look more toward Australia. Unlike British immigrants, these settlers from southern Europe were not offered government assistance for travel or settlement.

Instead they depended on the support of kith and kin and the links of chain migration with their villages or towns. Throughout the country towns of regional Australia, Greek cafés appeared; in the cane fields of northern Queensland Italian communities formed in such centers as Ingham. Many of these European settlers went west to Kalgoorlie, leading to antiforeigner riots during the Depression of the 1930s. Only slowly did the Australian-born begin to accept these new arrivals. By the late 1930s the Australian government had at least agreed to accept a small number of Jewish refugees from Germany and central Europe.

The events of the Second World War had a major effect on Australian immigration policy. Threatened with the prospect of a Japanese invasion, Australian governments embarked on a postwar nation-building exercise to increase population. It was hoped that migrants would secure the future of the nation, contributing to economic growth and providing a bulwark against a possible threat from Australia's Asian neighbors. Despite turning more to the United States for protection and investment, Australia still looked principally to Britain to fulfill the need for new citizens. Indeed, until the 1960s, British immigrants, supported by assisted passage schemes, constituted at least half of those who arrived in Australia.

British immigration began to revive after 1945, and the war in Europe also provided a new source of potential immigrants. Coming principally from the former Baltic states of Estonia, Latvia, and Lithuania, or from Poland and parts of central Europe, people who had been displaced from their homes—or DPs (displaced persons)—formed the first major wave of postwar non-English speaking migrants to Australia. Contracted to work for two years, many were sent to camps in regional Australia. They formed the bulk of the workers who built the great Snowy Mountains Scheme, which remains the most dramatic Australian postwar nation-building project.

During the 1950s immigrants came to Australia from all across northern and southern Europe. The prewar migration chains were revived among some early settlers from the Mediterranean, but there were also new patterns of migration from mainland Greece and southern Italy. Other settlers arrived from Germany, Holland, and even from Hungary in the wake of the revolt against Soviet control in 1956. With Britain and Europe still recovering from the war, Australia once again seemed a land of opportunity, which, if not as attractive as North America, still provided prospects for secure employment and opportunities to buy a house and bring up a family.

Australian homegrown industries now depended on both skilled and unskilled migrant laborers who, in turn, became the new consumers to maintain economic growth. Almost 60 percent of the increase in the Australian work force from the 1950s to the mid-1960s was the direct result of immigration. These new settlers from Europe began to transform the pattern of Australian cities, forming enclaves if not neighborhoods in which English was not always the first language spoken in the streets and shops. Outside the cities new mineral discoveries of the 1960s brought immigrants to mining towns in Queensland and Western Australia.

By the 1970s the old Anglo-dominated Australia was slowly being transformed by these new waves of immigrants. There was still a close link between knowledge of the English language, recognition of skills, and employment opportunities. Immigrants from Britain had little problem in having their trade and other qualifications recognized. Coming from already mature industrial economies, immigrants from Germany and Holland also found that their skills were highly paid in Australia.

British immigrants as well as those from northern or even Eastern Europe were more often to be found in the affluent suburbs of Australian cities. In contrast, many of the immigrants from southern Europe, who came from rural areas in their homelands, became the foundation of the blue-collar, unskilled industrial work force. In generally low-paying jobs, southern Europeans lived in inner-city areas close to their workplaces or had to move out to the fringes of the cities. Yet many still made fortunes in such areas as construction, which was helping build the skyscrapers that were transforming Australian urban landscapes.

Home ownership among Australia's new immigrants in the 1950s and 1960s was particularly high. Having acquired a house, many of the new settlers sought to invest in the future, helping their children and grandchildren go on to further education in colleges and universities.

The earlier postwar expectation was that the new arrivals should simply assimilate to their new environment. By the 1970s, and as part of an emerging welfare state, Australian governments had adopted a new policy of multiculturalism. There was growing recognition of the need for new arrivals to retain their languages and customs from their homeland and appreciation that many needed assistance in such areas as education, health, and housing. The migrant voice was now heard in politics, although proportionately few recent arrivals became parliamentary representatives or assumed leadership in the major political parties.

The new ethnic diversity of Australia was associated with the end of the old White Australia Policy. Under the Colombo Plan of 1951 Australian governments allowed a number of young people from the British Commonwealth to come to Australia to study. With their skills in demand as the economy expanded, many stayed on.

Also admitted were refugees from China, although these were principally White Russians from Manchuria who had first left their homeland in the wake of the 1917 Russian Revolution.

As the economies of Western Europe recovered from World War II, Australia had to broaden its search for immigrants to include lands closer to the Asian region. By the late 1960s there were new arrivals from Yugoslavia and Turkey. In the 1970s refugees from armed conflict in Lebanon arrived in Australia.

A changing economic and political relationship with the Asian region helped transform the pattern of migration to Australia. By the end of the 1960s Japan had already replaced Britain as Australia's chief trading partner. Australia's involvement with the United States in the Vietnam War also left a legacy. By the late 1970s boat people fleeing from the new Communist regime in Vietnam had begun to arrive on the shores of Northern Australia. This crisis led to the first major government-sponsored migration scheme of large numbers of arrivals from an Asian country. Settled initially in camps on the fringes of Australian cities, most of these refugees from Vietnam had to take up unskilled and low-paying jobs. Some struggled to adapt to the new circumstances, but within a decade many of their children had gone on to attend university.

The arrival of Vietnamese in Australia was a watershed in the history of Australian immigration. For the past two decades ethnic origin has not been an official criterion of who shall be allowed to immigrate to Australia. While the old forms of assisted passages that existed for British migration are now gone, those arriving in Australia have come for purposes of family reunion, as refugees, or with their skills in demand. Of some 85,000 immigrants to Australia each year, less than one-fifth now arrive from Britain or Europe.

Today, settlers migrate from throughout the world, although more than half come from the Asia-Pacific region. Included among these are people from the Pacific Islands and Australia's neighbor, New Zealand, from which migrants have been coming since the 19th century. From such areas as Hong Kong and Malaysia have arrived many with highly developed skills that are in demand in the new global economy. Unlike most of those early postwar arrivals from Europe or the refugees from the wars in Lebanon or Vietnam, these new arrivals often brought in capital and invested in residential and other real estate in Australian cities.

At the end of the 20th century the multicultural nature of Australia is clearly visible, particularly in its cities. In the new shopping arcades are seen the faces of people from many nations. In the suburbs, mosques and Buddhist temples are found near older churches of the Roman Catholic and Protestant traditions and newer cathedrals of Eastern Orthodoxy.

Of the Australian capital cities, Sydney is the most cosmopolitan, receiving almost 40 percent of new immigrants. More than half the Greek postwar immigrant population of 250,000 settled in Melbourne. The city retains much of its colonial heritage but also takes pride in being the city with the largest Greek population in the world outside Greece. Brisbane, Perth, and Darwin are growing with new settlers from the Asia-Pacific region. Even Adelaide has a mixture of older and newer populations. Only Tasmania's Hobart, on an island that is losing people because of lack of economic opportunities, holds on to much of the Anglo-Australian colonial past.

For many of those who see themselves as part of the Old Australia, the new Australian multiculturalism in a global era has brought uncertainties about national identity. In effect the Old Australia was principally an assimilation of the Anglo-Australians and Irish-Australians that took almost a century to achieve.

There is now far greater diversity but also complexity in the New Australia. Less than half the people in Australia can now trace their direct descent on both their paternal and maternal lines from the British and Irish settlers of the 19th and 20th century. Those with direct descent from non-British and originally non-English speaking settlers now make up about one-quarter of the population. The fastest growing group in Australia consists of people of mixed descent—from both 19th- and 20th-century settlers, from English-speaking and non-English speaking immigrants, from Aboriginal and non-Aboriginal background.

The Australian people are now remaking themselves in a variety of ways, which may lead to new forms of identity that will transcend the old nationalities and ethnic associations they brought with them from overseas.

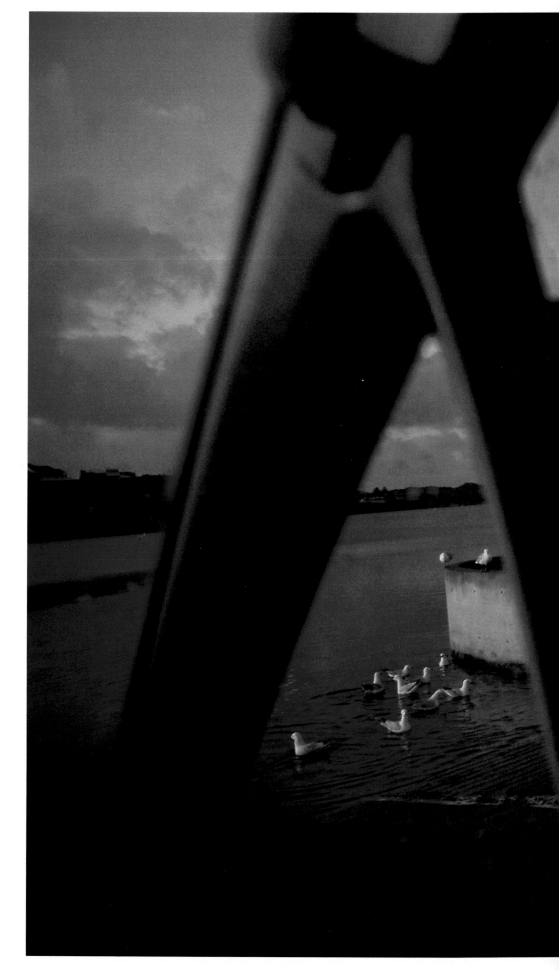

Cool and damp, dawn rises over the lovingly restored waterfront of Warrnambool. A boisterous haunt of sealers and whalers in its early days, Warrnambool became a major farming and wool-milling town, yet preserved enough of its historic maritime flavor to be a holiday mecca for sightseers traveling along the spectacular Shipwreck Coast.

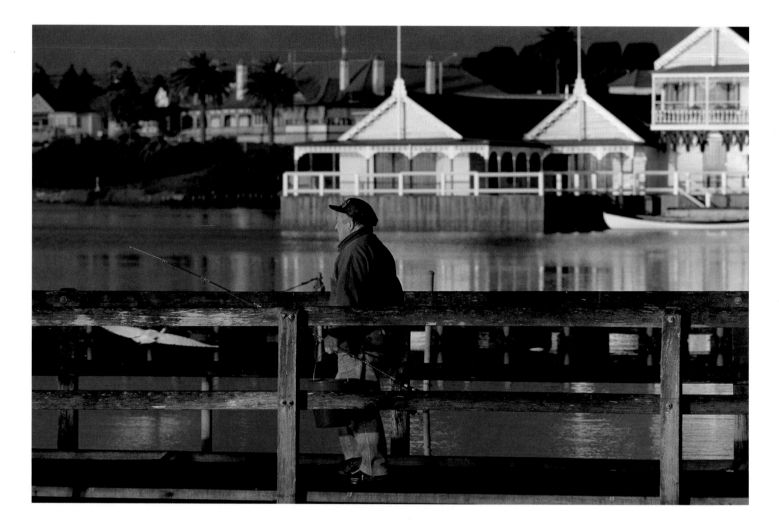

In the quiet of the morning, a fisherman lugs his bait bucket and rod to
the end of the jetty in Warrnambool.
The cold waters of the Southern
Ocean, washing up from Antarctica,
teem with enough fish to keep jetty
fishermen and a fleet of commerical
trawlers in action. In June endangered southern right whales migrate
to the area to breed.

Oblivious to the sun-splashed streets of Melbourne passing by the window, a girl has eyes only for her book. Pretty and peaceful as most country towns are, limited job prospects and the adventure of life in the "big smoke" of cities mean that many young people see their futures in Melbourne, Sydney, or even overseas.

As dawn breaks over Sydney, a solitary swimmer completes a few laps in a seawater pool in the beachside suburb of Coogee. Sydney is a city of sports fanatics. With its sheltered waters and breezy family atmosphere, Coogee, southeast of the city, has long been one of the beaches most popular with Sydneysiders.

Players break for a hearty lunch in the clubroom of Sydney's century-old Randwick Districts Cricket Club. Still wearing his leg pads, Chinese-Australian team captain Richard Chee Quee reflects the changing face of Sydney and the traditional British game of cricket. Quee has represented his state, New South Wales, in the Sheffield Shield national competition and has led cricket coaching clinics in Hong Kong.

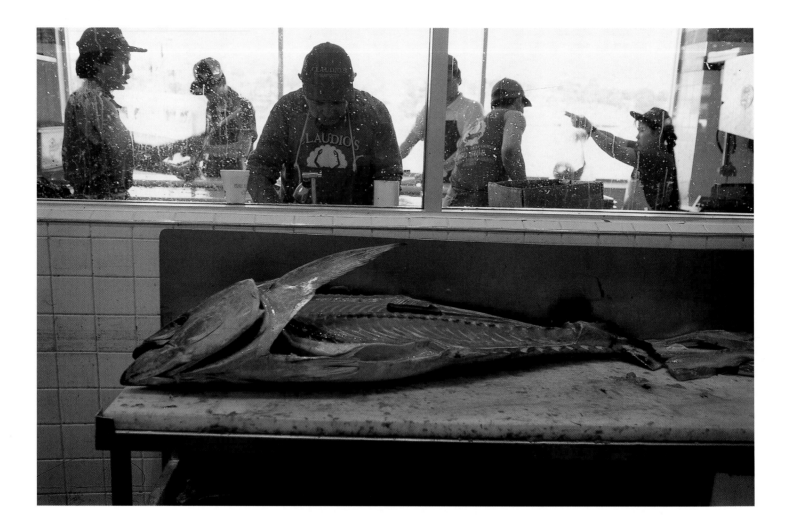

Bluefin tuna meets the filleting knife at Claudio's Quality Seafoods in the Sydney Fish Market. Early on week-days shopkeepers and chefs crowd the market on Blackwattle Bay, clamoring for the freshest and best fish. Sydney's thriving and cosmopolitan restaurant scene owes its existence to an influx of immigrants from Asia and the Mediterranean.

Like a giant beachside slumber party, Wylie's Floating Film Festival lures hundreds of arts buffs yet reflects Sydney's relaxed and humorously informal atmosphere. Spectators at the seaside baths at Coogee can watch from deck chairs or paddle around on their own rubber dinghies.

Luna Park's rictus grin, a Sydney landmark since 1935, still beckons fun lovers to the city's harborside. The amusement park closed for reno- vation in the 1980s, reopening in 1995. Sydney's lights and action attract the nation's brightest, richest, and raciest to Australia's largest and most glamorous city.

Following pages: *Sail-like roofs of the Opera House and the graceful arch of the Sydney Harbour Bridge create a romantic backdrop for a couple strolling the promenade along Farm Cove at twilight.*

A
Golden
Land

CHAPTER SEVEN

I love a sunburnt country
A land of sweeping plains,
Of ragged mountain ranges,
Of droughts and flooding rains.

Countless thousands of classrooms of Australian schoolchildren have recited Dorothea Mackellar's patriotic classic "My Country" since it was published in 1911, learning it by heart almost like a pledge of allegiance. But while Australians may love a sunburnt country, it is an abstract love; few choose to live in the dry interior.

When it comes to the views they see every morning from their kitchen windows, Australians very much prefer green lawns and leafy suburban streets. More than 80 percent of the population lives in the fertile strip of land between the Great Dividing Range and the east coast, and generally within a 60-minute drive of a beach. A brick home in a nice suburb, on a well-watered quarter acre, is far closer to the Australian dream than droving cattle in the Kimberley or shearing sheep in the Darling Downs.

Australia's Golden Land starts in Sydney's sun-drenched beaches and stretches through the seaside holiday towns of northern New South Wales, the ritzy Gold Coast, and north into the sugarcane and rain forests of tropical Queensland. Its warm, clear seas are home to Australia's jewel-like Great Barrier Reef. For most immigrants, visitors, and the steady flow of rural Australians moving to the coast, this is the promised land—the Australia of surf and sun and long, beachy weekends.

For many, the welcoming arms of Sydney Harbour are Australia's gateway to the world. Nothing better sym-

bolizes Australia's sunny prosperity than the Harbour Bridge, the Opera House, glimpses of yachts in secluded coves, and the terra-cotta-roofed mansions nestled in the palms and gums along its waterfront. While seven- and eight-digit real estate prices put harbor views beyond the reach—but not the aspirations—of most Sydneysiders, the city's 20-odd beaches offer everyone in this fiercely egalitarian city the inalienable right to swim and surf and bronze themselves basted in coconut oil.

The most famous of Sydney's beaches is at Bondi, a half-mile-long crescent of sand fronting the Pacific Ocean in Sydney's southeastern suburbs. Bondi Beach is the birthplace of the sunny beach culture for which Australia is so famous. Here in 1906 the world's first surf lifesaving club was formed—in response to a spate of drownings as Sydneysiders tried out their new-found freedom to swim in the sea. Incredibly, until the turn of the century, Australia's prim public decency laws forbade bathing from 6 a.m to 7 p.m., and even in the Swinging Sixties, dour inspectors patrolled the beaches looking for too-skimpy costumes. Surf lifesavers today are an Australian tradition, their distinctive yellow-and-red caps emblems of a long, hot Australian summer. There are now 260 clubs around Australia, and their members rescue about 11,000 swimmers each year. In between rescues they compete against each other in grueling competitions for big prize money, often here on Bondi Beach in front of crowds of thousands, broadcast live on national TV.

This is a sports-mad city in a sports-mad land, and Sydney's balmy subtropical weather, coupled with Sydneysiders' strong play ethic and love of leisure, mean that the calendar here is never empty. Cricket, Rugby League, and Union and Australian Rules football draw huge crowds on the weekends, while families and mates play matches on side streets and in parks and backyards across the city. Baseball, basketball, and soccer are popular. So are racehorses and greyhounds. The beaches are bright with surfers, the rivers busy with kayakers. Cyclists and joggers and in-line skaters crowd Centennial Park and the foreshores of the beaches. Every December—on Boxing Day—the harbor is bright with scores of racing yachts and hundreds of spectator craft for the start of the Sydney to Hobart Yacht Race, one of the world's great blue-water yacht races. New Year's Day sees the Sydney Cricket Ground full of spectators for the traditional holiday cricket match. Every August more than 30,000 runners cover the 8.7 miles from Hyde Park to Bondi Beach in the City to Surf, Australia's biggest and gaudiest footrace. And in September 2000 Sydney will host the first Olympics of the new millennium.

Since it was completed in 1932, the ornamental iron arch of the Sydney Harbour Bridge has been the gateway to holiday adventure and, often these days, new lives for many Australians as they head up the coast to the sun and promise of Queensland. The bridge stands like an invitation. I arrived in Australia on March 19, 1982, on the 50th anniversary of the opening of the bridge, and spent my first day in my new country walking across it, savoring the bracing, salty breeze off the harbor and the spectacular view of the city skyline. That now familiar skyline has grown by a good few skyscrapers since I first saw it, but familiarity has not tarnished the mile-long walk or the breathtaking harbor view. Whenever I come to Sydney, even if I'm there for only a day, I rise early and make my pilgrimage across the bridge.

North of the bridge the road becomes the Pacific Highway, a ribbon of mostly narrow, old-fashioned highway that stretches up the coast 1,500 miles to the lush tropical rain forests of Cairns. After rolling through Sydney's prosperous northern suburbs, the road winds past the forests and coastal inlets of the Ku-ring-gai Chase National Park and on a hundred miles to the heavy industry, steel, and coal city of Newcastle.

Newcastle suffers a bit unfairly from its sooty, smokestack image, although the battleship gray industrial sprawl with its towering chimneys does tend to dominate

this blue-collar city of nearly 275,000. It also has some of New South Wales finest surfing beaches, wide streets, colonial buildings, and a harbor with accompanying lighthouse that feels a bit like Maine. The city was founded in 1804, when a few prisoners and guards were sent to the outpost to mine coal. The location was presumably a convenience for the authorities, since the bolters generally ran in this direction anyway. Today, the city at the mouth of the Hunter River is a gateway for thousands of visitors heading into the vineyards of the Hunter Valley.

The Hunter Valley is a quirky mix of coal mining, racehorse studs, and some of Australia's oldest wine country. The first vines were planted by settlers around 1830, but it was an enterprising Scot named James Busby who put the industry on a commercial footing. In 1832 Busby, who had studied viticulture in France, imported hundreds of clippings from European vineyards and planted them on his property along the Hunter River. Over the next few years, as his own vines grew, he arranged for 20,000 cuttings to be distributed to his neighbors. Now the valley is home to some 50 wineries, including well-known labels such as Tyrell's, Lindemans, and McWilliams. It is also a popular weekend retreat for Sydneysiders. The scenic town of Scone, in the upper Hunter Valley, is famous for the more than 40 thoroughbred studs in the area. Some of Australia's wealthiest pastoral families—the seriously old wealth in this young nation—have elegant homesteads here. Among them is Belltrees, the stately manor of the White family since 1831. Australia's elite come to play at the charmingly old-fashioned polo grounds at Gundy and Elliston.

Far greater, if less glamorous and scenic, wealth lurks under the Hunter Valley's vines and pastures. It was an escaped convict in 1791 who stumbled upon what would become one of Australia's richest natural resources—coal. A few years later Lt. John Shortland, who was tracking down more escaped convicts, found a rich seam of it along the Hunter River. By 1799 Australia was exporting coal, sending its first shipment to India. Today, Australia is the world's biggest coal exporter, shipping nearly 300 million tons overseas each year. Much of it comes from here, where it is dispatched out of Newcastle.

North of Newcastle the Pacific Highway winds past a string of pretty little fishing and holiday villages along the

New South Wales coast. Towns such as Port Macquarie, Nambucca Heads, and Coffs Harbour are nestled in estuaries or at the mouth of rivers. The temperatures here grow warmer and the landscapes more tropical. The Great Dividing Range veers closer to the coast, its rain forest-cloaked eastern flanks brooding over the coastal villages below.

About 50 miles inland is World Heritage-listed Barrington Tops National Park. A wilderness atop two massive, 5,000-foot-high plateaus, it is dramatically cut by gorges and waterfalls, flanked by rain forest, and crowned by an alpine environment of snow gums, peat bogs, and moss. Weather is notoriously fickle up here, with occasional snow flurries even in the summer months.

Another 50-odd miles farther north and considerably closer to the coast is Dorrigo National Park, with its dense subtropical rain forests. This World Heritage site sits on the edge of the Great Dividing Range. Waterfalls spill over the rim of the plateau and feed the Bellinger River, which ultimately flows into the sea at the town of Urunga. The road that switchbacks its steep way inland, up the flanks of the range, is one of the most breathtaking side trips to be had along the northern New South Wales coast.

The stretch of the Pacific Highway along the northern New South Wales coast feels more and more like a tropical version of U.S. Route 66: narrow and potholed, with roadside kitsch and cheap motels. And for many Australian families, especially during the hard economic years of the early 1990s, the Pacific Highway was very much a migrant road, taking them away from the bleak skies of the southern industrial cities toward the sunny promise of Queensland—new jobs, new lives.

Along this highway about two miles north of the tropical town of Coffs Harbour is one of Australia's classic pieces of Route 66-style roadside camp—the Big Banana. This giant concrete piece of fruit is a monument to the main local industry, and Coffs Harbour is an amiable tourist trap that offers a banana museum, tours of a banana plantation, banana milk shakes, and banana souvenirs. Australia's roadsides are uniquely rich in this sort of kitsch. Nambour, Queensland, about 180 miles farther north, is home to the Big Pineapple. In South Australia the coastal town of Kingston has Larry, the Big Lobster; the Big Merino can be gawked at in Goulburn, New

South Wales; and Glenrowan, Victoria, has a 20-foot-high mock-up of the town's favorite felon, Ned Kelly.

The lighthouse on Cape Byron marks the easternmost point on the Australian continent, and the nearby summit of 3,794-foot Mount Warning—known as "Cloud Catcher" to the Aborigines—is the first place in Australia to feel the sun's rays each morning.

To the north the architecture begins to change to the relaxed, tropical informality of the old style Queenslander home. These elegant, highly ornamental, and uniquely Australian houses are typically built of timber, have corrugated iron roofs, and are raised several feet off the ground on hardwood (termite-proof) stumps to allow cooling air to circulate under the floor. Deep, shady verandas surround them on all sides, helping to keep the inner rooms cool. They are further protected from blazing summer heat and torrential tropical rains by decorative wooden lattice and slatted blinds but are still open to any available breeze. The first time I saw one of these beautifully designed tropical masterpieces I was cycling through the little sugar-growing town of Bauple. The owners came out and, with characteristic Queensland hospitality, invited me in for dinner and to stay the night.

Queensland is Australia's holiday state and a honey pot for its sun-seeking retirees. Its status is obvious the moment you cross the border, which marks the beginning of the famed Gold Coast Stretching from Coolangatta in the south to Beenleigh in the north, this tropical coastline is blessed with 26 miles of golden, sandy beaches and more than 300 days of sunshine each year. Australians have come here for holidays for more than a century, at first in coaches from Brisbane and later by train, but it has been only since the 1950s that the strip really began to flourish. Today, it is the most glittering and shamelessly commercial beachfront in Australia, a real estate jungle of high-rises, glitzy hotels, more than 500 restaurants and nightclubs, and a cavalcade of theme parks such as Sea World, Warner Bros. Movie World, and the Disney-like Dreamworld. More than half a million people live along the Gold Coast, and there are beds for another 100,000 visitors. It is Queensland's second largest population center after Brisbane, whose extreme southern suburbs end just a few miles from where the Gold Coast begins.

Surfers Paradise, originally the name of a local hotel in the 1930s, is the heart of the Gold Coast. Here towering high-rise hotels and apartments crowd the beach so closely that by mid-afternoon most of it is in shadow. Increasingly, that hardly matters. Much of the focus is away from the surf: to the annual IndyCar Race, nightclubs, luxury resorts, casinos, golf courses, convention centers, and designer shopping arcades. The golden sand and hard blue Pacific have become a sort of luxuriant, mood-setting backdrop.

It is a matter of a surprisingly few miles from this getaway holiday ambiance to the suburban world of Brisbane. Like most of Australia's capital cities, Brisbane was founded as a penal settlement. In 1823 the governor of New South Wales, Thomas Brisbane, decided to look around for an outpost that would discourage escape. The tropical heat and remoteness of a little known coast 460 miles north seemed the very spot, and he dispatched his surveyor-general, John Oxley, to scout out a suitable site. The next year a party of convicts and soldiers was sent north aboard the brig *Amity.*

The first site, on the coast of Moreton Bay, had to be abandoned because of poor soil, and the penal camp was shifted 27 miles up the winding Brisbane River to where Brisbane stands today. As is the case with most of Australia's penal colonies, this settlement's early history was one of hardship, brutality, dysentery, scurvy, heavy leg irons, merciless floggings, and sadistic guards.

In her 1975 historical novel, *The Commandant,* Brisbane-born writer Jessica Anderson gives a description of the penal colony, as seen through the eyes of a visitor in 1830: "Then a sudden bend in the river disclosed another kind of country: on one bank pleasant wooded hills, and on the other low fields swarming with men in yellow hoeing between rows of very young wheat. They were so close that Frances could hear the unrhythmic sounds of their shifting irons and the collapsing links of chain. Overseers, carrying heavy sticks, lumbered over the unsettled soil among them, and on the perimeter of the field moved red-coated soldiers, crosses of white webbing stark against their breasts, and bayonets shining and precise against field and sky.... It was their great number perhaps or the clumsiness of their fettered movements that made them appear sub-human, like animals adapted to men's work or goblins from under the hill."

Not many civilians would have seen this prison camp, since they were not generally permitted to travel within 50 miles of the place. The penal settlement was closed in 1839, and three years later Queensland was thrown open to free settlers. They came in droves. In 1859 the new colony separated from New South Wales, and Queen Victoria named it Queensland.

Although it is close to the coast, Brisbane is very much a river-oriented city, its commercial heart enclosed in a serpentine loop and linked by seven bridges to prosperous suburbs on the opposite bank. One of the most scenic of these bridges—the Story Bridge—was the creation of John Bradfield, the designer of the Sydney Harbour Bridge. Brisbane is rich in colonial architecture: Its sumptuous Italian Renaissance National Bank Building (1885) and even grander Treasury Building (1888) are testimony to the great mining wealth that came out of Queensland after the big gold strikes in the 1870s.

For most of this century Brisbane dozed in tropical sunshine. For a few tense years during World War II it was the headquarters of Gen. Douglas MacArthur and the Allies' Pacific forces, but afterward it returned to its slumbers. As late as the 1960s the tallest building in Brisbane was the 200-foot-high clock tower on its town hall. Brisbane's fortunes changed forever in the 1980s, when it hosted two international events—the Commonwealth Games of 1982 and the World Exposition of 1988—which exposed Brisbane to the world and the world to Brisbane. Both apparently liked what they saw, and in the years since Brisbane has bloomed into a vibrant cosmopolitan city—the third largest in Australia and growing rapidly. One of the fastest growing areas is the some 90-mile-long stretch of beaches an hour's drive north of the city. It is marked on maps as the Sunshine Coast.

Caloundra, Maroochydore, and Coolum Beach— once quiet holiday towns—became some of the nation's fastest growing communities during the 1990s. In what was probably Australia's biggest internal migration since the gold rush days, thousands of families and businesses flocked north to the sunbelt. New housing estates and real estate developments are sprouting up all along this breezy stretch of coast, and the highways are busy with suburban commuters and the vans of contractors servicing the housing boom. Resort towns such as Maroochydore are now small cities with their own burgeoning satellite suburbs.

For Queenslanders, who proudly considered themselves a breed apart yet were sensitive to the way southern city folk dismissed them as provincial, the population boom was a mixed blessing. Smugness at being discovered was tempered with dismay as throngs of newcomers added their hustle and pace to the Sunshine Coast's laid-back holiday atmosphere.

The hinterland is still quiet, tropical farmland: lush fields of pineapples, sugarcane, and macadamia nuts. Rising dramatically more than a thousand feet above these plantations are the Glasshouse Mountains. Capt. James Cook sighted these sheer volcanic necks from the deck of his ship as he sailed up the coast in 1770.

The exclusive resort town of Noosa Heads marks the northern end of the Sunshine Coast, where an upscale sort of holiday tranquillity still prevails. With its beautiful north-facing beach on Laguna Bay and regular, big waves, the sleepy town drew surfers from all over Australia in the 1960s and has never looked back. Now it is one of the most fashionable seaside retreats for Australia's rich and glamorous. Its streets are lined with classy restaurants, boutiques, and cafés. A zoning edict that forbids buildings to be any taller than the trees has helped maintain its small beach-town atmosphere. It helps too that its beach is protected by century-old Noosa National Park, with its thousand acres of rain forest. On the other side of the bay is the haunting coastal wilderness of Cooloola National Park, with its towering eucalypt forests, streaked cliffs, and beaches of colored sand.

World Heritage-listed Fraser Island sits a few miles off the northern end of the Cooloola Coast, accessible by ferries from Inskip Point or Hervey Bay. It is the world's largest sand island, more than 75 miles long, dotted by some 40 crystal-clear lakes and covered with lush forests, including the satinay, a rain forest tree that is found almost nowhere else. Marvelously rot resistant, the prized satinay was sought by the ship-building industry.

Logging on the island ceased in 1991. During the 1970s Fraser Island was at the center of a bitter struggle between conservationists and the sand-mining industry. The conservationists carried the day, and the island remains wild. The northern half of it forms part of Great Sandy National Park.

Because of its isolation from the mainland, Fraser Island is home to Australia's last pure strain of wild dingoes, whose bloodlines have never been mixed with dogs. In recent years their numbers have boomed, and, unable to find enough to eat, roving dingoes have become a menace. Several attacks on tourists have been reported.

Fraser Island takes its name from Eliza Fraser, the wife of the captain of the *Stirling Castle*, which was wrecked on Swain Reef, near Rockhampton, in 1836. After her husband was speared by Aborigines, Fraser and a party of survivors made their way to the island in an open boat. The Kabi Aborigines adopted her, convinced that she was the spirit of a local woman named Mamba who had somehow lost both her color and her language in the process of reincarnation. Among her new tribesmen was John Graham, an escaped convict who had been similarly adopted a year earlier. Graham, who by then spoke fluent Kabi, vouched for Fraser's Aboriginality.

A search party from Moreton Bay found the castaways two months later. Fraser's story became the basis for a series of paintings by artist Sidney Nolan and Patrick White's novel *A Fringe of Leaves*.

The rum and sugar town of Bundaberg, about 50 miles north and west of Fraser Island, is a popular port of call for round-the-world yachtsmen. A five-hour cruise from here brings the traveler to Lady Elliot Island, a tropical coral cay teeming with birds and sea turtles. Its sharp corals are littered with shipwrecks dating back to the early 19th century and stretching into the 1990s.

Small and pretty in its own right, Lady Elliot Island is also the southern starting point for one of the world's greatest—and Australia's most prized—natural wonders: the Great Barrier Reef. From here it stretches 1,250 miles along the tropical Queensland coast—a chain of brilliantly colored coral reefs, dazzling white sandbars, and green tropical islands. Although it is commonly referred to as the world's largest living thing, the Great Barrier Reef is composed of 2,500 individual reefs. Some are tiny motes only a couple of acres in size, while others extend for 38 square miles. Another 600 islands are scattered along the coast, each typically surrounded by its own fringing reefs. Altogether this World Heritage site covers 135,000 square miles.

The reefs are made of billions of tiny, brilliantly colored coral polyps, which flourish in the sunlight and warmth of these shallow, crystalline seas. Polyps form a hard exterior by excreting lime. When they die, their skeletons remain, forming limestone-like building blocks for the next generation. And so, over time, a reef gradually grows. The deepest bedrock foundations for the Great Barrier Reef go back about 18 million years, but most of the modern reef—as tourists and divers know it—was formed since the end of the last ice age about 15,000 years ago. As the world's glaciers melted, rising sea levels crept over Australia's coastal plain, flooding the lowlands and creating archipelagoes—such as the 70-odd Whitsunday Islands—from hilltops. Coral rarely grows in waters more than a hundred feet deep since, like flowers, polyps need sunlight and warmth. The rise in sea levels was slow enough for the corals to keep pace. Gradually, over centuries, the reef assumed its present shape to accommodate the changes in sea level.

There are two varieties of reefs—barrier reefs and fringing reefs. The Great Barrier Reef flanks the outer edge of the continental shelf, forming a barrier to the open ocean and creating a channel between the reef and the coast. Fringing reefs build up around the edges of islands. Most of the Great Barrier Reef islands that adorn tourist brochures are actually not on the reef at all. They are continental islands on the lee side of the barrier reef that are encrusted with fringing reefs. Lady Elliot Island is a notable exception, its cay forming a part of the reef itself, and at low tide visitors can walk its coral ledges. Heron Island, near Gladstone, and Green Island, farther north near Cairns, are also part of the Great Barrier Reef.

The language of biology and geography cannot begin to capture the sheer beauty of the reef. I had never snorkeled before visiting Cairns, in far northern Queensland, and nothing could have prepared me for the magical moment when I first put my face mask into the water. The colors that bloom in these warm waters defy description: Lurid reds and vibrant pinks mingle with yellows,

purples, and shades of white to create a dreamlike fantasia. Staghorn corals, brain corals, mushroom corals, and organ pipes—more than 400 species in all—flourish here. The spectacle becomes even more fantastic for a few moonlit nights early in summer when the corals spawn, releasing countless billions of kaleidoscopic eggs.

The labyrinthine reef complex provides food and shelter for an incredible variety of creatures: More than 1,500 species of fish, in every conceivable shape, color, and size live here. Hundreds of species of anemones, marine worms, sea stars, sea urchins, and sponges add their vibrant colors and flowing motion to the Technicolor dreamscape. The nooks and crannies in the coral shelter millions of crustaceans. More than 4,000 species of mollusks live here, including dazzlingly colorful nudibranch sea slugs and rare giant clams that can grow more than 3 feet across and weigh as much as 400 pounds. Whales, dolphins, and dugongs play in these seas. Swimming in these waters gave me the odd sensation of having dived into a particularly beautiful aquarium.

The Great Barrier Reef was declared a marine park in 1975 to protect it from—and preserve it for—the other species that was increasingly drawn to its dazzling spectacle: *Homo sapiens*. Millions of tourists flock to the reef, the islands, and far northern Queensland's tropical coast every year. Northern towns along the coastal highway project a sunny, breezy, salty image, jumping-off places for the paradises over the horizon. Rockhampton, where the Bruce Highway crosses the Tropic of Capricorn, is the gateway to Great Keppel Island, one of the coast's hard-partying island resorts. Farther up the coast Mackay and Airlie Beach are popular springboards to the Whitsunday Islands, a chain of more than 70 beautifully forested islands scattered in a passage rich in vibrant coral reefs. Townsville has nearby Magnetic Island, named by Captain James Cook because his compass behaved erratically as he sailed past in 1770. Long a popular picnic spot for tourists, Magnetic Island is rapidly becoming a rustic satellite suburb for burgeoning Townsville, with commuters taking a 20-minute catamaran ride to work.

This is Far North Queensland, or "F.N.Q." in local slang: The Deep North to the rest of Australia, who often compare it with America's Deep South. The Tropic of Capricorn serves as an antipodean Mason-Dixon line. Like Dixie, F.N.Q. has had a troubled racial history. In addition to its relations with Aborigines, in the mid-19th century Kanakas, Pacific Islanders, were imported to work the cotton and sugarcane fields in conditions of virtual slavery. Kanakas were brought over in 1863 for Robert Towns, the Sydney real estate developer who underwrote the development of Townsville. In all, more than 60,000 were brought into the country until the practice was abolished in 1904.

Nearly 200 miles north of Townsville is Cairns, with its backdrop of jungle-clad mountains, often shrouded in mist, and the blood-warm waters of Trinity Bay. This once sleepy sugar town is now a city approaching 100,000 inhabitants, and it is slowly challenging Townsville for the distinction of being Australia's biggest tropical city. Its international airport and the fact that the reef here is no more than 30 miles offshore—as opposed to more than 100 miles offshore farther south—have made Cairns the prime gateway to the Barrier Reef.

Its harbor and marinas gleam with yachts and glass-bottomed boats; the Esplanade is crowded with travel agents offering cruises or flights to the resort islands. Shop fronts are bright with diving gear. Breathtaking posters of the kaleidoscopic reefs lure visitors to booking desks for reef excursions or classes to earn diving certificates. Every evening tanned faces at the sidewalk cafés are marked with the telltale lines of divers' masks. Breathless table talk is of giant sea turtles, brilliant schools of tropical fish, and the exhilarating sense of "flying" over the edge of a coral precipice and perhaps seeing a giant tortoise slowly swimming in the rich, blue depths far below.

But Cairns looks inland as well, to the rain forests of the Atherton Tableland. One of Australia's most spectacular train journeys departs from here and switchbacks up the steep, jungled flanks of the Macalister Range and through Barron Gorge National Park to Kuranda. Every

day the 130-year-old steam train, reputedly the oldest still operating in the Southern Hemisphere, makes the 21-mile journey. One of the most breathtaking sights along the way is 800-foot-high Barron Gorge waterfall, which becomes even more thunderous after heavy rains. These rain forests—with those in Tasmania—are the wettest places in Australia. Nearby Mount Bellenden Ker received a record 36.9 feet of rain in 1979.

The colonial railroad station at Kuranda, with its landscaped gardens and banks of bright tropical flowers, is possibly the most picturesque depot in Australia. Nearby is the Australian Butterfly Sanctuary. Of its more than 2,000 tropical butterflies, many are rare, including the giant, iridescent blue Ulysses.

It was this steam railway that secured Cairns fortunes. Built in 1888, it linked the city with the Hodgkinson River goldfields and with the rich volcanic farmland on the Atherton Tablelands, with its bounty of macadamia nuts, tobacco, corn, peanuts, and coffee. Given this commercial advantage, Cairns quickly overshadowed rival Port Douglas, another 45 miles up the coast. Today, residents of the tranquil and tropical village of Port Douglas might think they got the better end of the bargain after all.

The drive to Port Douglas along the Cook Highway is one of the most spectacular and unspoiled in Australia. The road hugs the shore, passes secluded white coral beaches, and dips through lush rain forests. An avenue of ornamental palms leads from the Cook Highway into the tropical village of Port Douglas. With a population of about 3,700, it is the last readily accessible town for anyone driving north. "Port," as it is known locally, was discovered in the 1980s, but despite the multimillion dollar Sheraton Mirage, three Radisson resorts, and fast catamaran service from Cairns, the village has retained its sleepy end-of-the-line atmosphere.

Almost as big a draw as the prime diving spots on the reef are the ancient rain forests of Cape Tribulation and Daintree National Park. These are some of the world's largest remaining tracts of virgin tropical rain forest and mangroves, and one of the few places in Australia where tropical rain forests meet the sea. More than 90 species of orchids grow in these dripping jungles, which are also home to such strange creatures as the cassowary, a flightless rain forest bird. The cassowary stands well over six feet tall, including a multicolored crown of bone on top of its skull. Vaguely comical looking and seemingly gawky, the bird can be extremely dangerous, easily able to kill with a kick or a butt of its plated head.

Cape Tribulation and nearby Mount Sorrow were named by Capt. James Cook, who had a number of tribulations and sorrows when he passed through here on his voyage up Australia's eastern coast in 1770. His was the first recorded passage of a European ship through the Great Barrier Reef—a venture described by later navigator Matthew Flinders as the equivalent of threading a needle. Incredibly, for the first thousand miles or so of his journey through the coral, Cook was unaware that the Great Barrier Reef existed, although he began to suspect that something was making the coastal waters unusually tranquil.

As the reef stretches northward, it veers closer to the coast, as Cook was to learn. By the time he had reached the stretch of coastline near where Cooktown is today, he found himself navigating a tortuous maze of razor-sharp coral. On the night of June 11, 1770, his ship, *Endeavour,* ran aground on the reef that now bears her name.

A frantic effort to lighten the ship by heaving ballast and six cannons overboard, as well as manning the pumps and the arrival of a high tide, allowed Cook's crew to free the ship and limp toward the coast. The drama, and the officers' sangfroid in the face of danger, mightily impressed landlubber naturalist Joseph Banks. "All this time," he noted in his journal, "the seamen worked with surprising cheerfulness and alacrity; no grumbling or growling was to be heard throughout the ship, no not even an oath (though the ship in general was as well furnished with them as most in His Majesty's service)."

The crew worked the pumps and waited for the tide. "The dreadful time now approached," reported Banks, "and the anxiety in everybody's countenance was visible enough….fear of death now stared us in the face. Hopes we had none but of being able to keep the ship afloat till we could run her ashore on some part of the main where out of her materials we might build a vessel large enough to carry us to the East Indies. At ten o'clock she floated…."

Two years earlier French explorer Louis-Antoine de Bougainville had avoided a similar grounding as he approached the north Queensland coast from the open Pacific. Hearing waves washing over the shallow coral reefs ahead—a sound he later described as "the voice of God and we obeyed it"—he veered his craft away and sailed instead into the Solomon Islands. Had he ignored the watery voice and negotiated a route through the coral maze, France might have "discovered" and claimed Australia's eastern shores.

As it was, the *Endeavour* spent the next seven weeks careened on the shore near Cooktown's present location while ships' carpenters repaired the hole in her hull. A keen naturalist, Banks enjoyed his unexpected interlude in the jungle immensely, cataloguing 186 new species of plants and writing up the first known scientific description of the kangaroo.

Before setting out again in the newly repaired *Endeavour,* the explorers climbed a coastal mountain to try to scout a passage through the maze of sharp coral. "Here we overlooked a great deal of the sea to leeward, which afforded a melancholy prospect of the difficulties we were to encounter when we came out of our present harbour," Banks wrote. "In whichever direction we turned our eyes, shoals innumerable were to be seen and no such thing as any passage to sea but through the winding channels between them, dangerous to the last degree." But, piece by piece, Cook did negotiate a passage through the reefs, sailed to the tip of Queensland's Cape York Peninsula, and there, on Possession Island, hoisted the flag and claimed the entire eastern flank of the continent on behalf of England. Binding his crew to secrecy about what they had seen along Australia's coast, he set sail through the Dutch East Indies on a course for home.

Cook's voyage, which revealed the richness, diversity, and wonders of Australia, was only the beginning. It marked the beginning of many other journeys—like mine—to explore a land that is as timeless as it is unique.

Following pages: *The moon at sunrise lends an otherworldly feel to the freshwater lakes and pearly sands along the edge of lonely Shelburne Bay, on the remote northeast flank of the Cape York Peninsula.*

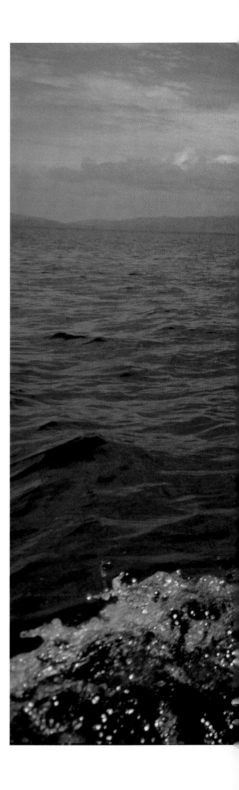

Tannin-stained waters of a nameless creek braid the sand as they meet the sea on the northeastern coast of Cape York Peninsula. Local Aborigines, who believe some of these waters harbor ancestral spirits and have traditionally hunted dugongs, turtles, and fish along these coasts, have laid claim to some areas; others have been targeted for conservation.

Heading home, Napoleon Short trails his catch, a dugong speared in the clean coastal waters south of the Lockhart River. A traditional food source for Cape York's Aborigines for eons, these gentle giants are declining in number today.

*Like an errant sparkle in a living
kaleidoscope, a brilliantly hued
blenny-type fish darts among corals
in the Great Barrier Reef. Australia's
crown jewel, the vast reef complex
stretches south more than 1,250 miles
from the continent's northeastern tip.
It hosts hundreds of species of corals,
mollusks, and tropical fish.*

With powerful teeth and a helmet-like brow it has adapted for life among corals, a Lord Howe Island doubleheader wrasse has flipped a sea urchin to feed on its meat and eggs. Smaller wrasses swirl around the encounter, waiting to scavenge scraps left over from the larger fish's feast.

Following pages: *At low tide shallow turquoise waters bathe Middleton Reef, creating a swirl of color and foam in an otherwise empty expanse of blue Pacific about 140 miles north of Lord Howe Island. Nearly awash at high tide, the coral-covered seamount has proven a deadly trap for unwary navigators and is littered with shipwrecks.*

Like flying over an alien landscape: A swim through the warm shallow waters around Agincourt Reefs, off the Queensland coast near Cairns, offers a glimpse into a bommie—*a submerged chunk of hard coral. Ancient worlds in themselves, bommies can be up to 2,000 years old.*

Beware of this beauty: A lionfish keeps the world at bay with a profusion of needle-sharp spines. The membrane-covered spines contain venom and can deliver an agonizing—although not lethal—wound.

Fickle coastal breezes on Queensland's Fraser Island expose trees long buried by shifting dunes. Some 76 miles long, Fraser is the world's largest sand island and the biggest island on Australia's east coast. Although Fraser is made up entirely of sand, rain forests cloak much of the island. Specially adapted aboveground roots allow the trees to thrive on shifting sands.

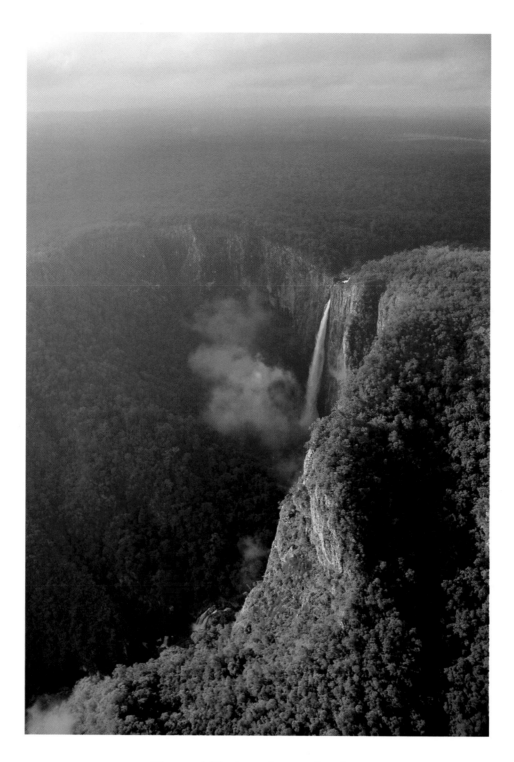

Diamond-like in an immensity of mountain and rain forest, Wallaman Falls plunges a thousand feet in Queensland's Lumholtz National Park. Most spectacular during the wet season, when Stony Creek is swollen by monsoon rains, Wallaman boasts the longest drop of any waterfall in Australia.

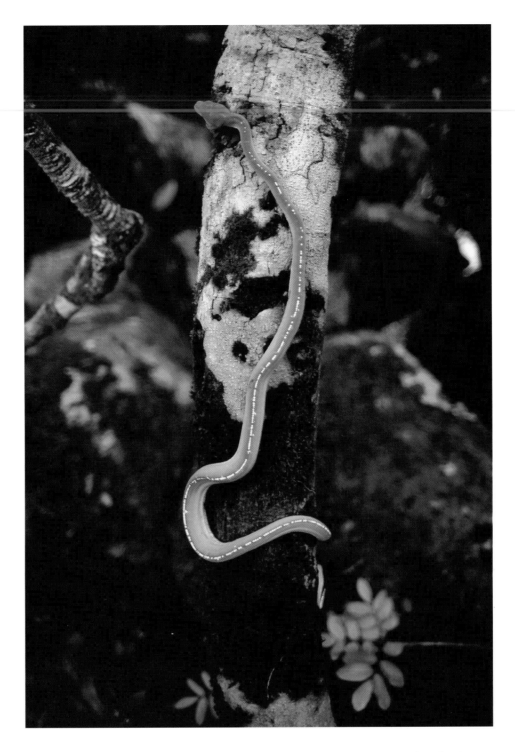

Toiling upward, a rare green python seeks a vantage point in Cape York's Iron Range National Park, Australia's largest remaining area of lowland tropical rain forest. Found only in this remote pocket of Queensland and farther north in New Guinea, the brilliantly colored snake is a legacy of pre-Ice Age days, when a land bridge linked Australia and New Guinea.

Following pages: *Wreaths of mist rise from the hollows of Queensland's Daintree National Park. Ancient rain forests along the Daintree River are living vestiges of those that cloaked the supercontinent of Gondwana more than a hundred million years ago. Flowering plants and ferns that flourished in the Age of Reptiles still thrive here today.*

Serpentine roots of a massive fig tree deep in Iron Range National Park hint at its vast, untouched wilderness. The park shelters such oddities as the striped possum, the northern quoll (a native cat), and dozens of species of tropical butterflies. Most are found only in Cape York and New Guinea.

Mosquito net, fan, and a six-volt battery to power it offer simple comforts in Brian Venable's pole-framed house at Cape Weymouth, on the east coast of the Cape York Peninsula. A sense of frontier and a desire for a self-reliant, alternative lifestyle draw an increasing number of Australians away from cities and into the tropical bush of far northern Queensland.

Following pages: *Early morning anglers greet the dawn at Byron Bay, the first point on the Australian coast to see the sun. The popular resort town on the New South Wales northern coast perches on a nearly unbroken chain of beaches that stretch 360 miles.*

by Harry Gordon

A Sports-Mad Country

When Australia's prime minister, John Howard, chose a couple of years ago to nominate the greatest living Australian, he did not single out a Nobel Prize winner, a World Bank president, a chief United Nations weapons envoy, an astronaut (although such people were eligible), or even a scientist, a judge, or a poet. Howard opted instead for a sportsman: a cricket player he had idolized since boyhood, Sir Donald Bradman. Bradman used to be a prolific scorer with the bat, and his deeds offered the nation comfort at times when it needed something to feel good about—during the Depression and immediately after World War II. As a captain of the Australian team, he once occupied the job that Howard considers to represent "almost the pinnacle of human achievement."

More recently, after it became publicly known that two Australian cricketers had taken money from an Indian bookmaker, Howard appeared on television, an Australian flag behind him, quite as grave-faced as when offering solace after disastrous floods and bushfires. Cricket is a game whose leisurely grace radiates a wholesome aura, and this revelation had provoked outrage and shame across the nation, even a sense of betrayal. An obviously affected Howard spoke on TV of the country's "intense feeling of disappointment" after an event he knew would "deeply disturb Australians." At this point a visitor from overseas might have been excused some degree of bewilderment. It would be truly hard to imagine any other world leader, or any other nation, reacting with such apparent agony to some shenanigans with a bookie by a couple of sportsmen. So what goes on?

The Australian prime minister is certainly an unrepentant sports buff, one who takes time on his way to visit Bill Clinton to wander around Yankee Stadium, one whose office—with its trophies, bats, balls, and photographs of champions—has the look of a small annex in a sports museum. But Howard is also a most conservative, sober politician. The truth is, his attitudes simply reflect those of his people. Australia, it needs to be understood, enjoys a serious love affair with sports. With a population of 19 million, an amiable climate, and endless beaches, the place positively pulsates with it.

To experience an Australian summer, which embraces the torpor of a long, hot Christmas holiday, is to be drenched by sports. The images of people at play are just about inescapable, which provides no problem, because most people are besotted by sports. The international cricket, tennis, and golf matches are watched on site by huge crowds—100,000 at the Melbourne Cricket Ground is fairly commonplace—and on television by millions more. On Boxing Day the entire nation watches an astonishing congestion in Sydney Harbour, as more than a hundred yachts begin the annual race to Hobart (630 nautical miles south), and a virtual confetti of small craft crowd every bay and inlet for some sort of view. The abundant beaches—and Australia is largely a coastal-dwelling nation—attract hordes: It is estimated that 8 million Australians are active swimmers. As they are buffeted in the waters around the continent, they are watched over by 27,500 unpaid surf lifesavers, 8,500 of them female. And when those on the beaches are not actually swimming, they're riding a board, sunbathing, picnicking, or playing a sandy brand of cricket that involves small children, parents, uncles, even grannies.

A 1998 survey suggests that Australians have trouble staying still. More than 2.3 million of them take to the water with some form of surfboard, 4.1 million regularly swing a golf club, and 937,000 play tennis. Twenty percent of the population (3.7 million) are active joggers, and one in three is a regular trekker through the bush. While most European nations support one code of football, Australia has settled for four—three imported, one indigenously invented—and all have large, fervent followings. The television audience for a single Australian Football League game can reach 3.5 million. For the three-minute running of a November horse race, the Melbourne Cup, the entire nation simply stops whatever it's doing, watches, and listens.

It could be argued that no other nation has defined its character and the values it cherishes more precisely through sports than Australia. These include a bluff camaraderie (known locally as mateship), a fiercely egalitarian attitude that asserts itself in a willingness to challenge authority, a tendency not just to confront adversity but to welcome it, a desire for a "fair go" (which amounts to an even break), and a laconic acceptance that you can't always win. One classic gesture and one defiant athlete have managed, in quite separate fashions, to sum up most of the distinctive elements.

The gesture involves a runner, John Landy, sacrificing an almost certain world record to go back to the aid of another athlete, Ron Clarke. Clarke had been accidentally tripped, spread-eagled on the track, then spiked as Landy leaped across his body. It happened in 1956, but the image remains etched enduringly into the Australian consciousness. Landy's action is seen not only as a sublime piece of sportsmanship, but also, romantically, as an act of mateship somehow evoking echoes of instinctive bravery among the trenches on the Somme. A sculptor, Mitch Mitchell, has immortalized it in a sculpture at the entrance to Melbourne's Olympic Park.

The defiant athlete, who happens to be the nation's most loved Olympian, is Dawn Fraser, winner of four gold medals and the first Olympic swimmer of either sex ever to win the same event three times in a row. Adversity was her beat. Discipline was her enemy. The youngest of eight children raised in a battling dockside suburb, Fraser played often as a child in a disused coal mine, suffered a variety of respiratory problems aggravated by coal dust, and was a truant and a tomboy. She left school at 14 to work in a garment factory, and by her own candid assessment was a potential delinquent. She never paid for a swimming lesson in her life, and went on to set 39 world records (27 of them individual). In 1964, during preparation for the Tokyo Olympics, she was involved in a car crash that killed her mother and injured her so badly that her neck and spine had to be encased in a steel brace for nine weeks. She won in Tokyo, but soon afterward was expelled from swimming for ten years. There had been some problems with discipline: She had marched in the opening ceremony against orders, stolen a flag, and been arrested by Japanese police.

She was 27, and the martyrdom implicit in that virtual life ban served only to enhance the legend of Fraser. Her serial conflicts with authority are seen, again romantically, to identify with those of gold miners who fought a bloody battle for their rights at the Eureka Stockade, Ballarat, in 1854.

Australia's preoccupation with sports has intrigued many visitors. A leading American sportswriter called it a land "completely surrounded by water and inundated with athletes." In the 1960s one newcomer to the country noted that being in Australia was "like living in a gymnasium. You can't look up without seeing someone practicing a sport of some kind...."

A New York writer declared in print, after a stay in Australia, that he was hard put to recall any conversation in which sports did not intrude. "If the other party is at all vulnerable," he wrote, "Australians will talk sport as if they existed for nothing else." The complaint is justified, but hardly new. As long ago as June 1892, a prominent Melbourne clergyman, the Reverend Dr. Bevan, was voicing publicly his annoyance about sport's domination of newspaper space and general conversation.

One aspect of this mania is that it doesn't play favorites. While other countries are known to go a little crazy about a single sport, such as soccer, Australia's passion pervades just about any activity that involves a contest. A measure of its intensity is provided by the knowledge that the name of Sir Howard Florey is far less well known in his homeland than those of shoals of swimmers, runners, rowers, cyclists, and tennis players. The swimmers, runners, and the rest have won gold medals, set world records, taken Wimbledon championships, enjoyed brief brushes with glory. Florey was a codeveloper of penicillin, which is credited with having saved millions of lives since 1944.

Australia's obsession with sports was seeded in the goldfields of the 1850s, where diggers indulged in bare-knuckle prize fights, footraces, and a brand of football that had a Gaelic accent but was unburdened by too many rules. It was nourished by antipodean distance, the sheer infancy of settlement, a sense of inferiority, and a yearning, in a land then split into colonies, for a feeling of oneness. Success in sport offered a kind of unifying glue, just as it helped many former convicts in that transplanted, strongly masculine society erase the awful sense of second-rateness that came with faraway memories of rejection, suppression, and poverty. By winning, it was possible to demonstrate, in the most basic way, that Australians *were* at least as good as people who lived in England and Europe. In a land with an ancient (yet seemingly brief) past and an uncertain future, sports offered rare scope for the settlers to thumb a nose at older, more established societies.

The feeling of inferiority was not just accepted: It was rubbed in. When teams from England first visited the colonies to play cricket during the summer of 1861-1862, they allowed the locals to play 22 men against their own 11. The reasoning was that the colonials might expect to be half as good as the British were. As the Australian teams improved, they fielded first 18, then 15 players, against the visiting Englishmen. When a team of 11 Australians finally beat the All-England Eleven in Melbourne in 1877 by 45 runs, the Sydney *Daily News* echoed the general mood of euphoria: "It may console them…[in London]…to note that the English race is not disintegrating in a distant land and on turf where lately the black-fellow hurled his boomerang."

The winning, and the euphoria, had in fact begun for Australia a year earlier, when a giant quarryman, a sculler called Edward Trickett, became the country's first undisputed world champion in a match race on the Thames. It took three weeks for the news to reach Australia, and when it did the *Sydney Morning Herald* reported that people didn't believe it, that it was too good to be true. When Trickett returned by ship four months later, 25,000 people waited at the wharf to greet him, along with several brass bands and all the firefighters of Sydney equipped with blazing torches. Such was the excitement that total strangers hugged in the streets.

If a moment in history might be isolated as representing the first real effusion of national pride, and the birth of a love affair with sports, "Ned" Trickett's return provided it. He was the first of a long line of heroes, and his feat offered comfort to countrymen who wanted desperately to possess an identity and share some sort of collective ego.

In the next 25 years, until the six colonies came together in federation as Australia, a variety of champions emerged. During this period, a time when those colonies were a loose bundle of neighboring territories, when there was no Australian flag, no postage stamp, and no anthem, the country made its first impact on the Olympic Games. A young accountant, Edwin Flack, who had been studying in London traveled to Athens in 1896 to take part in Baron Pierre de Coubertin's bold experiment, a revival of the ancient Greek Olympics. The experiment was hugely successful, and so was Edwin Flack.

At a time when national Olympic committees had not yet been established, Flack ran in a vest carrying the emblem of his old Melbourne school and won both the 800- and 1500-meter races. His solo expedition to Athens had another, unlikely benefit for Australian sport. Because of it, the country is able to make the rare boast that it has attended every summer Olympics of the modern era. At the 1900 Paris Games, less that a year before nationhood formally arrived, three Australians competed, and they all won gold medals.

It was in the first half of the 20th century that Australia began to develop a reputation as a nursery of sport. One pioneer was Norman Brookes, who won the Wimbledon championships in 1907 and 1914, played Davis Cup from 1905 until 1920, and began an illustrious tennis lineage. Through all this period, with odd exceptions such as opera singer Dame Nellie Melba (who happened to be the aunt of another Wimbledon champion, Gerald Patterson) Australians made little world impact in the arts.

Novelist Tom Keneally has observed that during his Sydney childhood in the 1930s, culture was something that came from another hemisphere: "What we could do was fight valiantly in wars that didn't very much concern us, produce exceptional wool and rust-free wheat, fly planes, and run, kick, swim, bat and bowl better than any race on earth." That accepted wisdom was reinforced in classrooms, where the pioneering legend of the Australian was celebrated, often in conflict with the land, the climate, the geography, and authority. It was a manly kind of legend, with little concession to the arts. Keneally detected some annoyance in the Australian cultural community toward sport, because it had been "so long seen as the appropriate response to the business of being Australian." Happily, Keneally later became one of a sizable group of Australian writers, artists, opera singers, dancers, musicians, actors, and filmmakers who made, and continue to make, a significant international impact on the arts.

The decade that still looms boldest in the landscape of Australian sporting achievement was the 1950s. A plethora of extraordinary performances occurred, one that caused the place to be recognized suddenly as a dominant force in world sports, with stature out of all proportion to its then population of some 9 million people (akin to those of Morocco and Peru). It was a period in which Melbourne hosted the 1956 Olympics (at which the home nation won a record 13 gold medals). It was a time when

Australian tennis players grabbed hold of the Davis Cup and refused to let go, simultaneously winning Wimbledon titles with what British newspapers called sad monotony.

The winning was contagious, diverse, and falsely suggestive of invincibility. Australian swimmers broke and rebroke *every* world freestyle swimming record and treated other strokes with similar contempt. John Landy and Herb Elliott ran the mile faster than anyone else, and a succession of lithe and graceful girls, from Shirley Strickland and Marjorie Jackson to Betty Cuthbert, challenged and beat the greatest Russian, Dutch, English, and German sprinters. Jack Brabham won three Formula One world driving championships, Peter Thomson took five British Open golf titles, and Russell Mockridge and Sid Patterson became world and Olympic cycling champions.

Most piquantly, rower Stuart Mackenzie echoed the deeds of the earliest practitioners of his sport by winning the Henley Diamond Sculls—the world championship of the time—not once but six times. Mackenzie, an ebullient character, was a throwback to the era when it seemed appropriate, metaphorically at least, to thumb one's nose at the British establishment, represented to him by the straw-boater gallery at Henley on Thames. Once he wore a bowler hat as he raced, and on another occasion he paddled across to a launch and splashed a spectator who had heckled him. While beating the triple Olympic champion Vyacheslav Ivanov, he took time to doff his cap and nod genially to a hooting crowd.

Inevitably the triumphs of the 1950s, particularly at the Olympics, invited theories from abroad. Factors credited for the wins included the climate, the high-protein diet, the sheer space (then around 2.3 people to the square kilometer compared to 64 in Europe), the migrant stock, even the classless nature of society. The coaching of Forbes Carlile (swimming), Percy Cerutty (athletics), and Harry Hopman (tennis) was also seen as significant.

Australia's extravagant success slowed a little in the 1960s and early 1970s, then came to a crunching halt. After John Newcombe, of Sydney, won his second consecutive Wimbledon title in 1971, the Americans, Swedes, and Germans took over. In 1976 a calamity occurred: The Australian Olympic team returned from Montreal without a single gold medal. It was the first such dismal result in 40 years, and there was much disquiet around the country. Of the many opinions to emerge from the subse-quent inquests, only two really counted. One was that, in terms of coaching and conditioning, other countries had simply caught up with Australia. The other was that, if Australia was to become a world force again, it could never rely on natural ability: It needed to spend money on overseas competition, training facilities, research, sports medicine, and the importation of coaches. Since winning the right in 1993 to host the 2000 Olympics—the second ever in the Southern Hemisphere—Australia has been spending hard and winning well, especially in swimming, rowing, shooting, and equestrian events. The women, particularly, have performed with distinction in hockey, netball, cycling, cricket, basketball, softball, basketball, and the new Olympic disciplines of the triathlon and female water polo.

Ah, those women. So long neglected, so long the victims of undisguised prejudice. For a long time Australian sport was like a stuffy club that shuddered at the thought of admitting female members. One woman, a kind of aquatic suffragette named Fanny Durack, stormed her way through a back door to raise her own fare to the Stockholm Olympics in 1912. There she won gold in swimming. Today, Durack is revered as a pioneer. Then she was a nuisance, quite as unpopular with administrators as Dawn Fraser half a century later. In the 1950s Fraser was a member of an invasion force whose superb performances caused women to be taken seriously in sport. Around her were world-beating sprinters Marjorie Jackson, Shirley Strickland, and Betty Cuthbert, closely followed by tennis players Margaret Court and Evonne Goolagong Cawley and the world squash champion Heather McKay (undefeated for 18 years).

Recent performances by athletes such as swimmers Michael Klim, Ian Thorpe, and Susie O'Neill and Aboriginal sprinter Cathy Freeman suggest that the Sydney Games, and the decade for which they will provide the overture, will echo for Australia the kind of success it enjoyed during the 1950s. Again, all kinds of theories will undoubtedly be rounded up to explain the triumphs, including those usual suspects of climate, space (a little less now, but still abundant), diet, and coaching.

In truth, though, the most significant factor will be that magnificent, enduring, and occasionally annoying obsession that had such raw beginnings on the goldfields 150 years ago.

As gray waves roll in at sunrise, a young surfer waits for her boyfriend and his mates to quit the waves off Byron Bay, on the New South Wales coast. With almost perfect beach weather year-round, the easygoing town has been a haven for surfers and backpackers since the 1960s.

A matter of perspective: Viewed through the windshield of one vehicle, a bikini-clad whale watcher uses her four-wheel drive as a crow's nest as she scans the waters off Fraser Island for humpbacks. Hunted nearly to extinction earlier this century, the whales have returned, and whale-watching has become popular with tourists and locals.

Known as the "Queen of the North,"
to the thousands of adventurers who
flocked here during the Palmer River
gold rush in the 1870s, Cooktown
boasted 65 pubs, 3 banks, and a population of more than 30,000. Today,
it is a sleepy hamlet on Queensland's
north coast and a jumping-off point
for adventurers bound for the tip of
Cape York.

Watching for his ride, a schoolboy
waits in the doorway of a shop in the
north Queensland town of Tully.
Made lush by more than 160 inches
of rain a year and rich volcanic soil,
Tully nestles in the heart of Queensland's sugar industry region. Despite
its ups and downs, sugar has largely
been sweet to the residents of Tully.
Local folklore includes a claim to
having more millionaires per capita
than any other town in Australia.

Supported by a single strand of rope, Kate Reid, artistic director of Circus Entroupe, practices violin in the northern New South Wales town of Lismore. The circus performs at nightclubs, festivals, and in Aboriginal communities around Australia. Towns in these rain forested mountains have been havens for artists and Australia's counterculture since 1974, when the Aquarius Music Festival was held in the area.

Following pages: *The pot of gold at the end of the rainbow for many Australians, Queensland's southern coast and the bustling promise of its capital city, Brisbane, lure thousands of job- and sun-seekers from around Australia. Once a distant country cousin to cosmopolitan Sydney and Melbourne, Brisbane and its suburbs now rank among the fastest growing communities in Australia.*

INDEX

NOTES ON CONTRIBUTORS

Roff Smith, a New Englander who now makes his home in Seppeltsfield, South Australia, wrote three articles for the National Geographic about his 10,000-mile bicycle trip around the continent. His other contributions to the Magazine include "Nebraska: Standing Tall Again" in the November 1998 issue and "New River's Deep Soul" in June 1999.

Sam Abell has photographed for more than 20 National Geographic articles and books since 1970, including two cover stories on Australia, "Journey Into Dreamtime" and "The Uneasy Magic of Cape York Peninsula." In addition to his editorial work he maintains a career as a speaker, writer, and teacher of photography. His work is collected in the book *Stay This Moment*, which was the basis of an exhibition at the International Center of Photography in New York City.

Frank Brennan, S.J., Director of the Jesuit Social Justice Centre in Sydney, is a lawyer who is the author of several books on the subject of Aboriginal land rights.

Harry Gordon, award-winning journalist, author, and editor, writes on the Olympics for *The Australian* and is a member of Australia's Sporting Hall of Fame.

John Landy, fascinated by natural history since his childhood in Melbourne, has written the award-winning *Close to Nature* as well as *A Coastal Diary*.

Geoffrey Sherington, professor and Dean of the Faculty of Education at the University of Sydney, has written extensively on the history of immigration to Australia.

ACKNOWLEDGMENTS

The Book Division wishes to thank the many individuals, groups, and organizations mentioned or quoted in this publication for their help and guidance. In addition, we are grateful to naturalist and photographer Kerry Trapnell for his help in identifying many of the photographs and to the following: the tourist bureaus of Derby and Broome, West Australia; the Launceston Reference Library, Launceston, Tasmania; and Dr. Paul S. C. Taçon, Australian Museum, Sydney. Our thanks also to consulting editors Martha Christian and Bonnie S. Lawrence.

ADDITIONAL READING

The reader may wish to consult the National Geographic Index for related articles and books, including *Surprising Lands Down under,* by Mary Ann Harrell; *Wild Shores of Austrlia* by Ron Fisher; and *Voyages to Paradise* by William R. Gray. The following sources may also be of interest: Jessica Anderson, *The Commandant;* Susan Bambrick, ed., *The Cambridge Encyclopedia of Australia;* Bruce Chatwin, *The Songlines;* John J. Cove, *What the Bones Say: Tasmanian Aborigines, Science and Domination;* Robyn Davidson, *Tracks;* Tim Flannery, *The Explorers;* Lonely Planet Publications, *Australia;* Robert Hughes, *The Fatal Shore: The Epic of Australia's Founding;* Mark Twain, *Following the Equator: A Journey Around the World.*

ILLUSTRATIONS CREDITS

Photographs by National Geographic Photographer Sam Abell unless noted below.
Introduction: p. 9, Francis Birtles/Alpha; p. 12-13, David Doubilet; p. 20-21, David Doubilet. **Chapter One—The Tropical North:** p. 42-43, Mike Osborn/Kimberley Vision; p. 46-47, David Doubilet; p. 58-59, Paul Chesley. **Chapter Two—The Outback:** p. 92-93 (both), Kerry Trapnell; p. 94-95, Medford Taylor; p. 96-97, Mark Cheater; p. 100-101, Joseph J. Scherschel; p. 104-105, Rick Smolan; p. 106-107 (both), Medford Taylor; p. 108-109, David Austen; p. 110-115 (all), Medford Taylor; p. 116-117, David Austen; p. 118, Carl Purcell; p. 119-123 (all), Kerry Trapnell. **Chapter Three—The Golden West:** p. 134-139 (all), David Doubilet. **Chapter Four—The Southern Shores:** p. 180-183 (all), David Doubilet; p. 184-185 (both), Kerry Trapnell; p. 187-189 (both), Kerry Trapnell; p. 190, David Doubilet; p. 191-192 (all), Kerry Trapnell; p. 192-193, William Albert Allard, National Geographic Photographer; p. 194-197 (all), Kerry Trapnell. **Chapter Six—The Heritage Coast:** p. 234-235, Kerry Trapnell; p. 238-239, David Austen; p. 240-241, Kerry Trapnell; p. 242-243 (both), Kerry Trapnell; p. 252-255 (all), Kerry Trapnell. **Chapter Seven—A Golden Land:** p. 272-277 (all), David Doubilet; p. 292, Kerry Trapnell; p. 296-299 (all), Kerry Trapnell.

AUSTRALIA
Journey Through a Timeless Land

By Roff Smith
Photographs by Sam Abell

Published by the National Geographic Society

John M. Fahey, Jr.	President and Chief Executive Officer
Gilbert M. Grosvenor	Chairman of the Board
Nina D. Hoffman	Senior Vice President

Prepared by the Book Division

William R. Gray	Vice President and Director
Charles Kogod	Assistant Director
Barbara A. Payne	Editorial Director and Managing Editor
David Griffin	Design Director

Staff for this book

Leah Bendavid-Val	Project Editor
Toni Eugene	Text Editor
Lyle Rosbotham	Art Director
Sallie M. Greenwood	Researcher
Carl Mehler	Director of Maps
Kevin G. Craig	Assistant Editor
Meredith C. Wilcox	Illustrations Assistant
Natasha Klauss	Research Assistant
R. Gary Colbert	Production Director
Lewis R. Bassford	Production Project Manager
Peggy J. Candore	Assistant to the Director
Connie Binder	Indexer

Manufacturing and Quality Control

George V. White	Director
John T. Dunn	Associate Director
Vincent P. Ryan	Manager
Phil Schlosser	Budget Analyst

The world's largest nonprofit scientific and educational organization, the National Geographic Society was founded in 1888 "for the increase and diffusion of geographic knowledge." Since then it has supported scientific exploration and spread information to its more than nine million members worldwide.

The National Geographic Society educates and inspires millions every day through magazines, books, television programs, videos, maps and atlases, research grants, the National Geography Bee, teacher workshops, and innovative classroom materials.

The Society is supported through membership dues and income from the sale of its educational products. Members receive NATIONAL GEOGRAPHIC magazine—the Society's official journal—discounts on Society products, and other benefits.

For more information about the National Geographic Society and its educational programs and publications, please call 1-800-NGS-LINE (647-5463), or write to the following address:

National Geographic Society
1145 17th Street N.W.
Washington, D.C. 20036-4688 U.S.A.

Visit the Society's Web site at
www.nationalgeographic.com

Library of Congress Cataloging-in-Publication Data

Smith, Roff
     Australia : journey through a timeless land / by Roff
Smith ; photographs by Sam Abell.
         p. cm.
     Includes index.
     ISBN 0-7922-7578-0 -- ISBN 0-7922-7579-9 (deluxe ed.)
      1. Australia--Description and travel. I. Abell, Sam. II. Title.

DU105.2 .S55 1999
919.404'65--dc21

99-023810